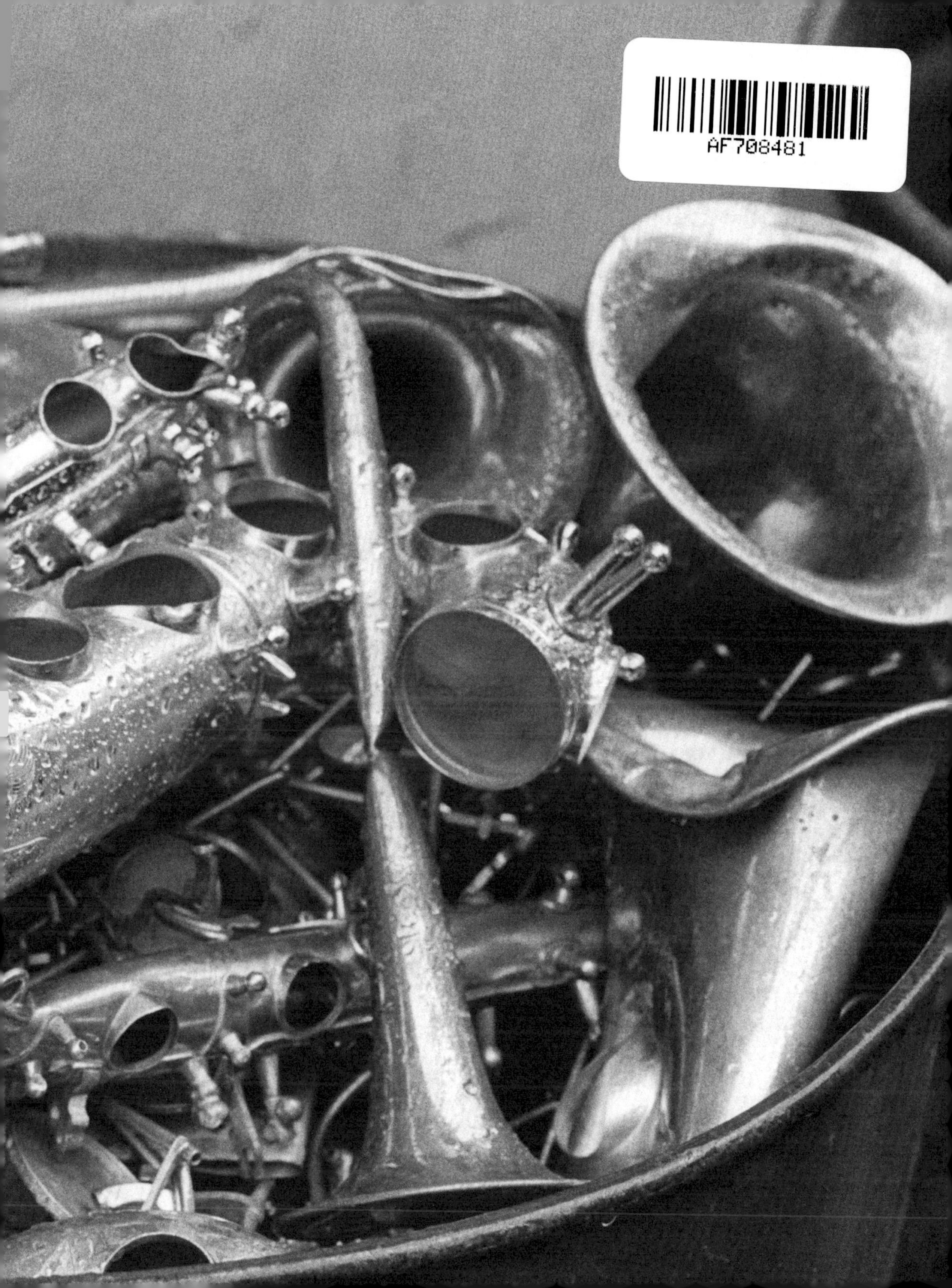

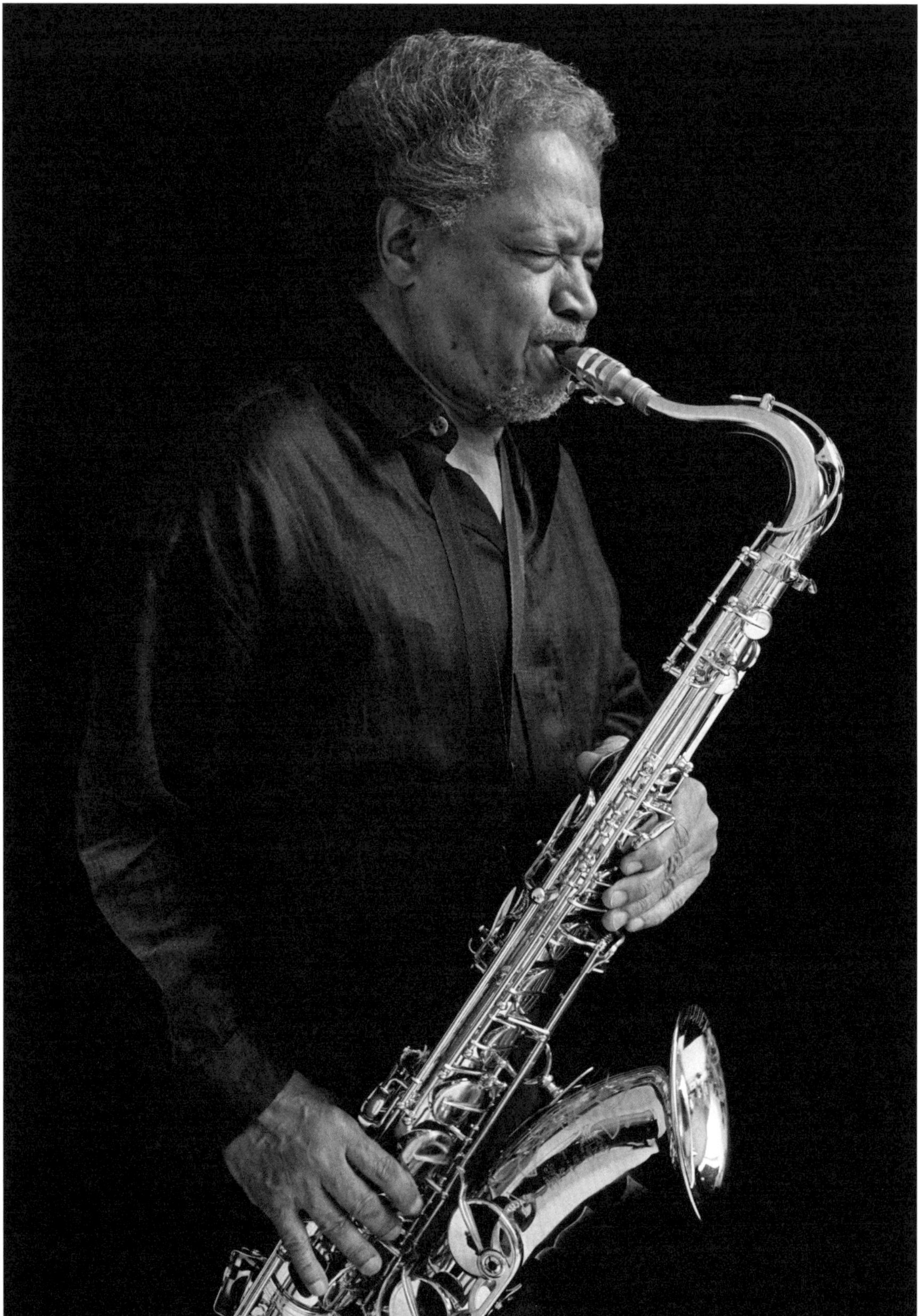

JAZZ

ARTHUR ELGORT

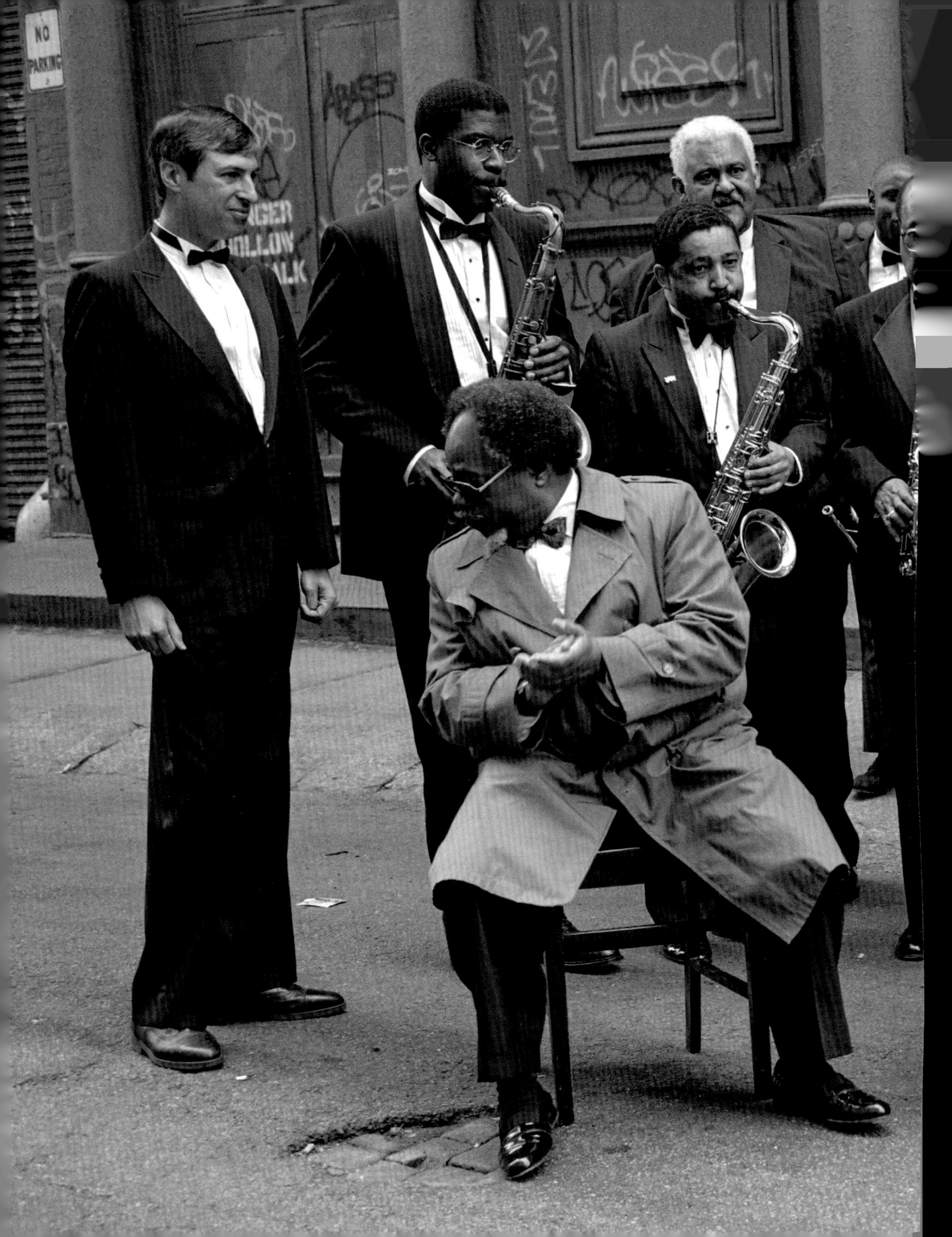
NO
PARKING

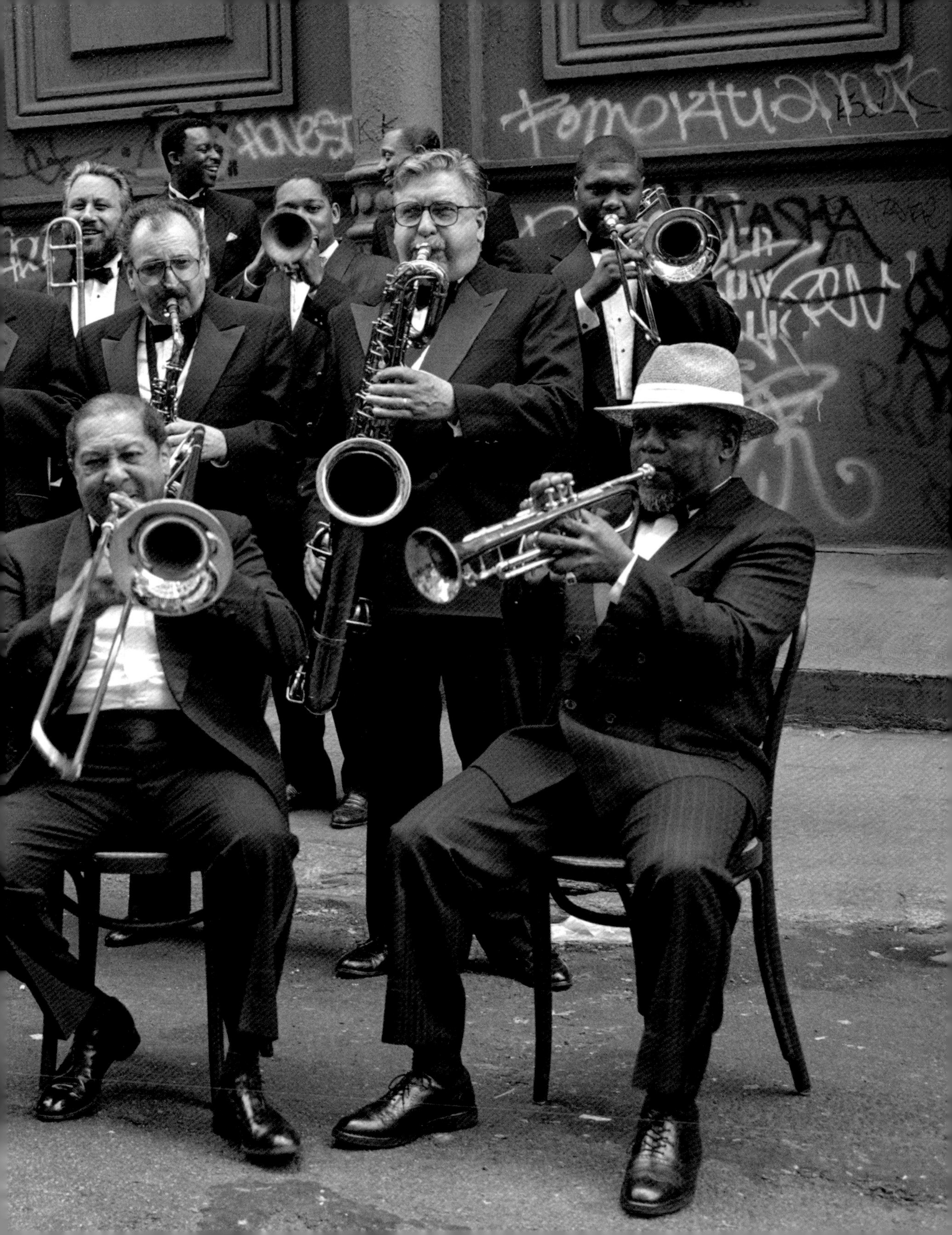
NATASHA

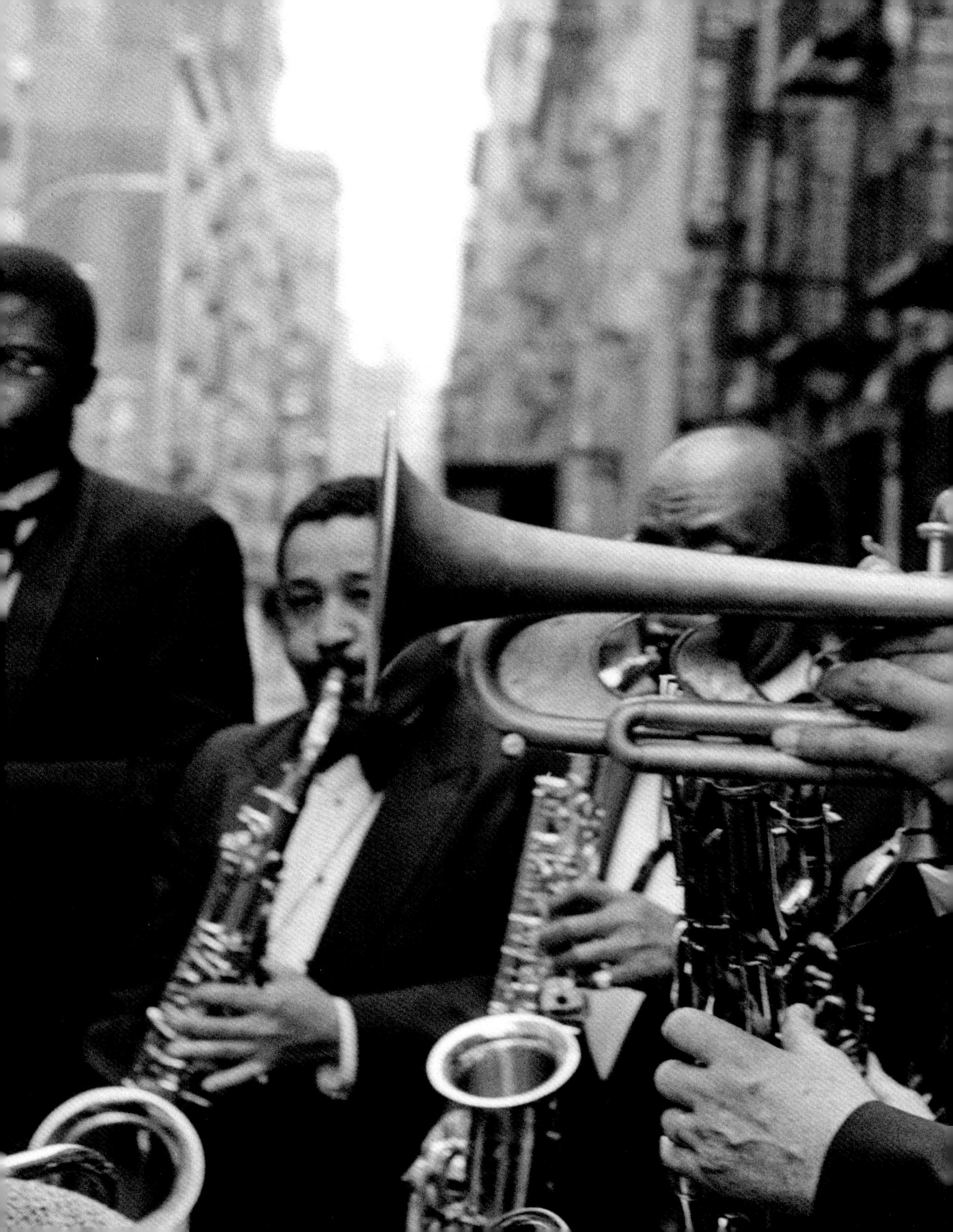

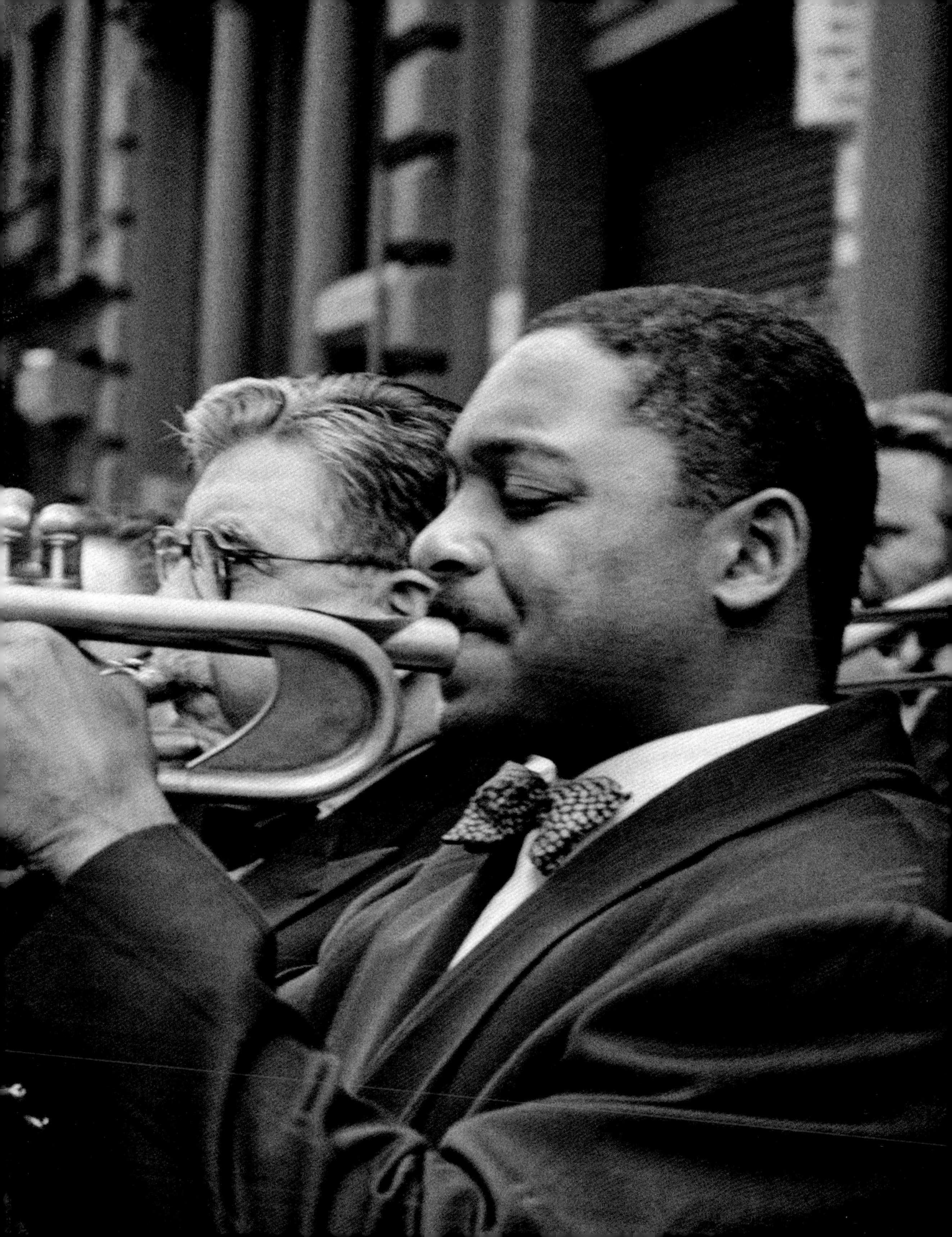

FOREWORD

BY WYNTON MARSALIS

Jazz is the art of now. Musicians anticipate the future to organize the present as it passes into memory. Though we are said to be playing, we are actually conjuring. We integrate a new mythology from our shared human heritage in the intensity of each passing moment. Horns fill up the center space with streams and streaks of improvised melodies, while the swinging cymbal and walking bass create the space itself. It is the time-space continuum. The dynamic 'to and fro' of cymbal and bass is called swing, but on the bandstand, it's reverently known as THE time. Dynamic and flexible yet impassive and unforgiving, 'the time' is the cutting edge of our truth. And it's very simple. You're in time...or you're not. Every passing moment is a snapshot of possibilities and actualities, negotiations and conclusions...and lying is not an option...there's only time to tell the truth. Together, we conceive and execute at the speed of instinct. What could be becomes, what is is, what was is forevermore.

In photography, the interplay of light and darkness, angle and plane, form and substance, point and counterpoint, all come to bear on a single moment. A flash of the shutter and everything present is accounted for. Click!

The ephemeral becomes permanent. What was a present moment, incomprehensible in its complexity, is now a clearly delineated and intensely personal recording, executed at the speed of instinct. The strict tempo and mercurial nature of light is equivalent to 'the time' in jazz. It forces the photographer's hand and eye to jump light itself and capture the perfect moment of balance between 'what will be' and 'what is' to give 'what was' the perpetual energy of present-ness. When that instinct is true, a timeless photograph forever leaps off the page.

Arthur Elgort's photos draw you into a world deep beyond the surface. He loves jazz and jazz musicians, and we love him. He knows that our notes, harmonies and rhythms are only introductions to feelings, gestures, and insights. His art reveals and reflects the telepathic empathy and soul that defines a jazz musician, and the not-as-common-as-you-would-think knowledge that jazz emanates from a way of life, an attitude about living and a recognition that what is, is.

Mr. Elgort captures telling moments in perfect rhythm and time. He is present and honest about what he sees: story, subject matter, position, balance with the setting, mood, dynamics, all work in perfect coordination to create a compelling visual counterpoint. He is able to find the unique lyricism and poetry of each musician and situation. The range and depth of the feelings in his photographs tells you that he is himself a jazz man with the same understanding, intention, and mythology. And to create meaningful work under the pressure of time, we must agree to some workable degree on our collective mythology. How we see it, hear it, and feel it.

Since the time of its birth, the essences and symbols of jazz have been assaulted with an overwhelming volume of misinformation. Every type of diversion has been enlisted to diminish its place at the center of our national story: from its whorehouse birth to the darktown fantasies of old Harlem, from its relationship to drug addiction to its political identity (which was considered subversive whenever musicians pressed for freedom and justice).

The last 30 years have seen a more subtle and successful philosophical attack that celebrates jazz for being every form of music in existence...except itself!! Mr. Elgort's book strongly suggests that jazz has an identity that is its own. He does the music a great service by showing so many of the great and charismatic older and younger musicians together. Jazz people know the elders, but it's a revelation to feel the younger musicians and their personalities. Through his eyes, we see our music as it is handed from generation to generation. We realize that jazz continued to produce fine musicians even as other styles of music occupied more and more of the nation's interest. Mr. Elgort presents us with a real jazz continuum.

Youngsters Stefon Harris and Javon Jackson dressed to the serious nines while veterans Doc Cheatham and Milt Hinton reflect the wisdom of the ages on the very next page.

The un-aging exuberance of Illinois Jacquet.

The youthful vigor and optimism of David Sanchez with his two-tone oxfords gettin' up against the backdrop of a locked down Harlem Avenue with the Striver's Row awning describing what you have to do to get through this period of corruption.

Roy Hargrove and James Carter demonstrating the transcendence of sartorial splendor.

Mona and Milt Hinton holding hands, the embodiment of community and love as James Carter receives the love they shared with so many of us.

Young Walter Blanding with the high-minded fire, optimism and seriousness of youth.

From the open-faced laugh of Benny Carter to the wry smile of Dizzy Gillespie.

Remembrances of those men and women who found the sexiness and sass of swing and the romance of dialogue in late night spots and who continue to (even as the pornographization of music, the segregation of night life and the assault of too loud volume on our sense of the intimate occupy center stage).

Michael Bowie in a moment of perfect inspiration meets perspiration.

Shoes, shoes, shoes.....

The sanctity of duets across time: from James Carter and Joshua Redman to Lionel Hampton and Illinois Jacquet to Dexter Gordon and Clark Terry.

Arnett Cobb says it all. Up on his crutches still pushing deep feeling into the world.

Donald Harrison, Olu Dara and Jesse Davis: high style and pure soul.

Arthur Elgort's work is expansive. It shows that jazz doesn't have to search all over the world for an identity that's already in your family album. All you have to do is open the book. And it's all here.

(preceding page)

Wynton Marsalis, 1992, New York City

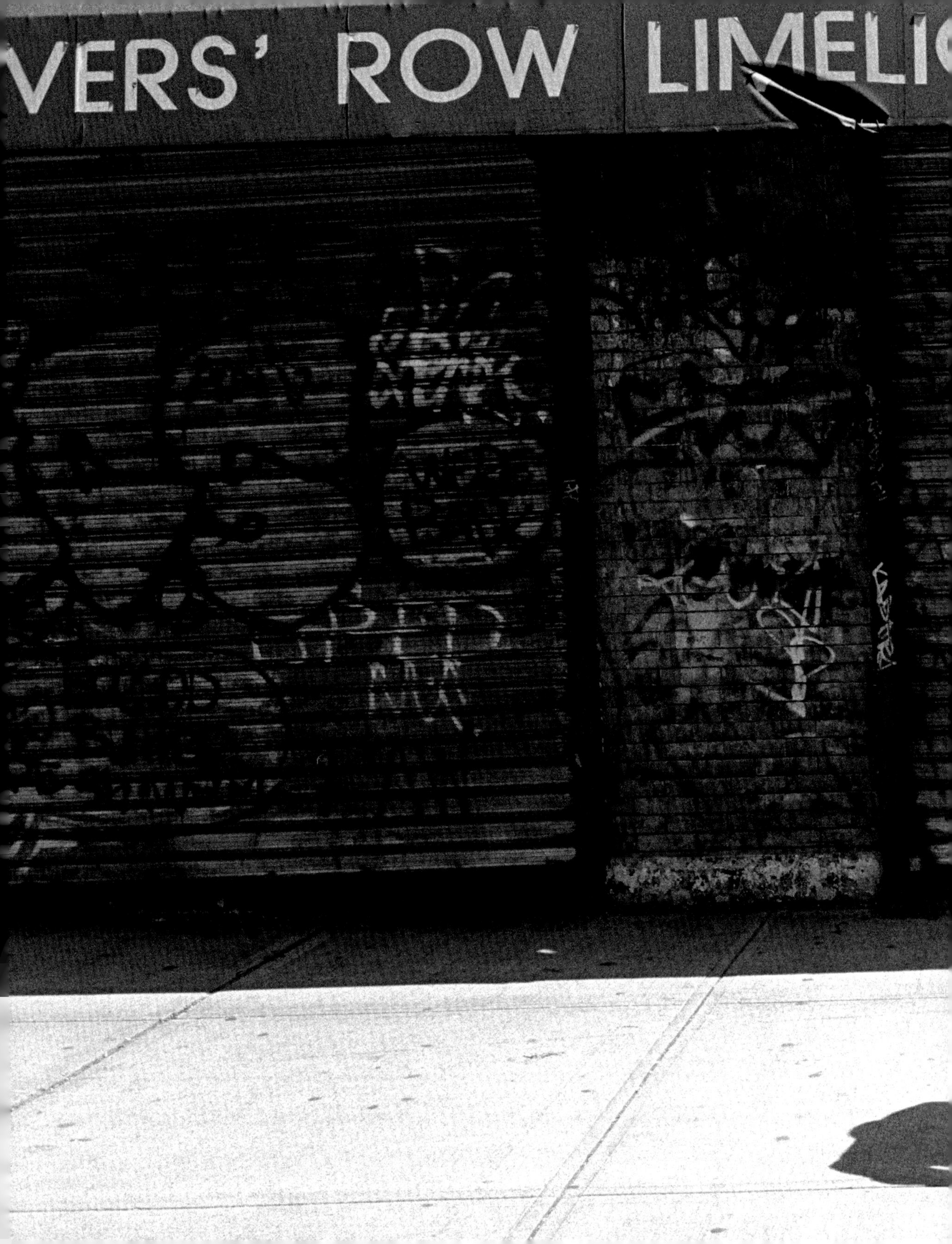
VERS' ROW LIMELI

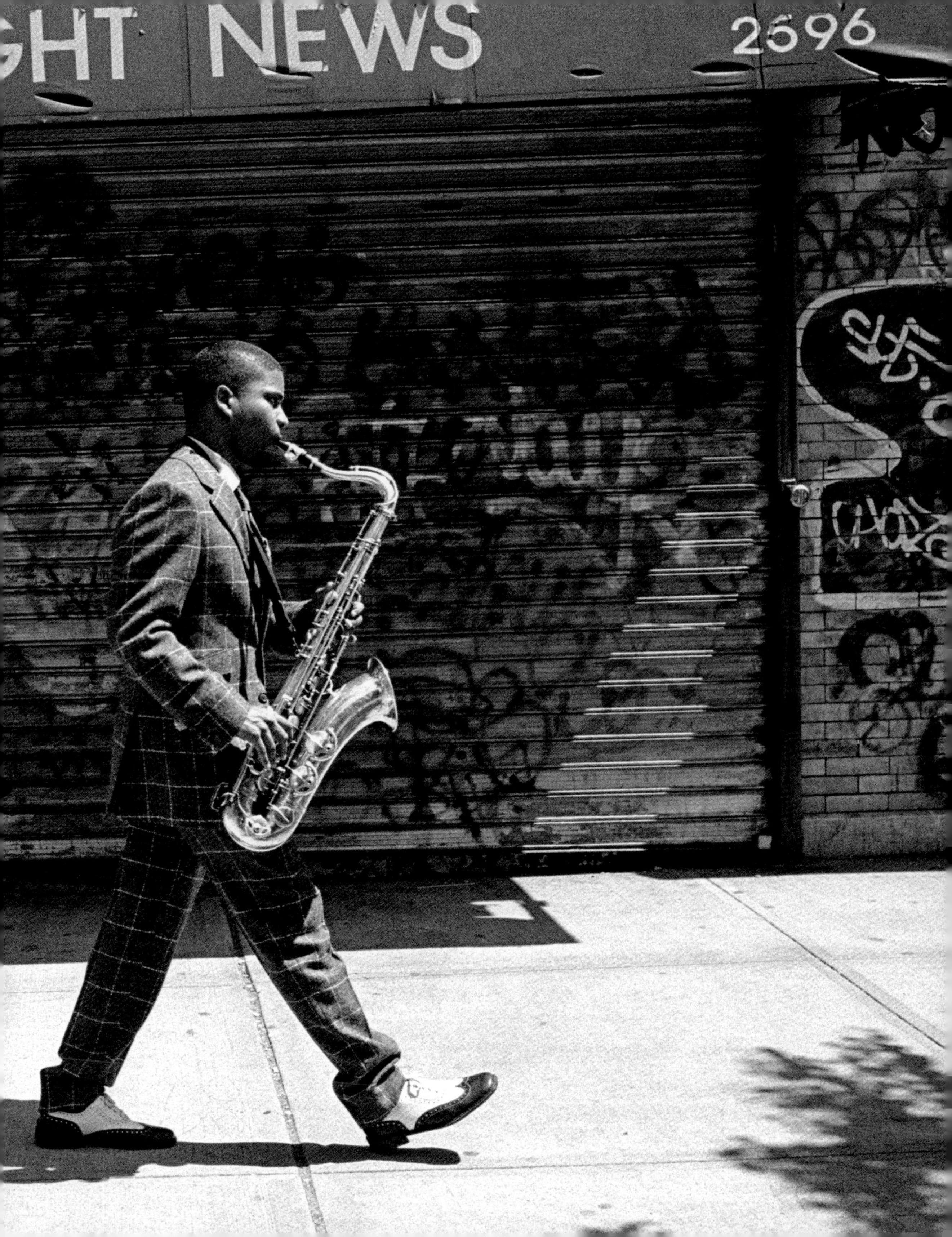
GHT NEWS
2596

INTRODUCTION
BY HANK O'NEAL

One of the first LPs I bought was a Columbia issued sampler in 1955 called I Like Jazz. It cost only one dollar, which I could only just afford. Arthur may have bought the same record at around the same time, or maybe he didn't, but he picked up the jazz bug just a few years earlier than I did. He was nine when he started listening and he doesn't just like jazz, he loves it.

Over the years Arthur has celebrated the way jazz is best created in his photographs, in the often spontaneous and improvisational nature of some of his finest work. Arthur can put a camera on a tripod, but often his best in-between-takes kind of photographs have the improvisational feel of a great saxophonist in action, when you don't exactly know what is going to come next or where he will go with his next chorus. The saxophonist will play off of something the drummer or pianist does, something unexpected and Arthur will play off something one of his models might do - a gesture, a tilt of the head, something spontaneous that makes for a more exciting photograph.

His love of music often creeps into his carefully stylized fashion photographs. One of my favorites is one he took of Christy Turlington and Naomi Campbell in 1991. The setting is a hotel bedroom in New Orleans. The girls are beautifully attired in black lace, lounging on a large bed. Christy is attempting to play a soprano saxophone. Naomi is pretending to read some sheet music. There is sheet music scattered around the girls. On either side of the bed, partially in view, are nightstands with lamps, a telephone, a beer bottle, and each has a small photograph; one of Dexter Gordon on the S/S Norway and the other of George Benson looking sharp on a Harlem street corner. When Arthur uses a jazz musician in one of his photographs, they always look sharp.

For twenty years Shelley Shier and I produced The Floating Jazz Festival. From 1983 until 2002 we handpicked the finest jazz musicians, assembled them on an ocean liner and once or twice a year sailed around the Caribbean or across the Atlantic. In 1988 we had Dizzy Gillespie, Clark Terry, Illinois Jacquet, Benny Carter, Arnett Cobb, Buddy Tate, and many more. Arthur had been given an assignment by Italian Vogue and wanted to come on board to do a fashion shoot combining beautifully attired models with jazz musicians. What Arthur didn't know was that we had a surprise guest, his all time favorite, Dexter Gordon, and as fate would have it, it was possibly the last time Dexter performed in public. Arthur got to do his fashion shoot while hanging with Dexter, using him in some photographs that were later published in magazines. In the process Arthur created a short film about his idol, Dexter On Vacation. It was on this voyage that Arthur also met Illinois Jacquet.

In 1990, Illinois Jacquet was back on board and so was Arthur with all his cameras loaded. That year he not only filmed Illinois and his big band for the movie, Texas Tenor: The Illinois Jacquet Story, but he created many wonderful photographs that were featured in French Glamour. This time the musicians featured included Illinois, Milt Hinton, Clark Terry, Doc Cheatham, Johnny Grimes,

Cecil Payne, Al Grey, many members of the Jacquet band, and Dorothy Donegan, the irrepressible and photogenic super pianist. In 1992 Arthur and the crew were back on board again with Dizzy, Jon Faddis, Al Grey, Clark Terry, and John Grimes to produce feature articles for German and Italian Vogue, and to begin work on a documentary about Dorothy which, regrettably, remains unfinished.

Jazz photography is all about skill and access. You must have both. Arthur has a unique kind of access, the access afforded by the knowledge of his subjects. And he has the skill that comes from his many years taking photographs for prestigious, often glamorous magazines, advertising campaigns, and elegant books, such as the one you are holding. I have often wondered, what is a jazz photographer? I once took a photo of Dizzy Gillespie and James Moody boarding the S/S Norway. To someone who doesn't recognize these two men, it is just a picture of two old guys smiling at a camera as they walk up a gangway. But to the editor and many of the readers of JazzTimes, when they saw it all those years ago, it was a great jazz photograph. I would argue that when Arthur has a jazz musician near the lens of his camera, whatever pops into that camera is a jazz photograph, not only because of the subject matter but because of the way Arthur works, how he thinks about his subjects, how he improvises with his camera as much as possible, and because of the spirit in which it was taken.

Just as Arthur broke new ground in the 70s when he took his models outside and photographed them in natural light while encouraging them to move, he took jazz musicians outside their natural settings of smoky clubs and concert halls. He put them on the streets of Harlem, in front of the clubs, on the decks of ocean liners, playing on tennis courts, in the middle of cobblestoned Crosby Street next to his studio, or bathed in natural light in his studio. Because of his use of natural light, if the musicians moved a little he could move with them and improvise with his camera, just as he did with the girls.

Arthur is unique among great photographers. He specializes in fashion but enjoys photographing jazz musicians at work, at play, or in their everyday life. He has taken thousands of jazz photographs, he is a fan of jazz, and even has a grand piano, a trumpet or two, and maybe a drum set in the closet. I have known many exceptional photographers who love jazz but none who can play it until I met Arthur. One of the reasons he is so good with jazz musicians is because he is one. Though he has never been a professional, he has played the trumpet and the cornet for years and while he has never been very good with the clarinet, in his dreams he is Sidney Bechet. Jazz permeates his studio, there are sagging shelves of CDs and one is always playing. And in between Vogue and other magazine shoots he has had musicians coming in and out of the studio snapping pictures all the while.

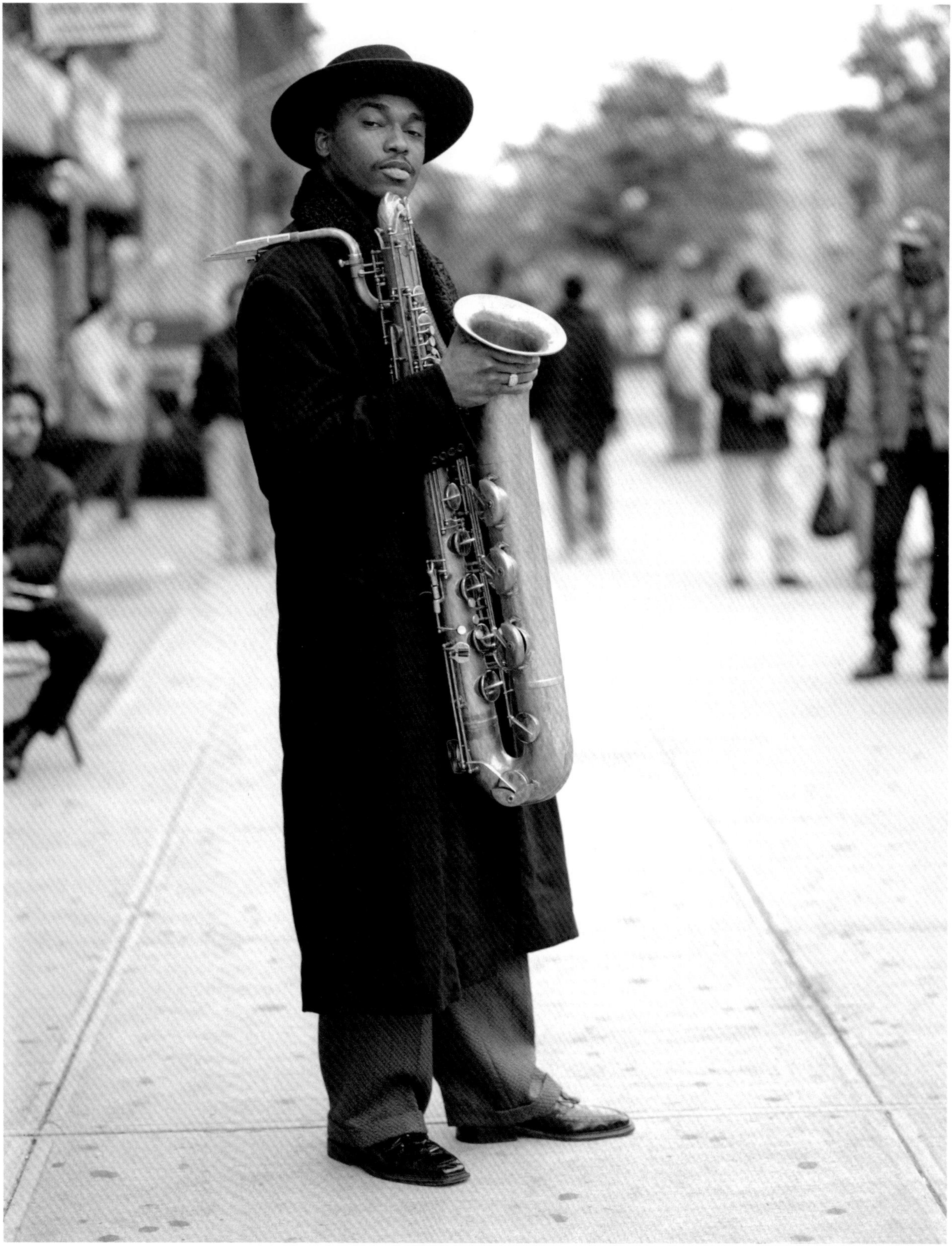

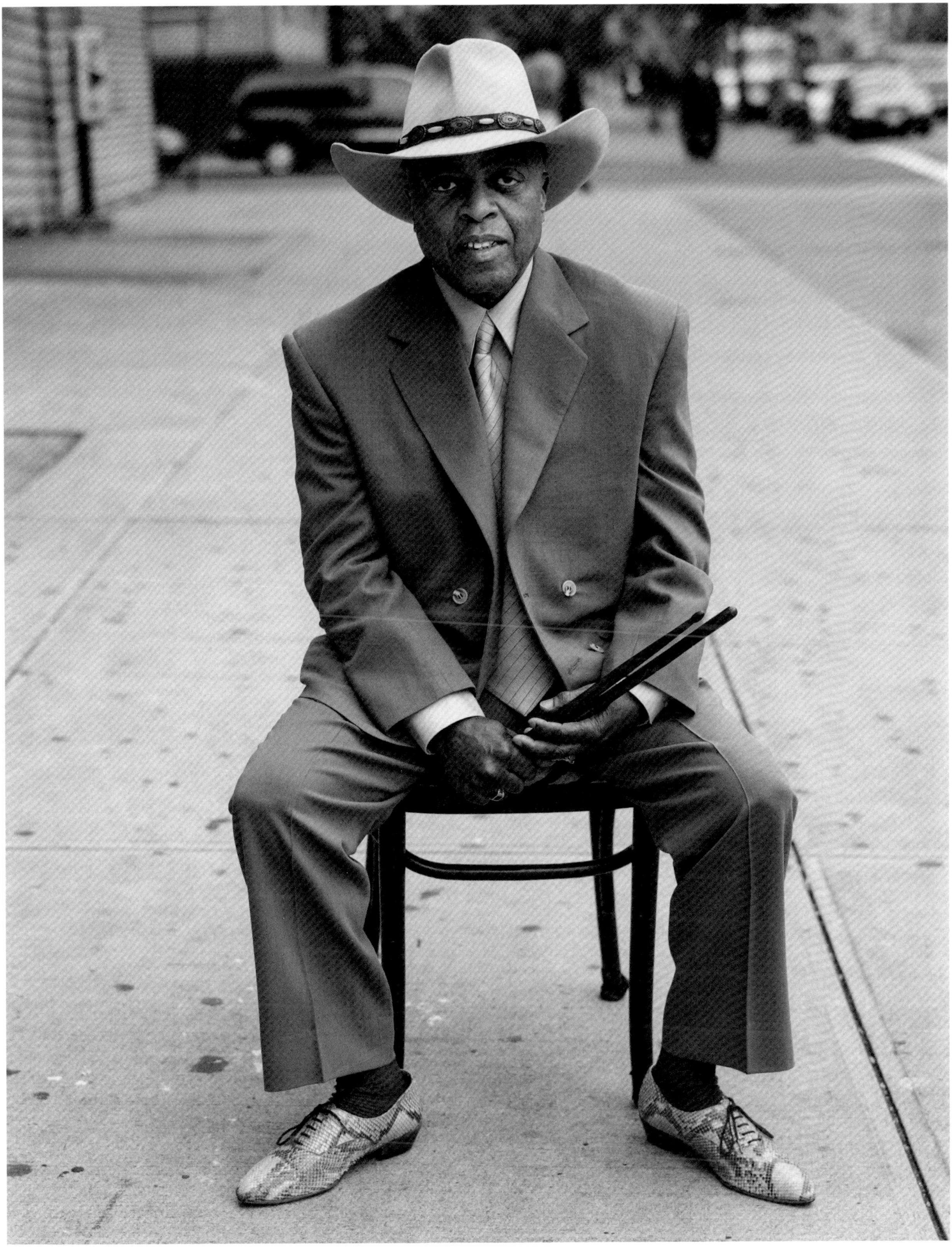

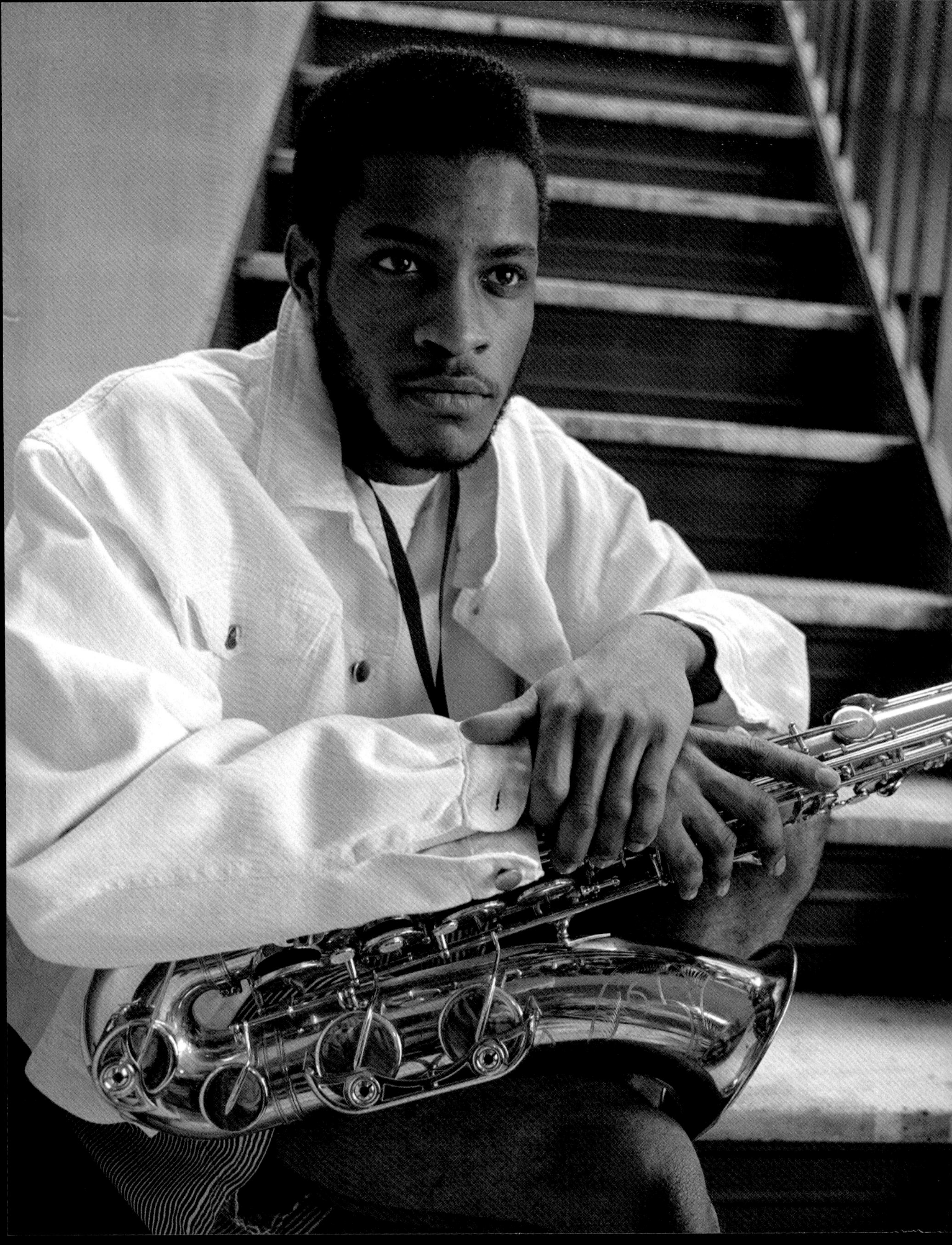

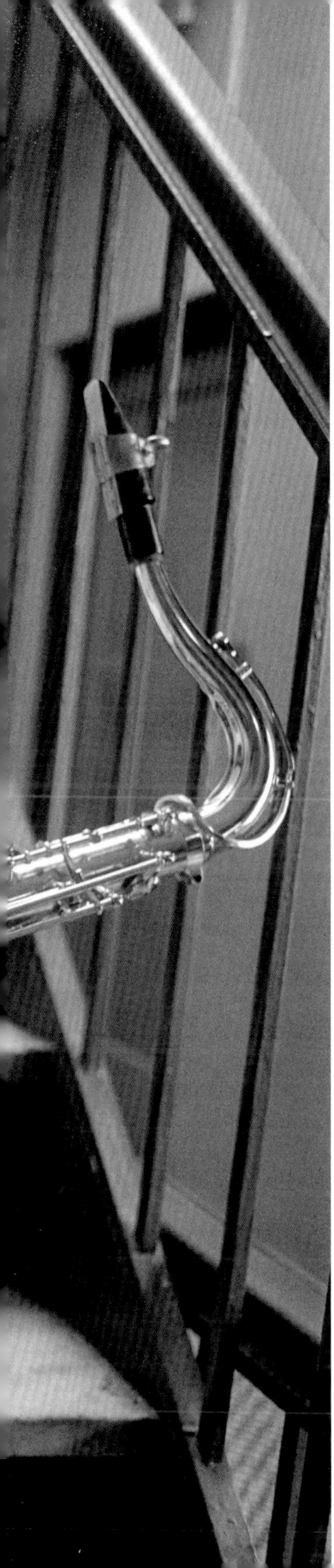

Walter Blanding
1992, Brooklyn, NY

(preceding pages)
James Carter
2000, New York City

Roy Haynes
2000, New York City

(following page)
Michael Bowie
1990, New York City

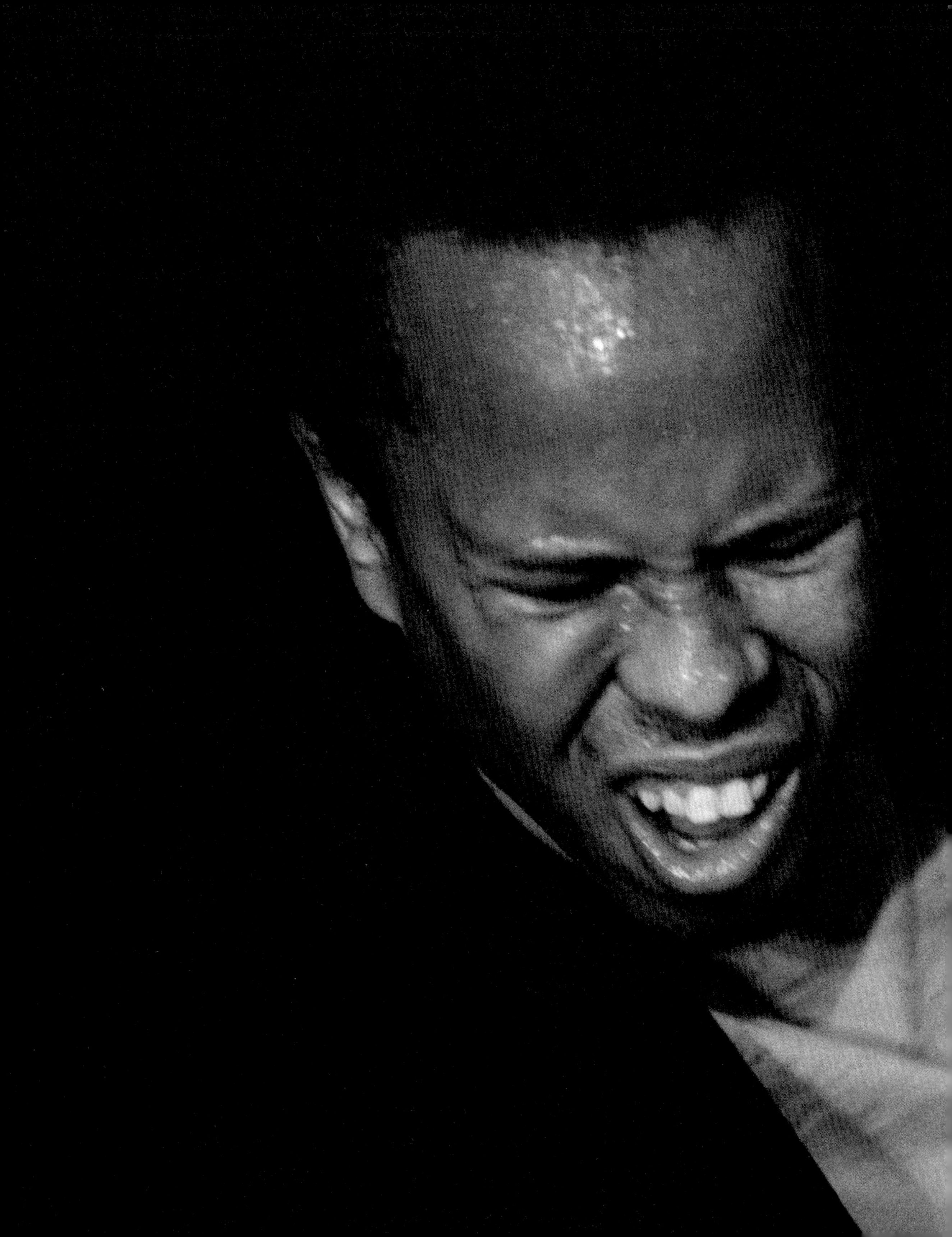

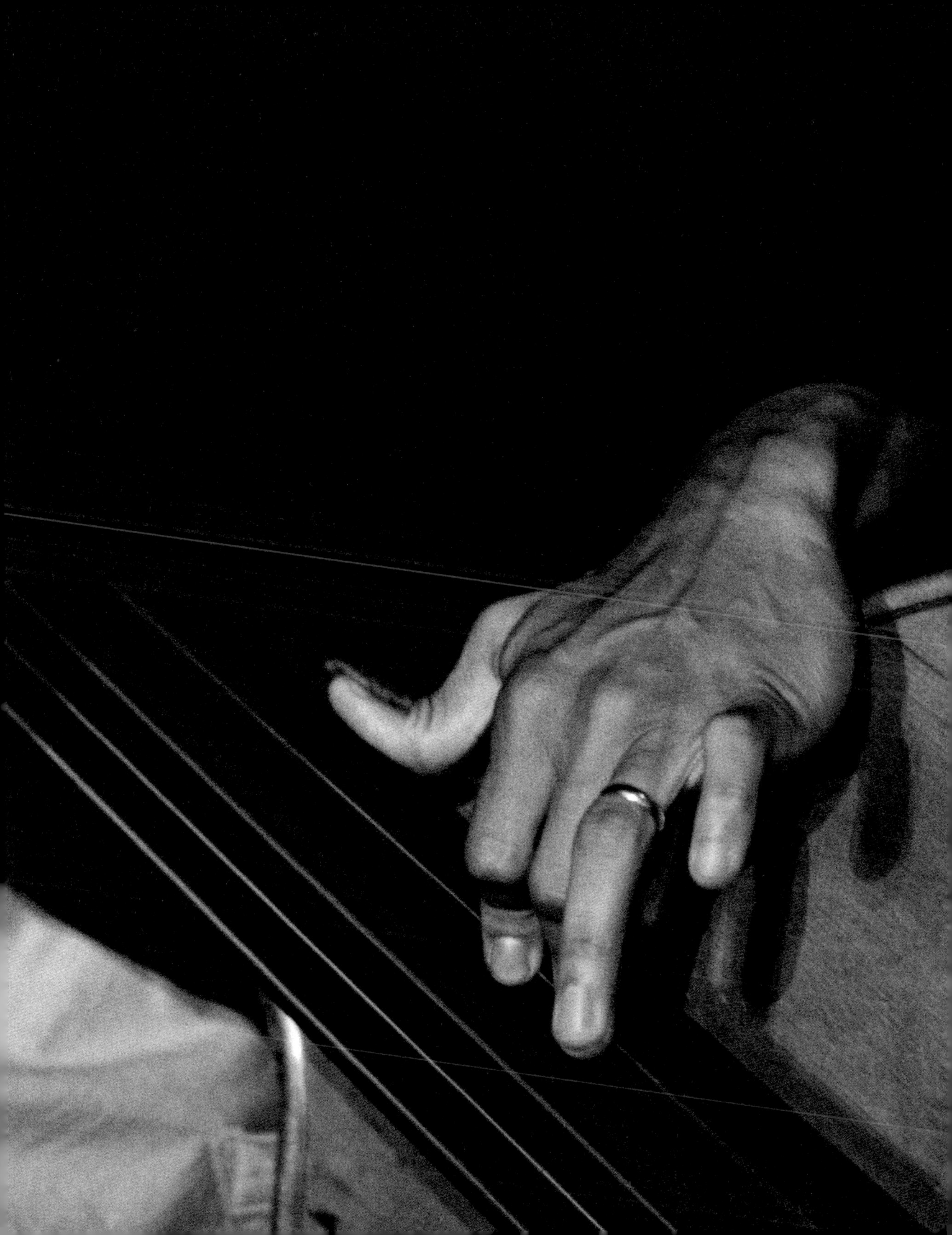

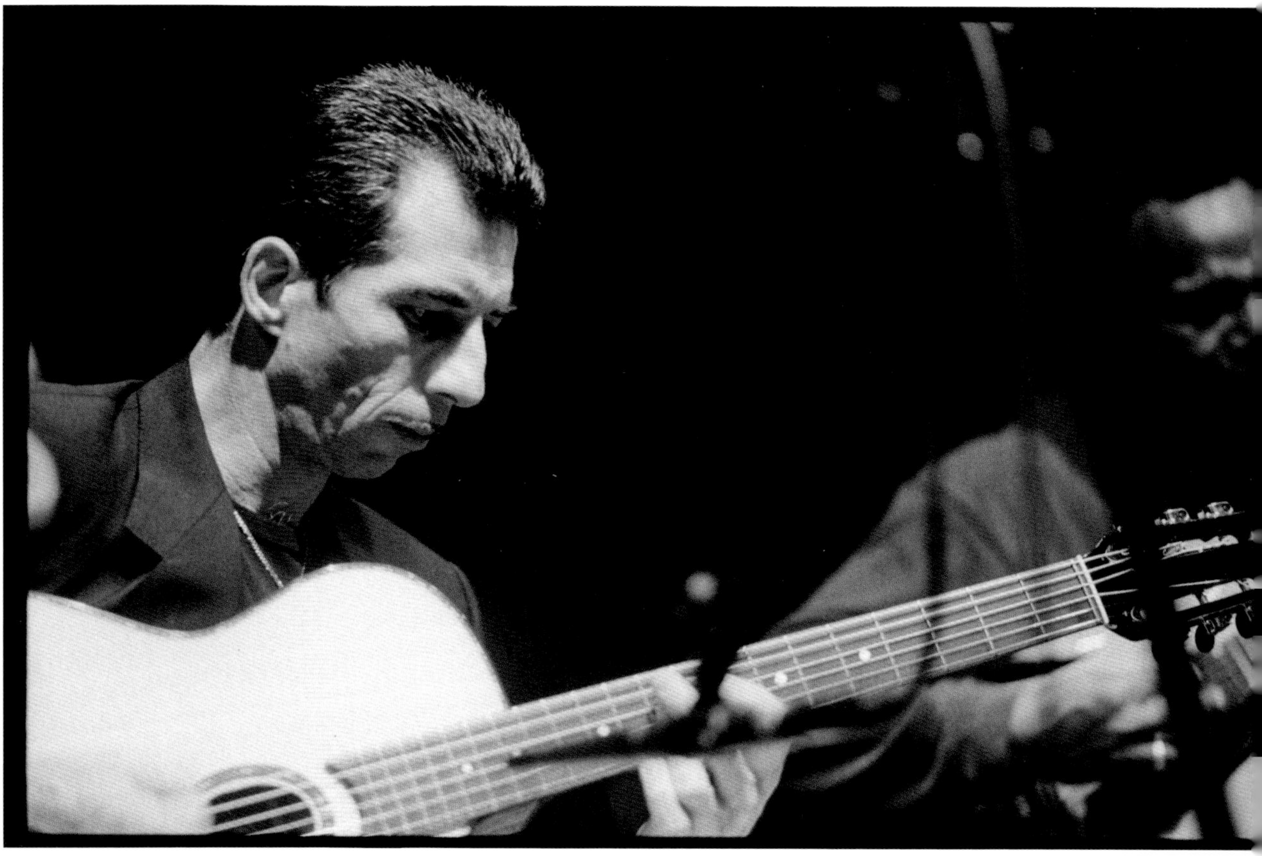

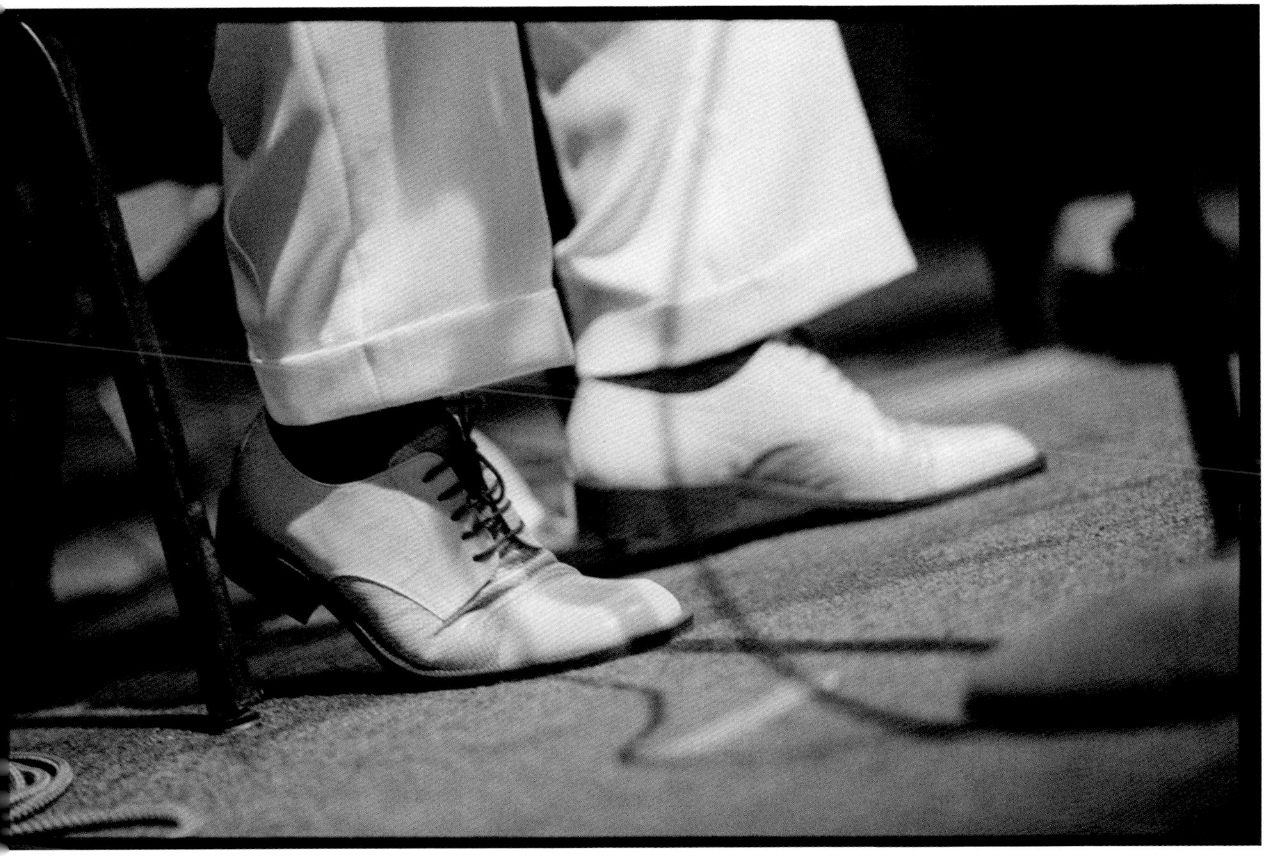

Angelo Debarre
2001, New York City

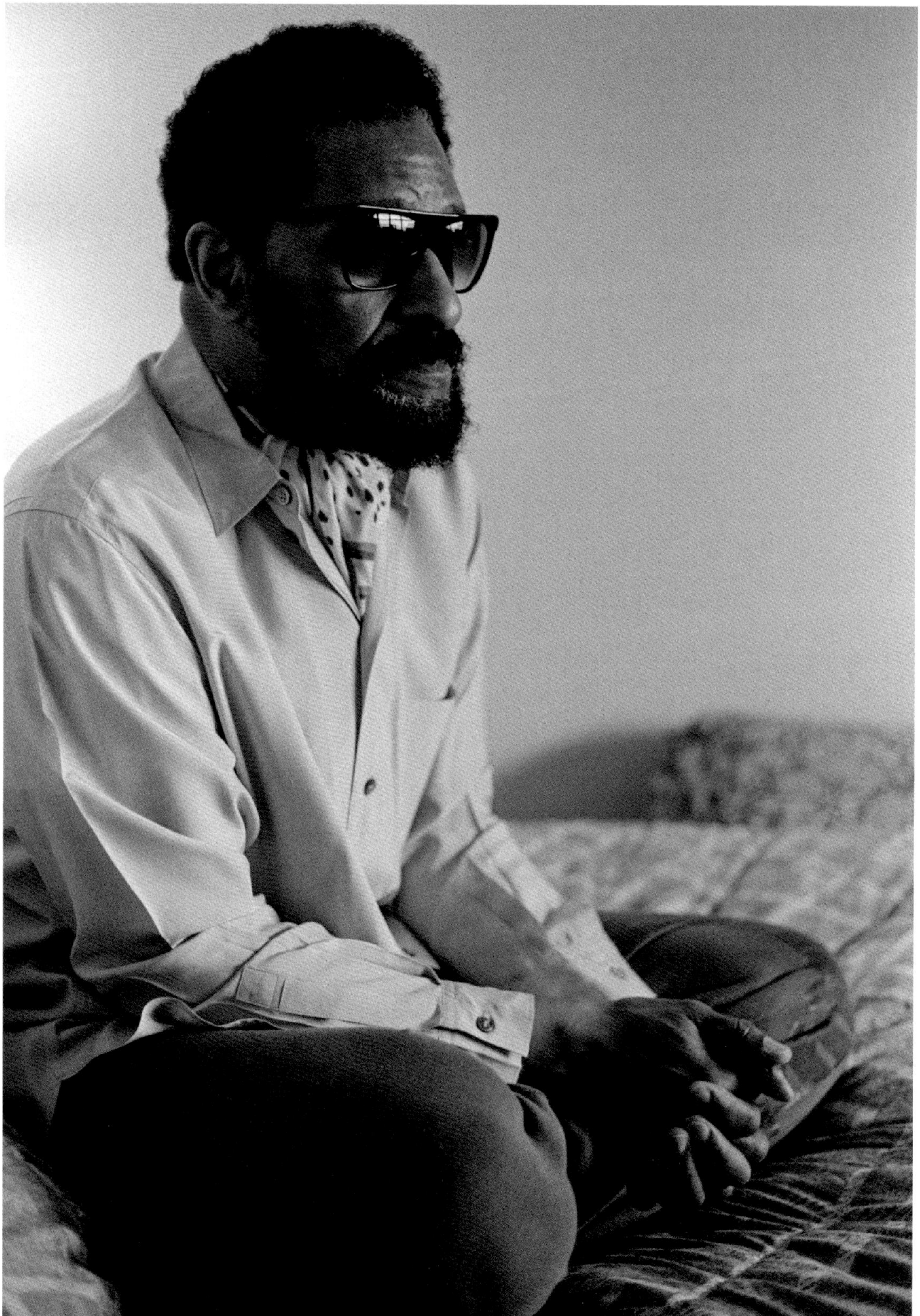

Sonny Rollins
1991, New York City

(following pages)
Dexter Gordon
1988, SS Norway

George Benson and Liya Kebede
2000, New York City

Milt Hinton and Jeny Howorth
1988, SS Norway

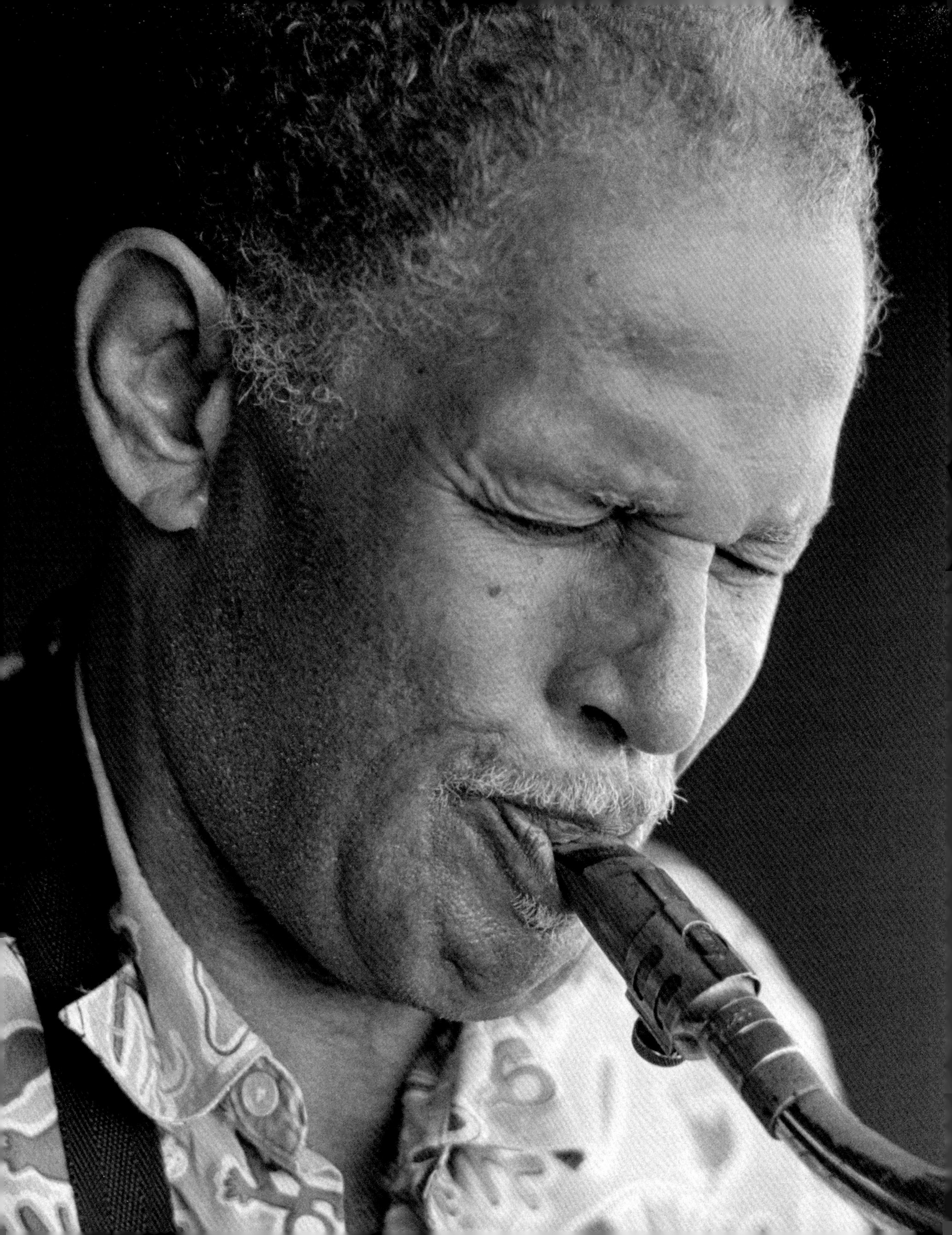

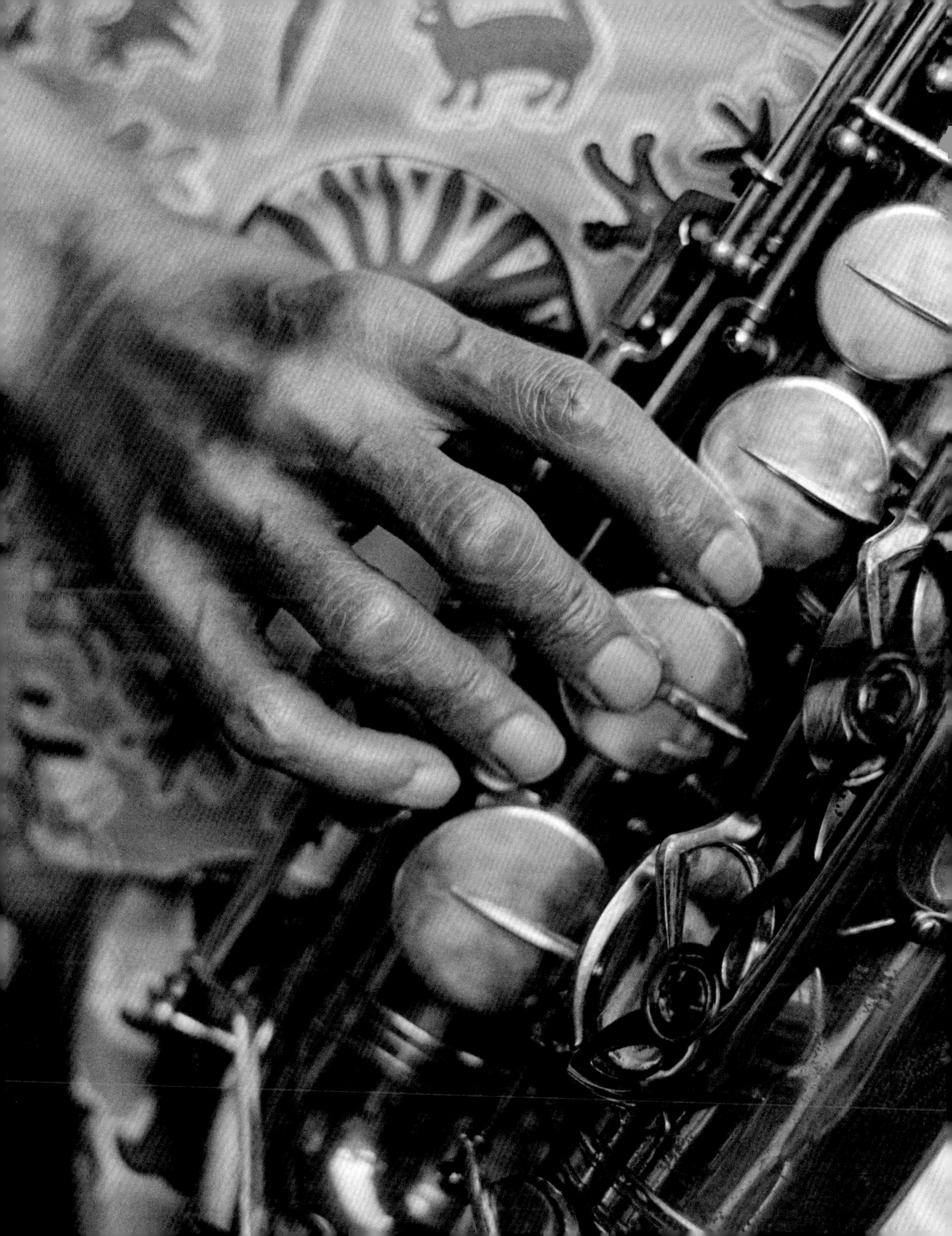

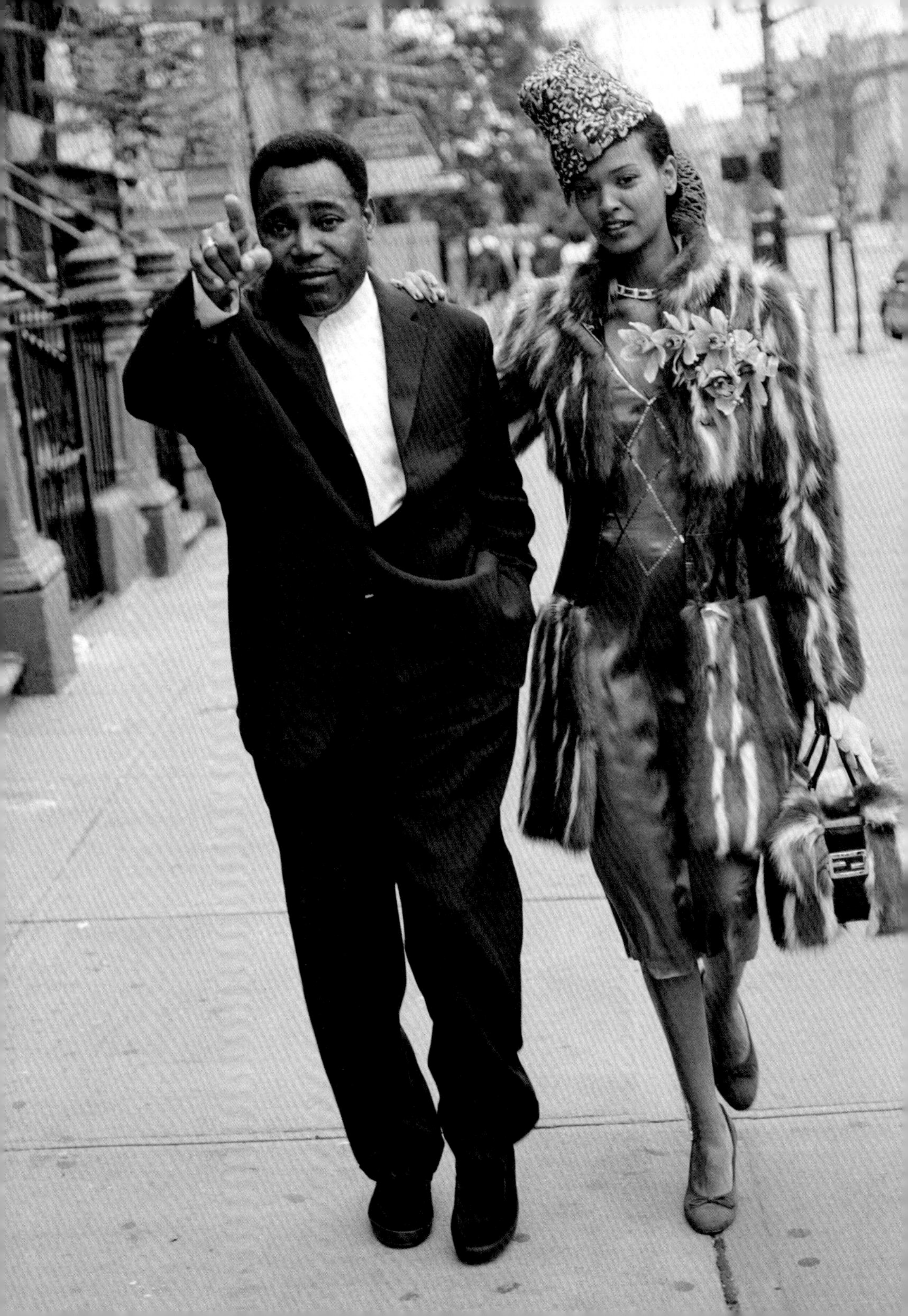

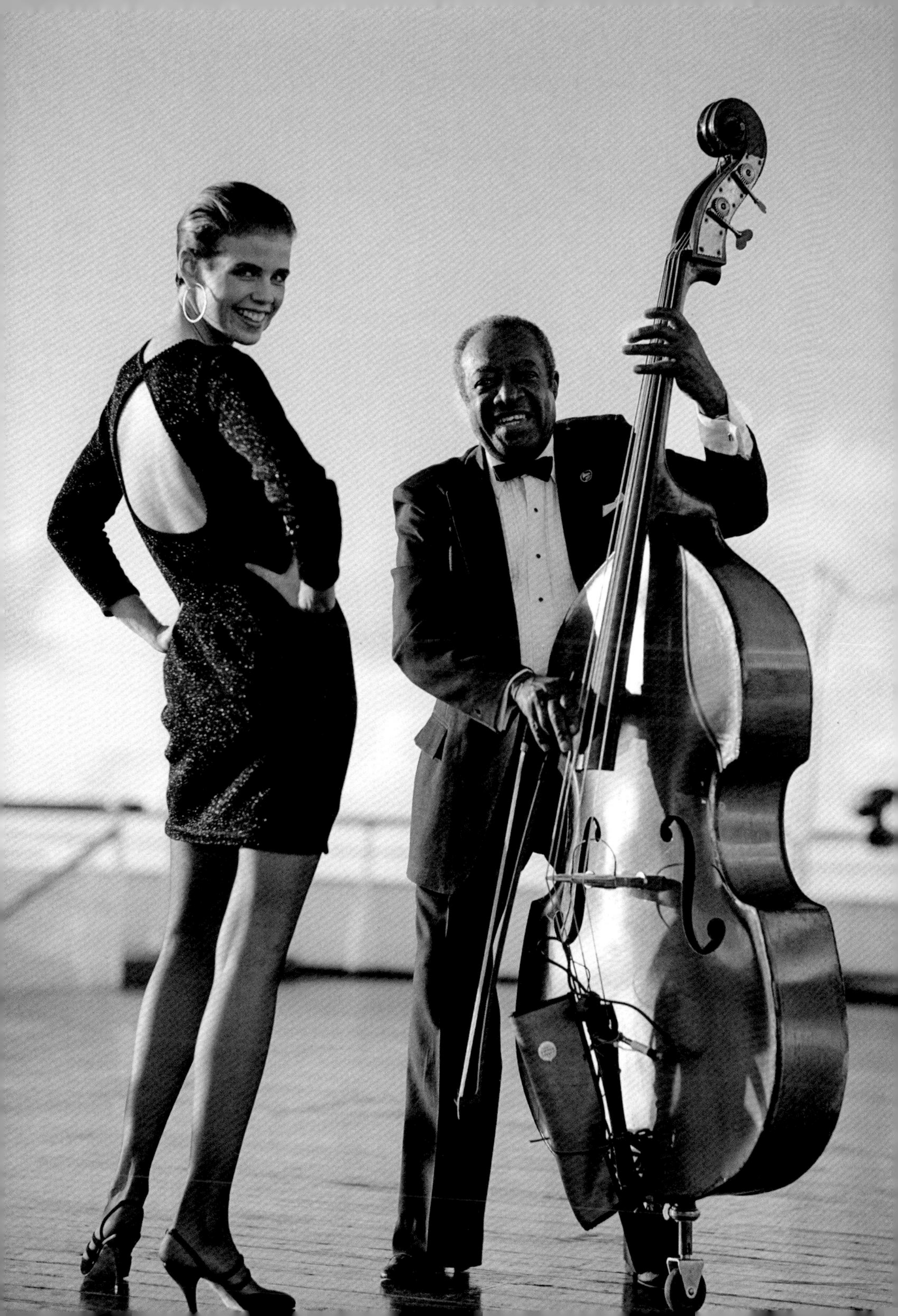

"Anytime, anywhere there was a piano Dorothy would sit down and play – at a concert hall, a church, or even a restaurant, like this picture. She loved to perform and she was such an amazing character – she wore a fake Chanel hat but real Chanel shoes, and she might have been the best female jazz pianist you've ever heard."

Dorothy Donegan
1991, New Orleans

(following pages)
Joshua Redman
1996, New York City

Cecil Payne
1990, New York City

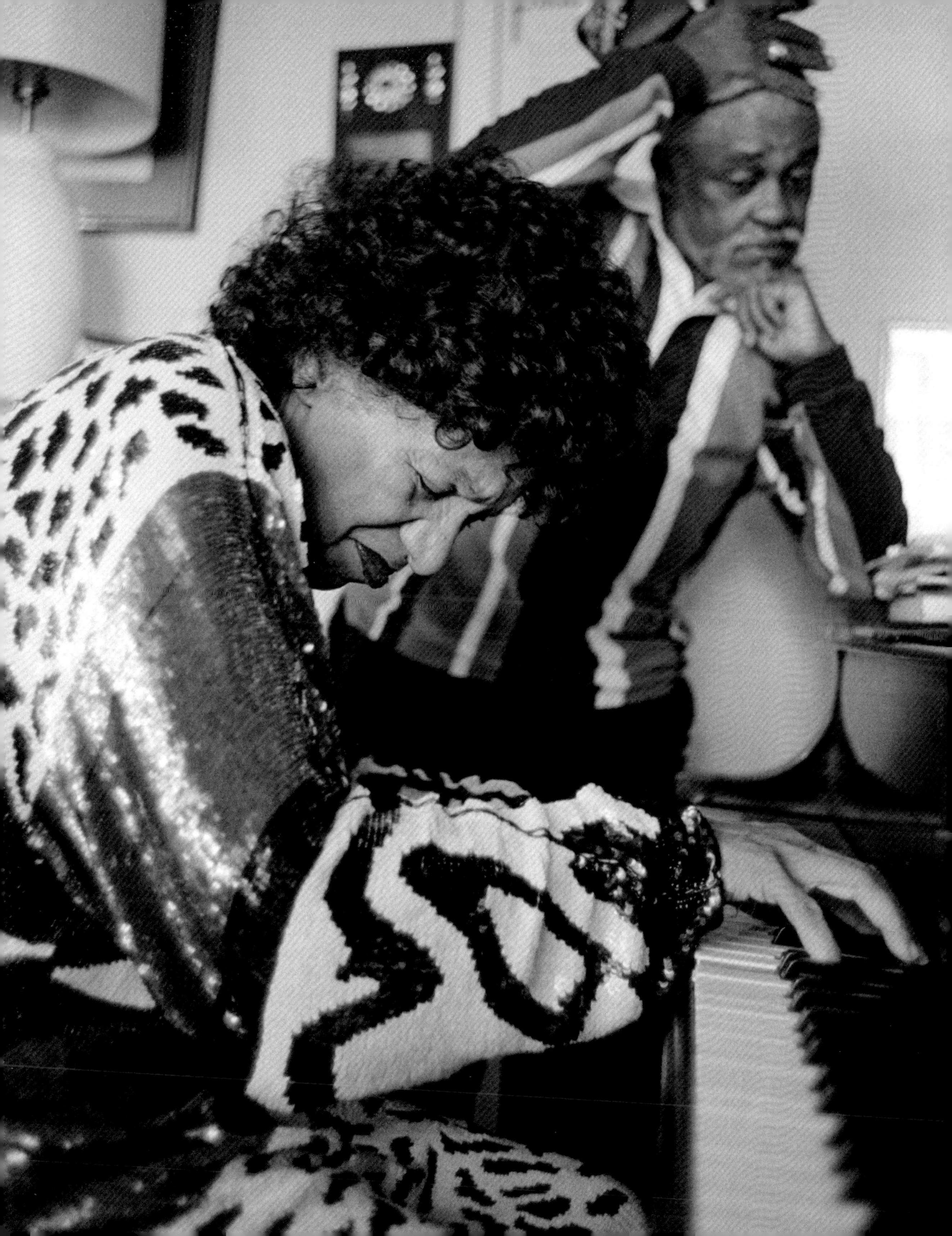

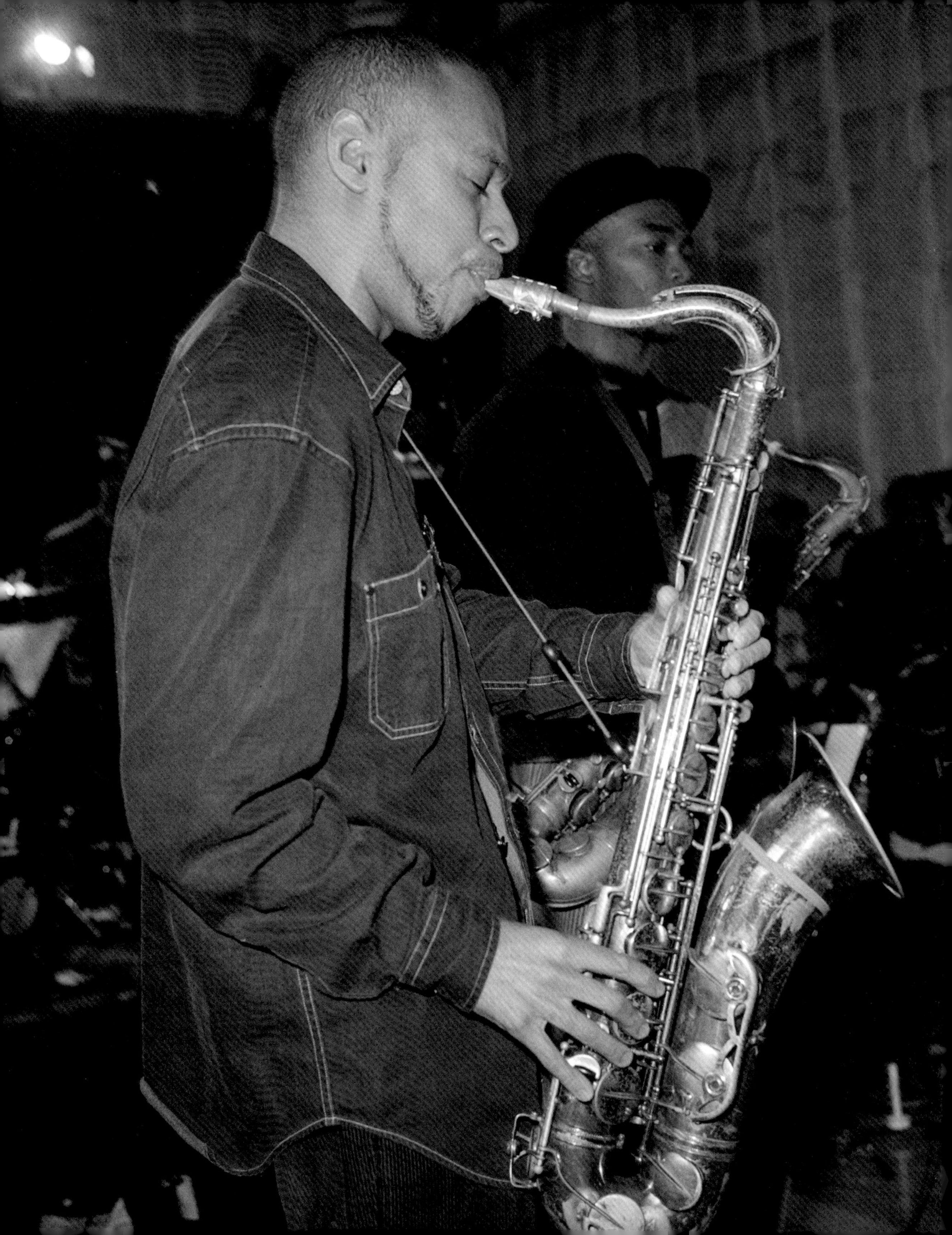

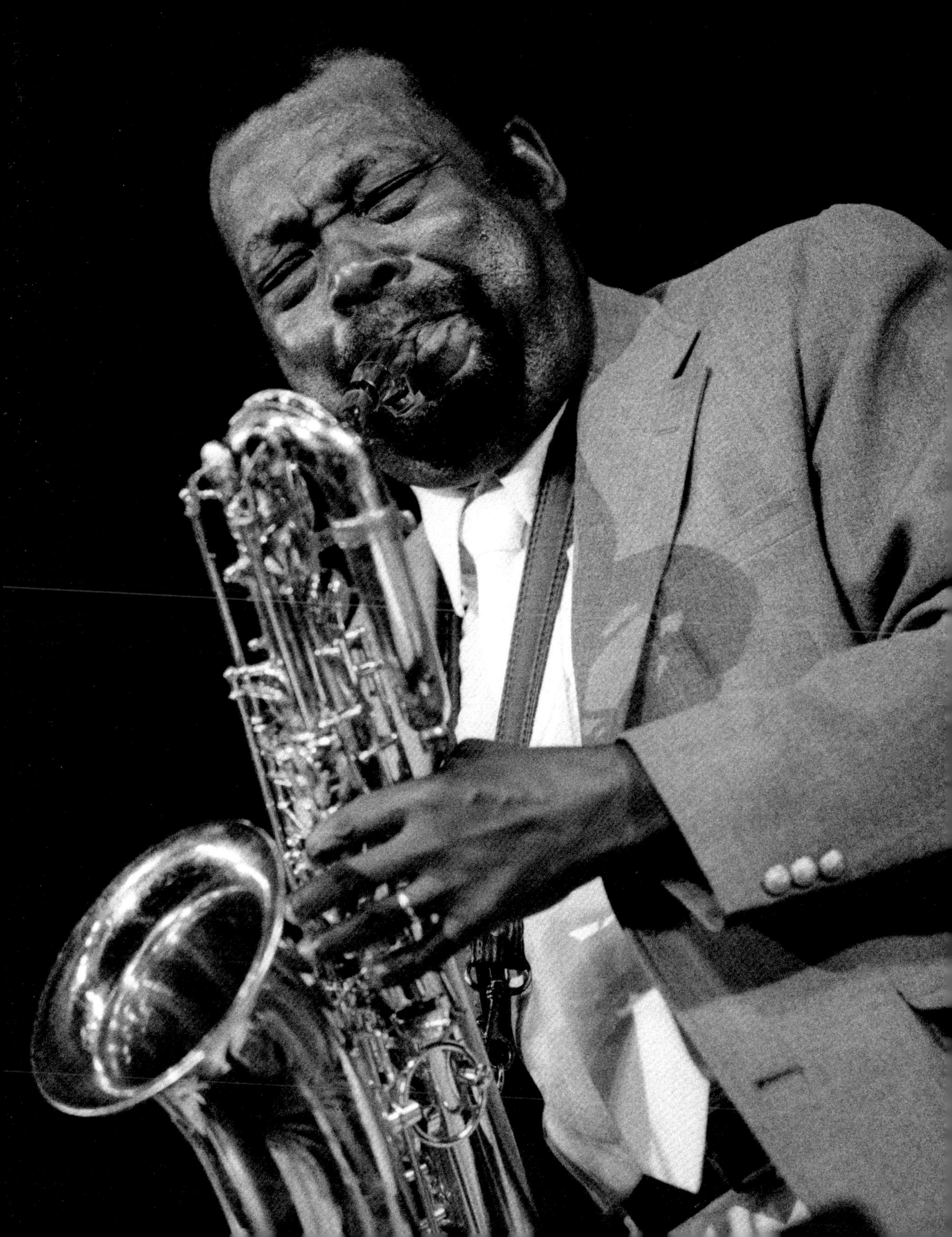

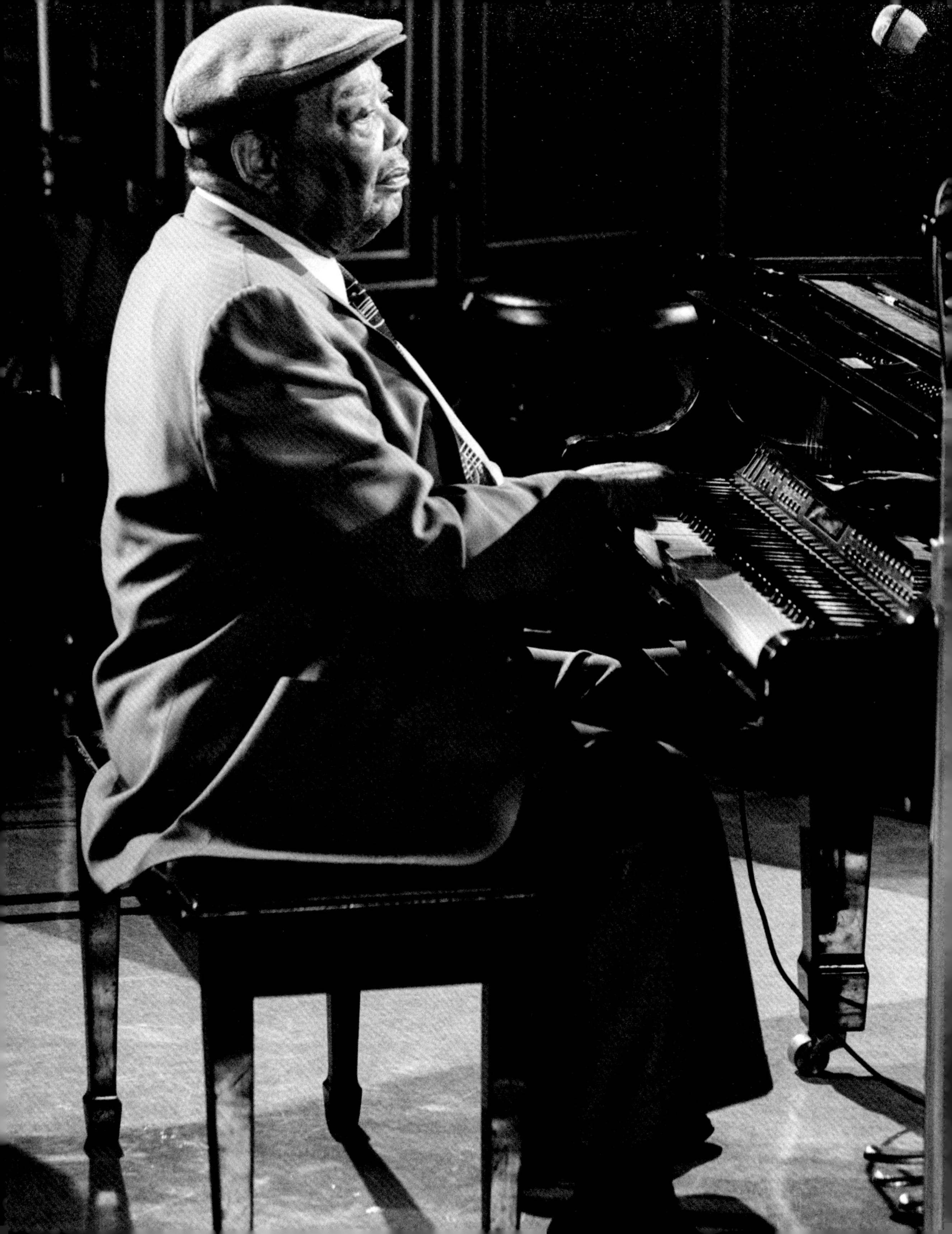

DEVELOPER, STOP BATH, FIXER & SWEAT

Jazz is what it looks like
when the quarter note
is an f-stop away,
when the shutter speed lays down
the bass line
and the conductor is not a man
in a three-piece pinstripe suit,
but the scat of light reflecting
off a brass instrument
glistening in a bead of sweat,
still visible from behind closed lids
concentrating only on the music.

These frames capture the frames
of horns carrying their players,
of bright metallic notes
and throats crooning to callused
fingertips
that dance up and up the down beat
between breaths
between lives and deaths
before and after velvet hurricanes
improvise *caul* and response
and spin spit and air back into gold.

When this visual griot,
this orchestra conductor of light
places his eye on the mouthpiece,
and wraps his heart around a box
built to capture souls,
the careful listener can hear the music
every time a jazz man shudders
or this man's shutter blinks.

--Frank X Walker

Jay McShann
1996, New York City

(following pages)
Pat Metheny
1992, New York City

Aaron Neville
2000, New York City

Don Byron
2000, New York City

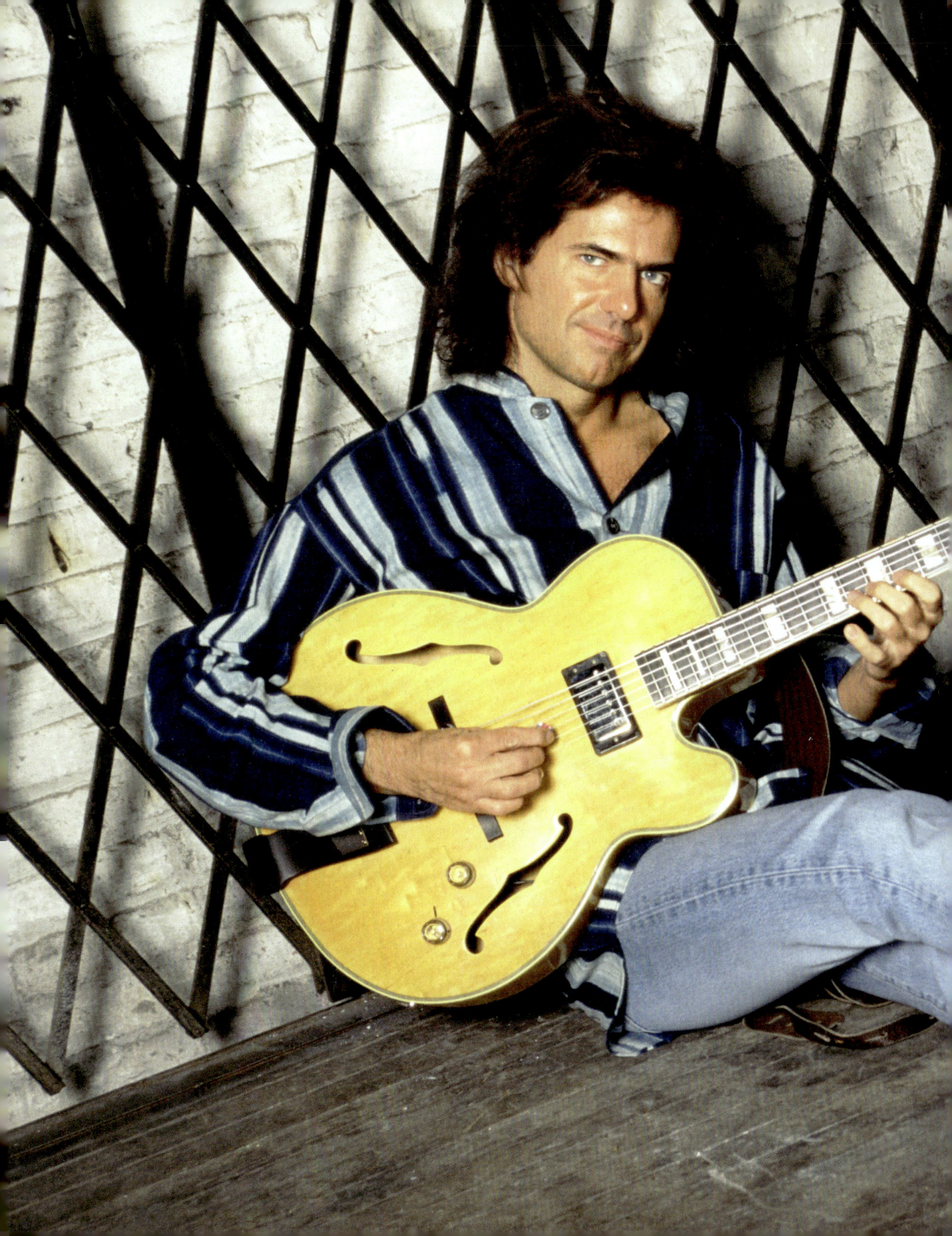

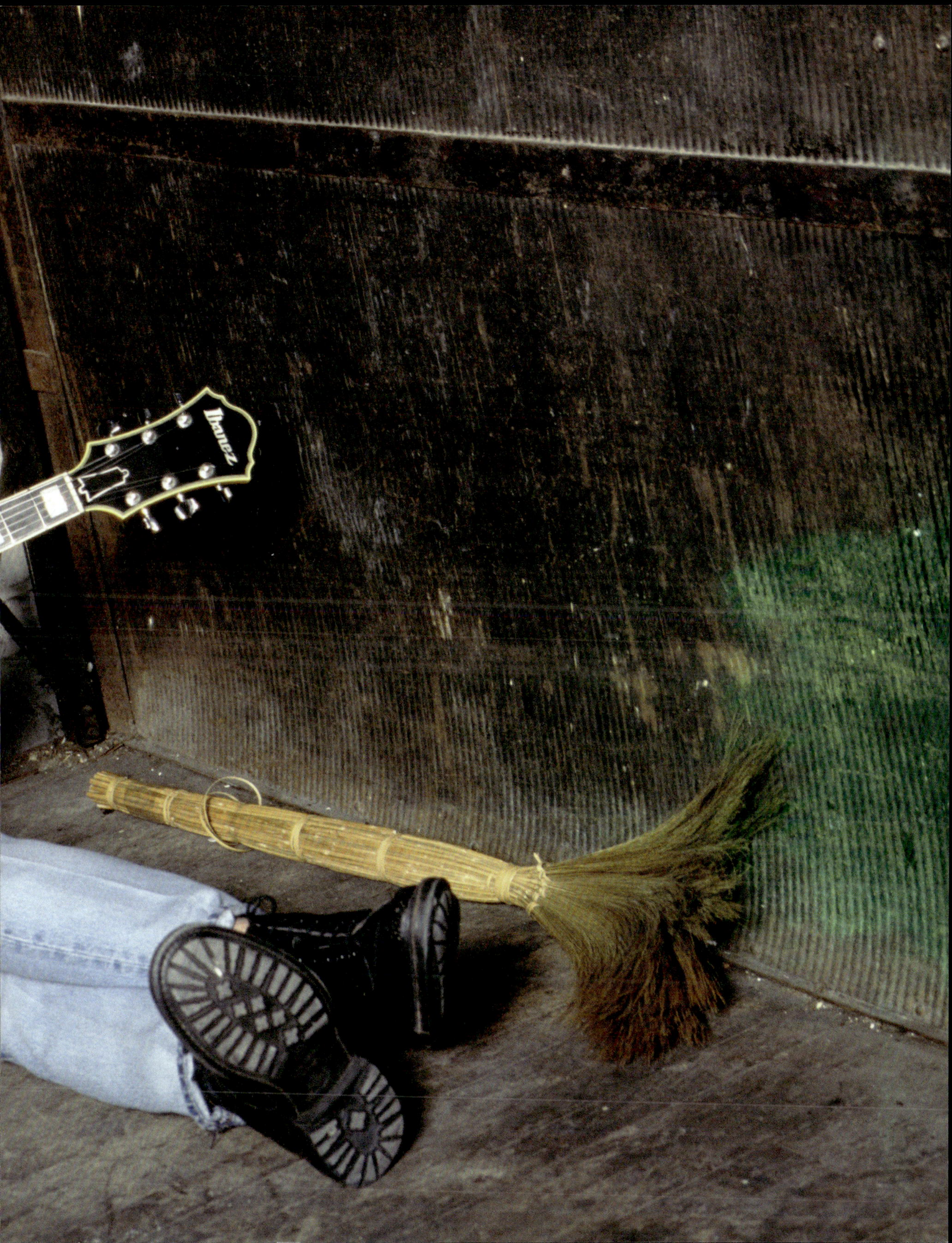

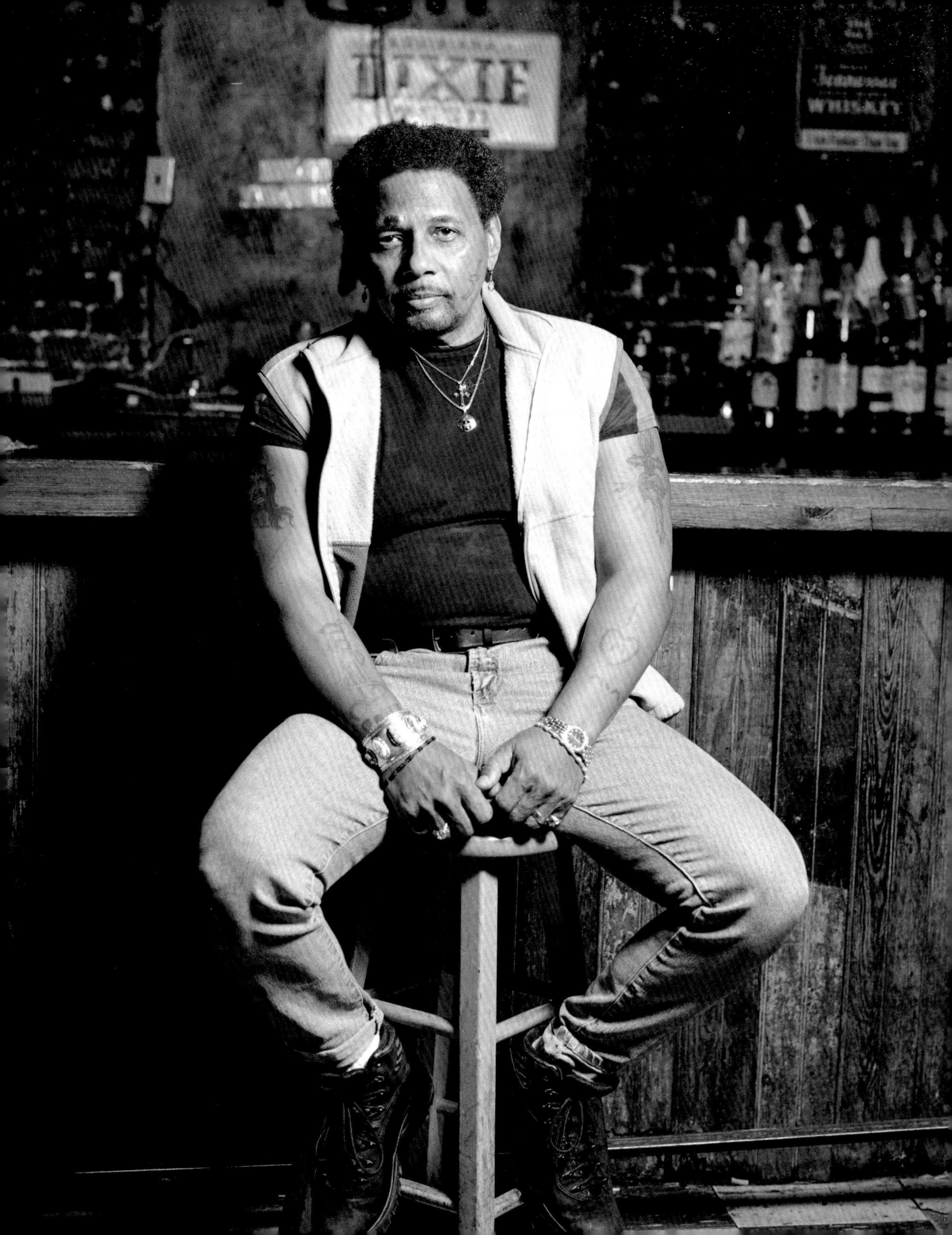
DIXIE

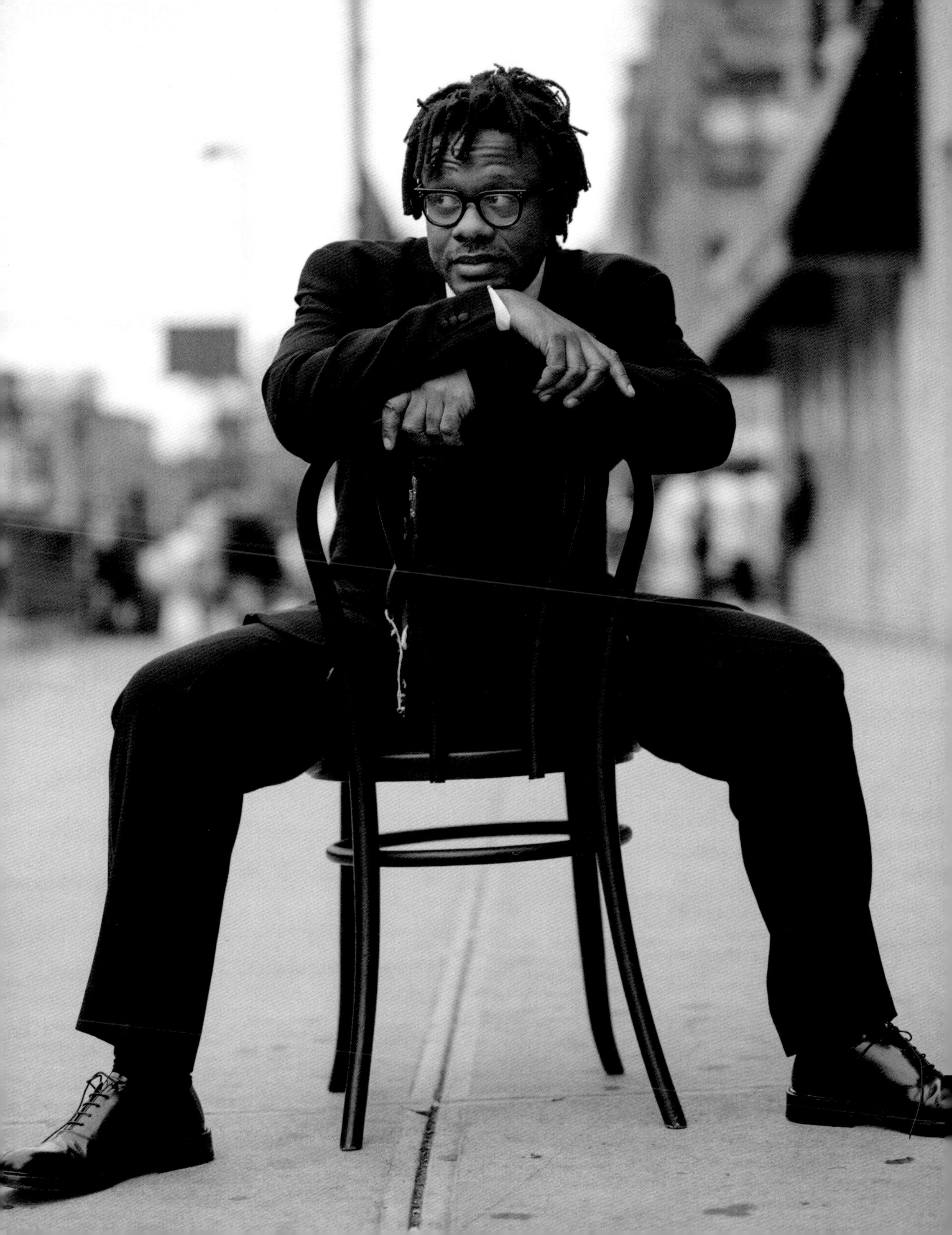

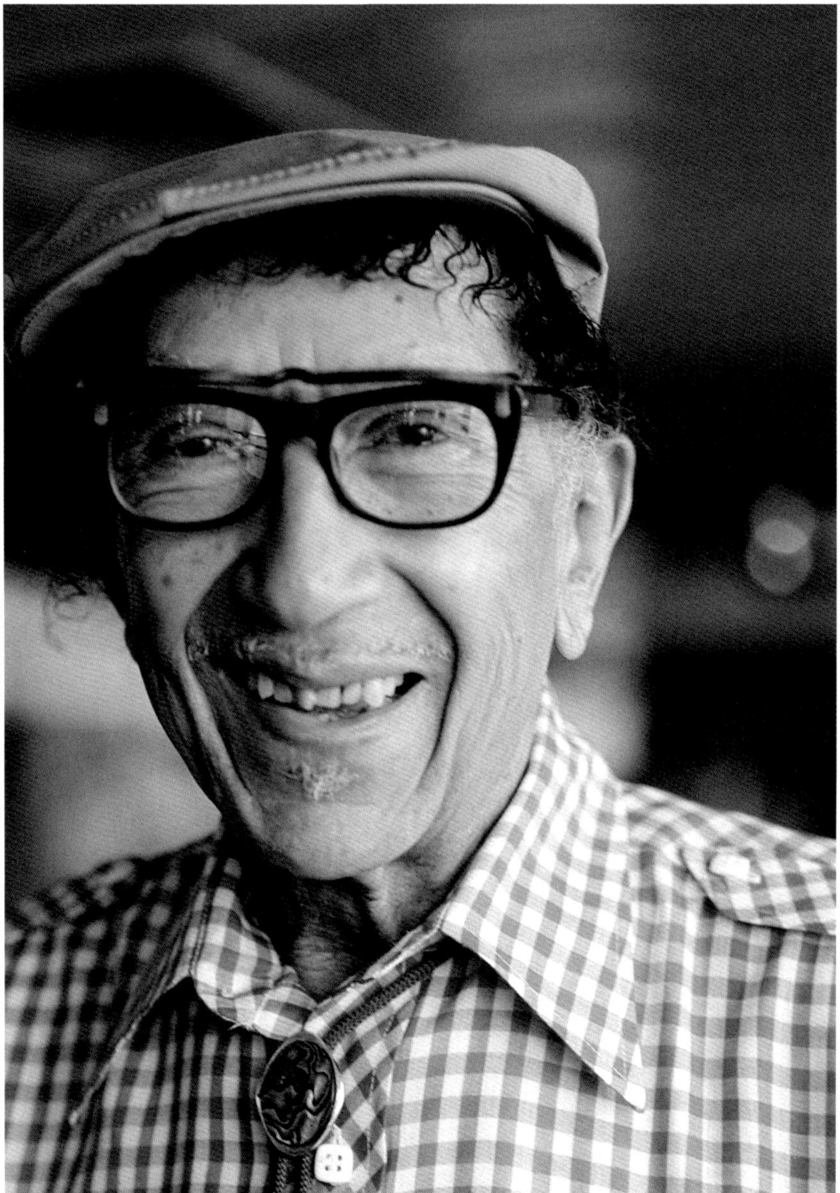

Doc Cheatham
1990, New York City

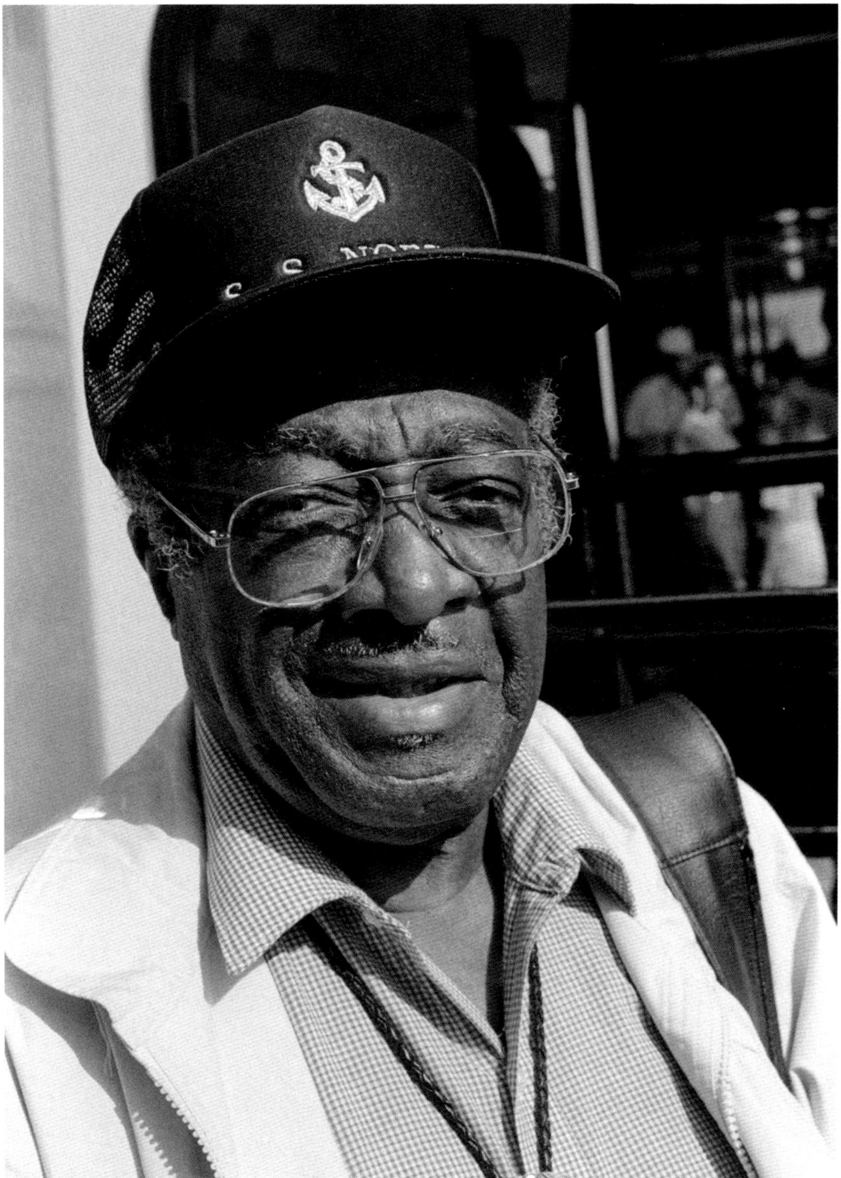

Milt Hinton
1988, New York City

Ornette Coleman
1988, New York City

(following pages)
Dizzy Gillespie and Jeny Howorth
1988, SS Norway

Thelonious Monk Jr.
New York City, 1998

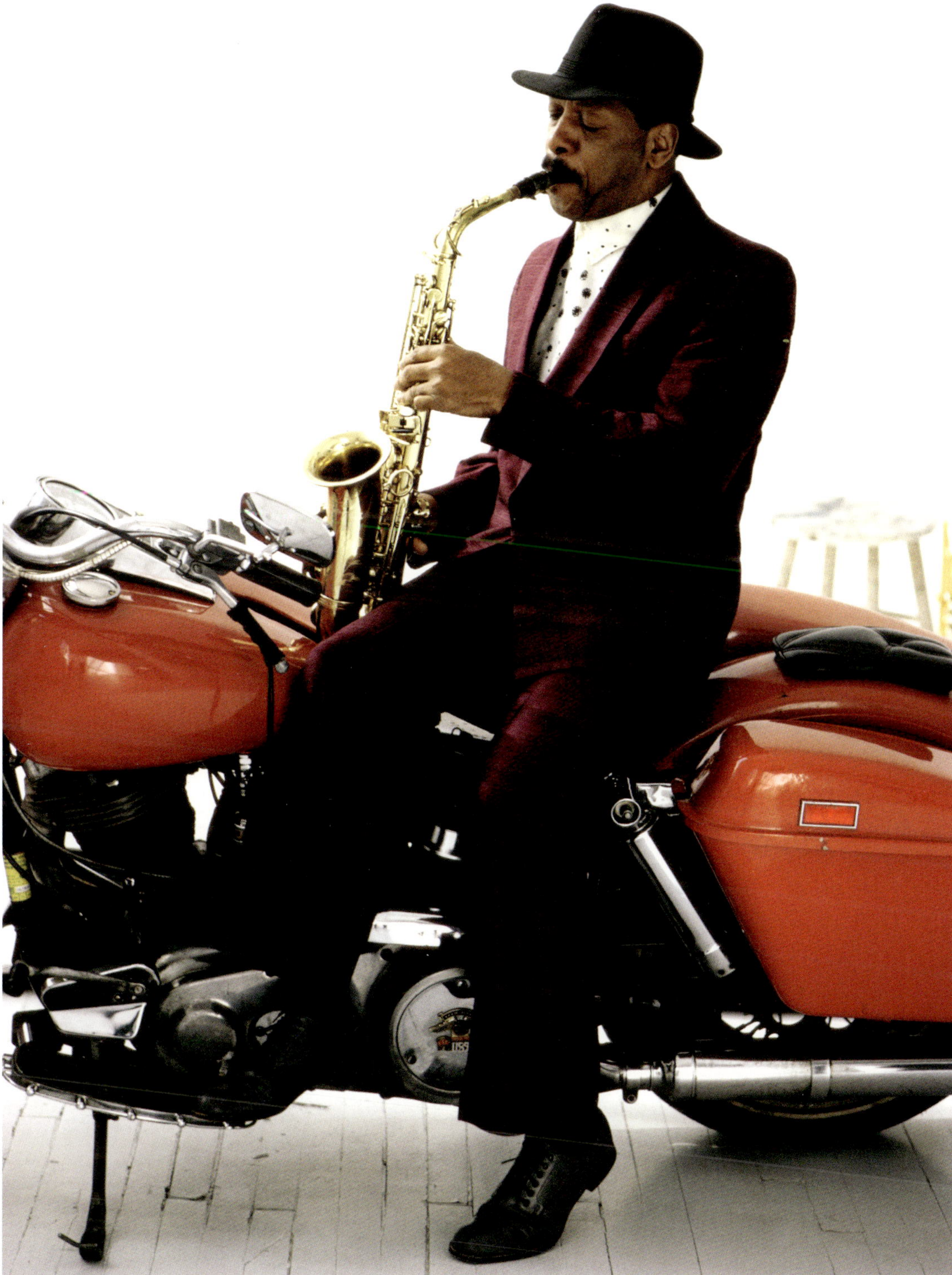

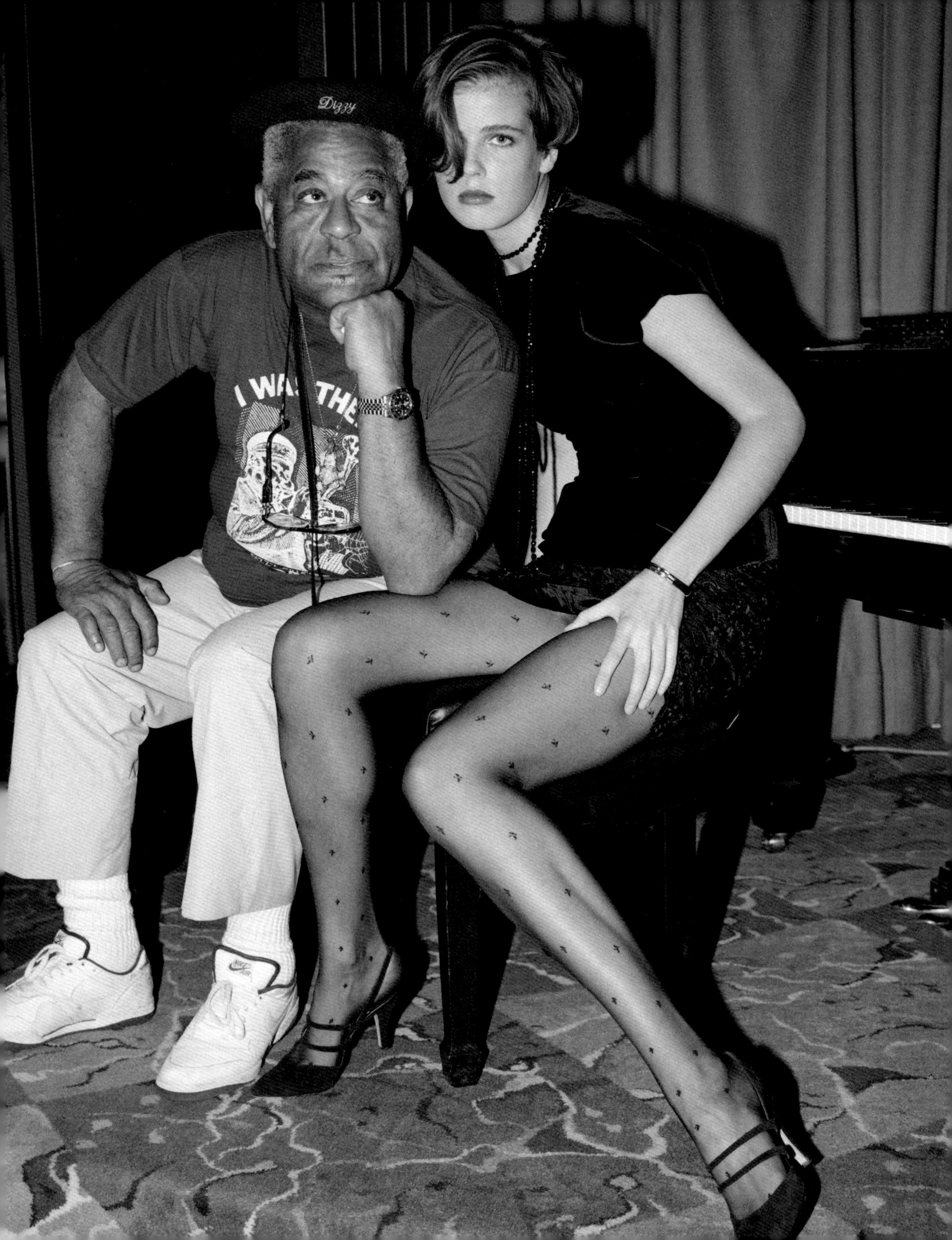
Dizzy

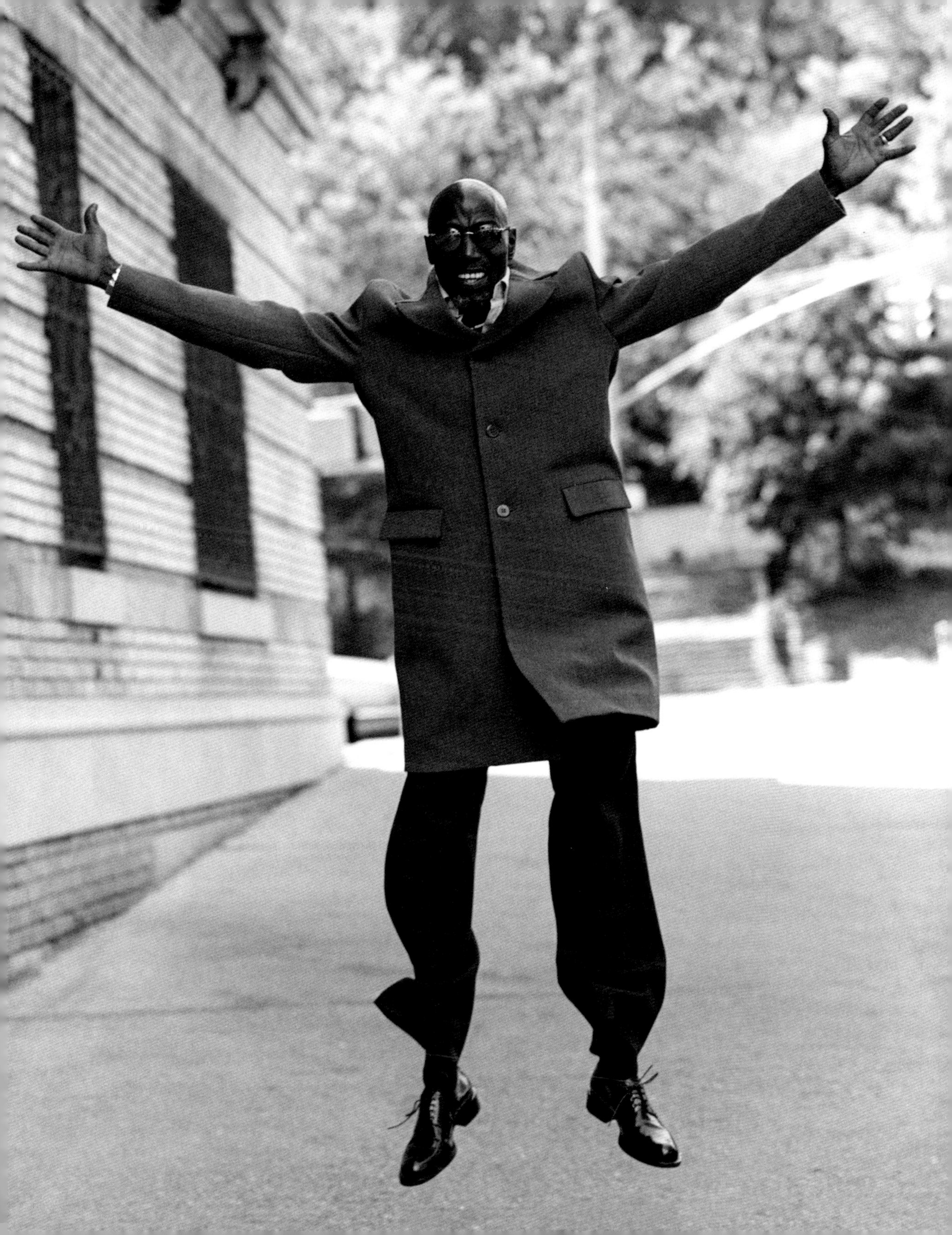

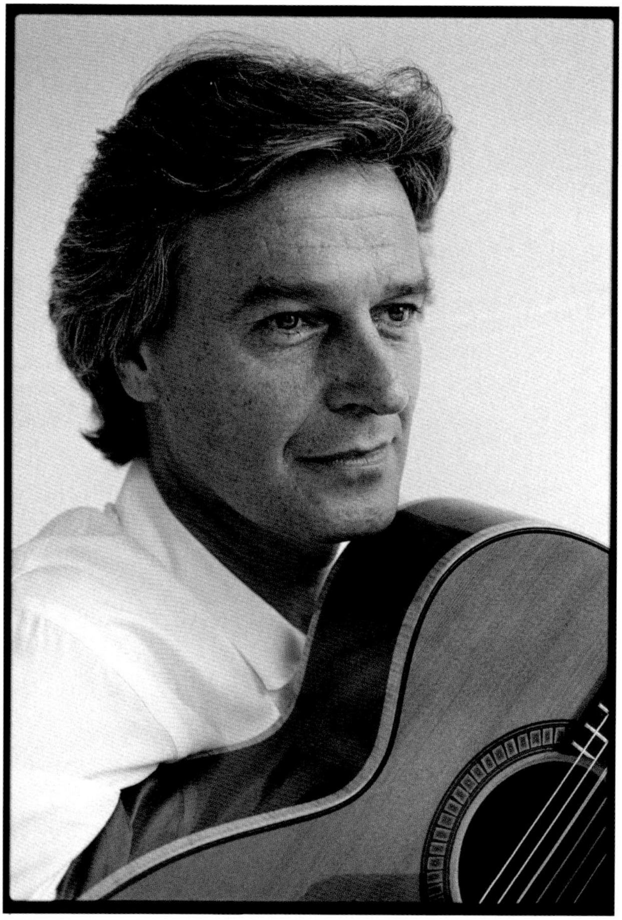

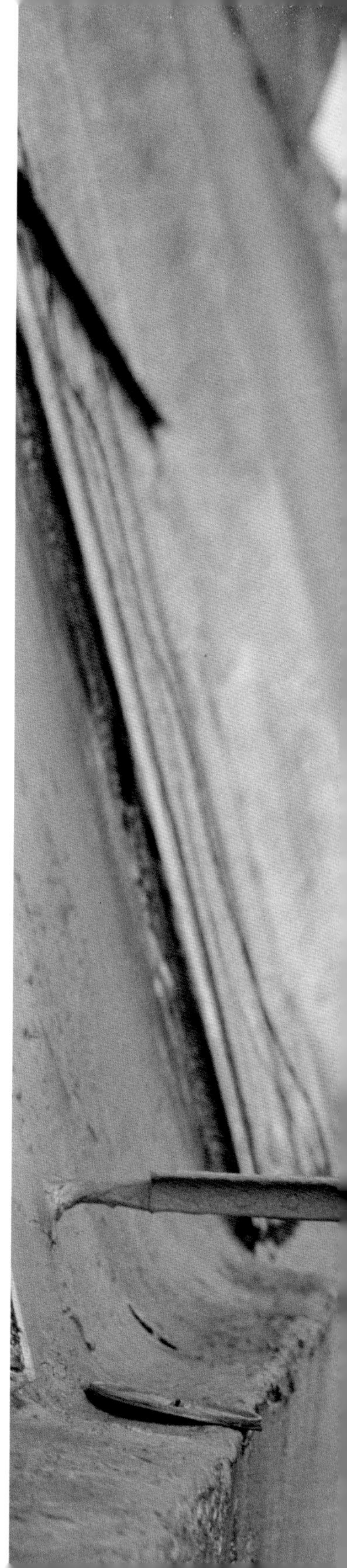

John McLaughlin
1989, New York City

John McLaughlin
1986, New York City

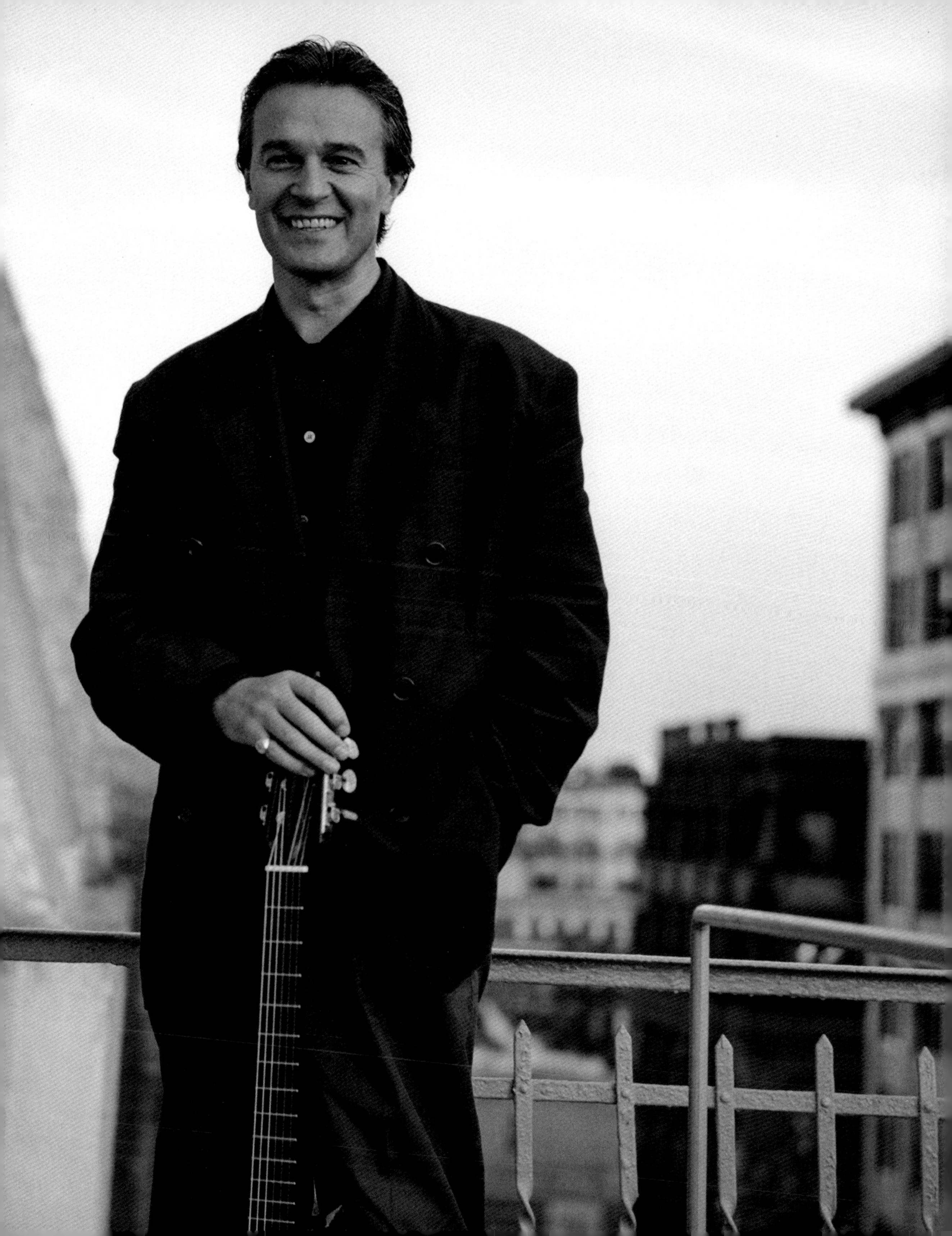

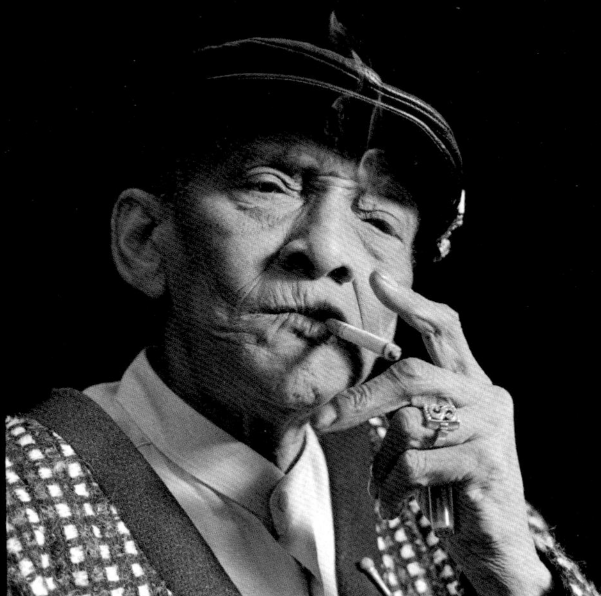

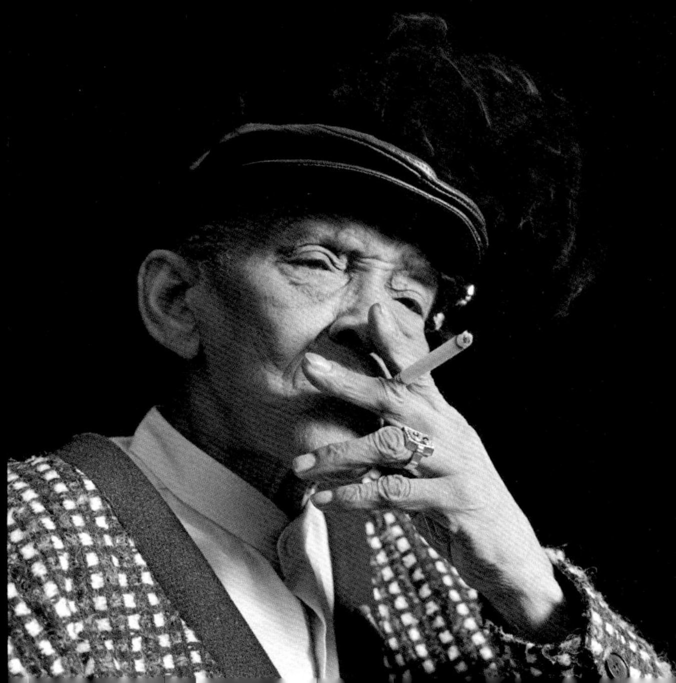

Jimmy Scott
1996, New York City

(following pages)
Jesse Davis
1991, New York City

Illinois Jacquet and Lionel Hampton
1991, New York City

Dexter Gordon and Clark Terry
1988, SS Norway

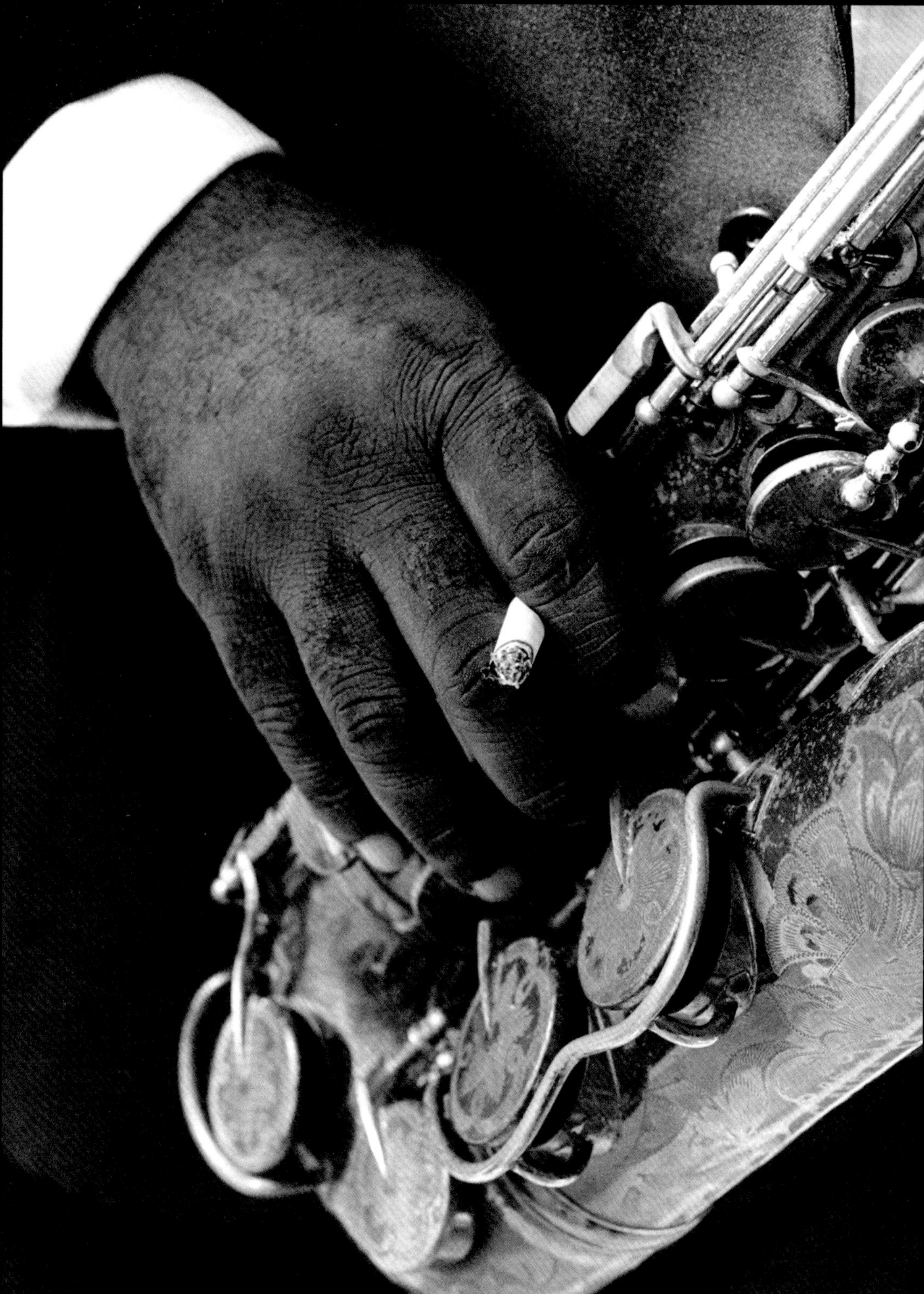

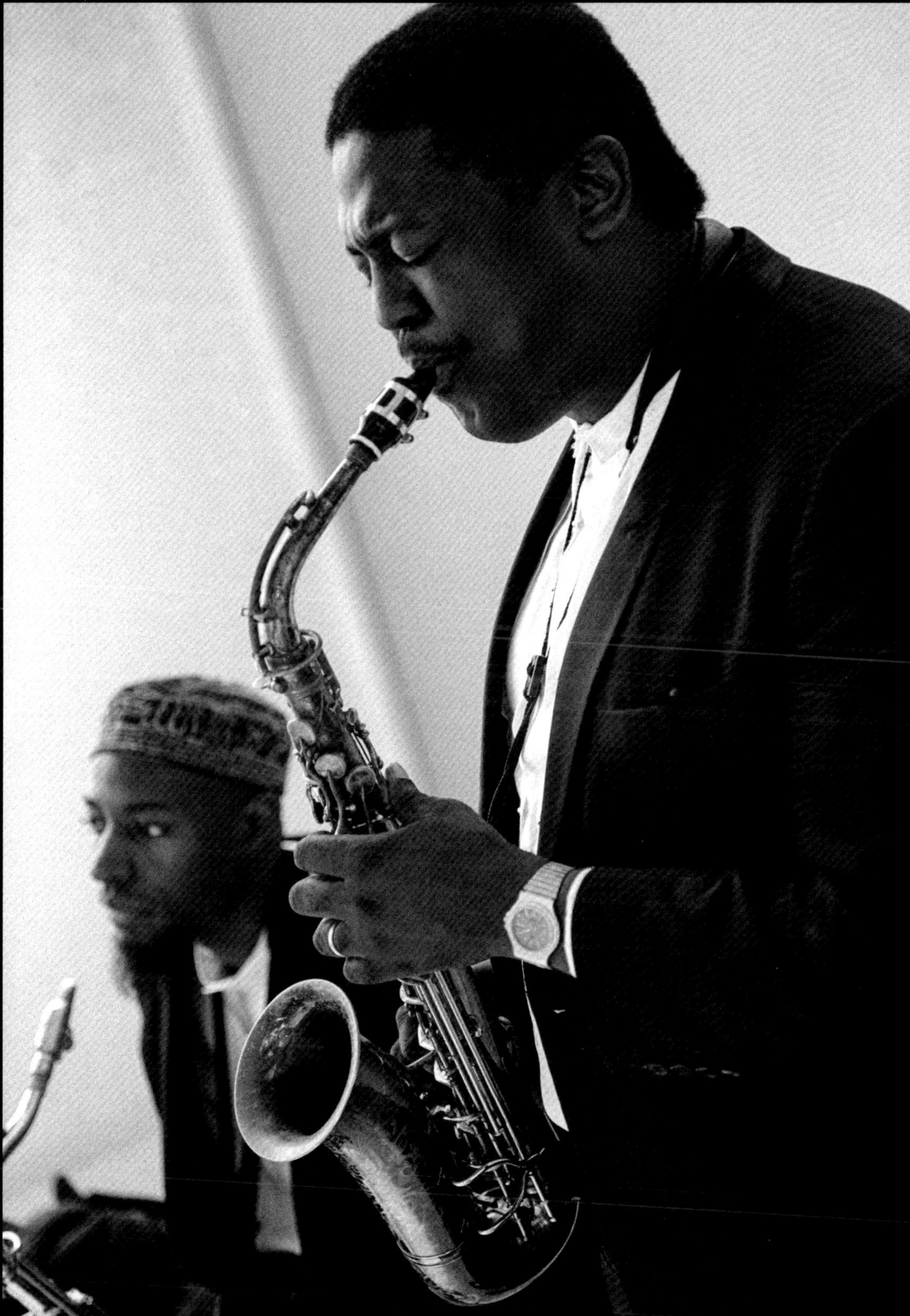

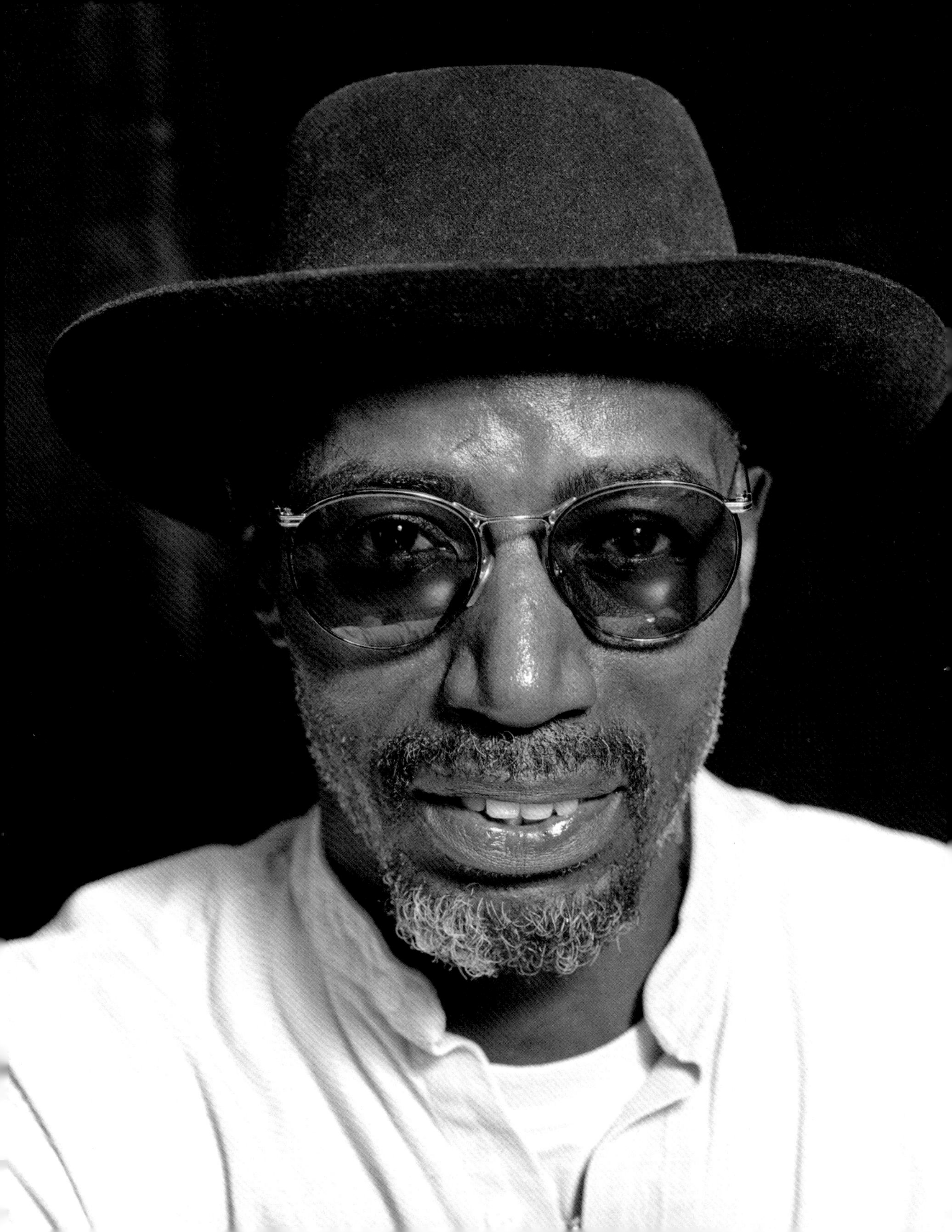

Thelonious Monk Jr.
1996, New York City

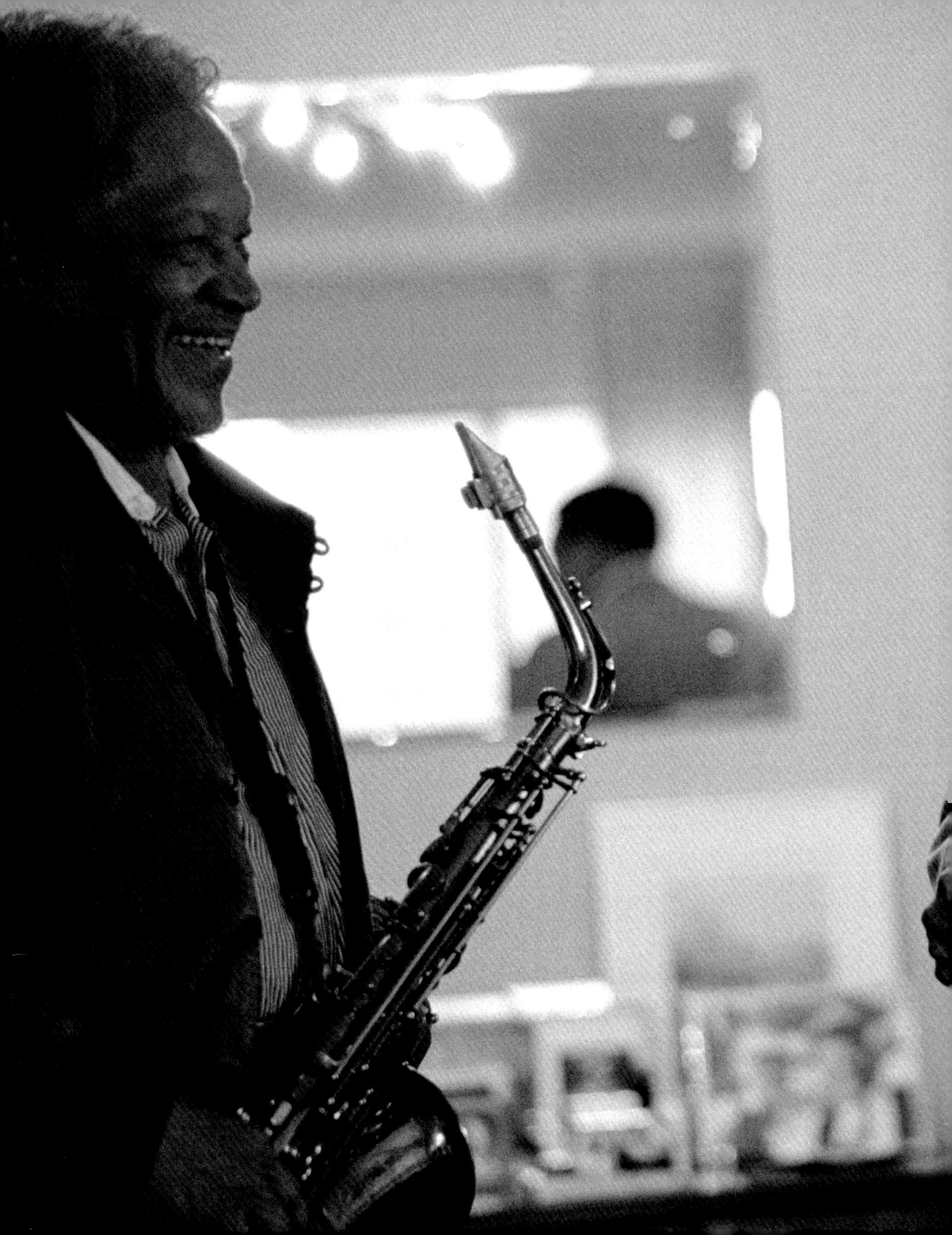

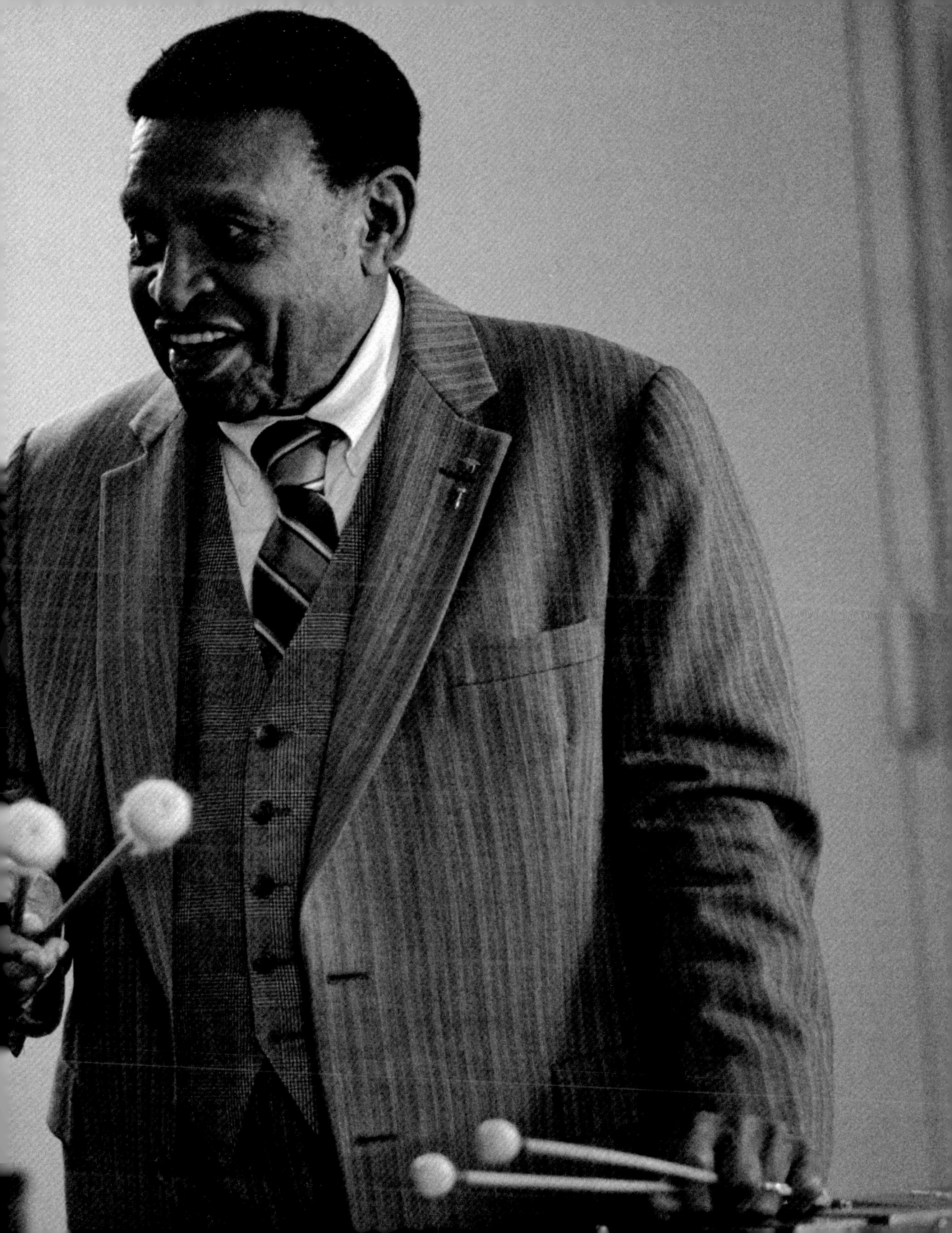

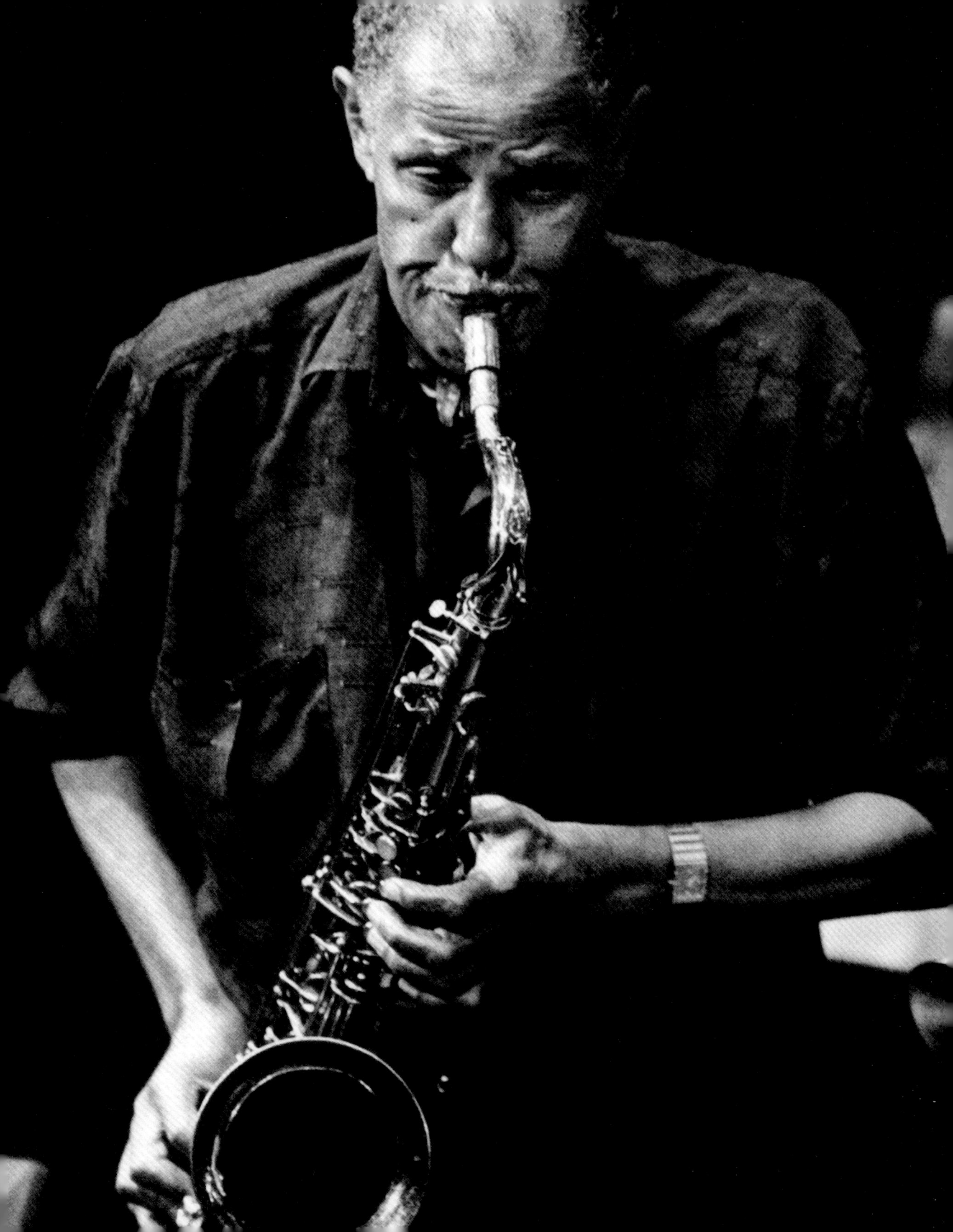

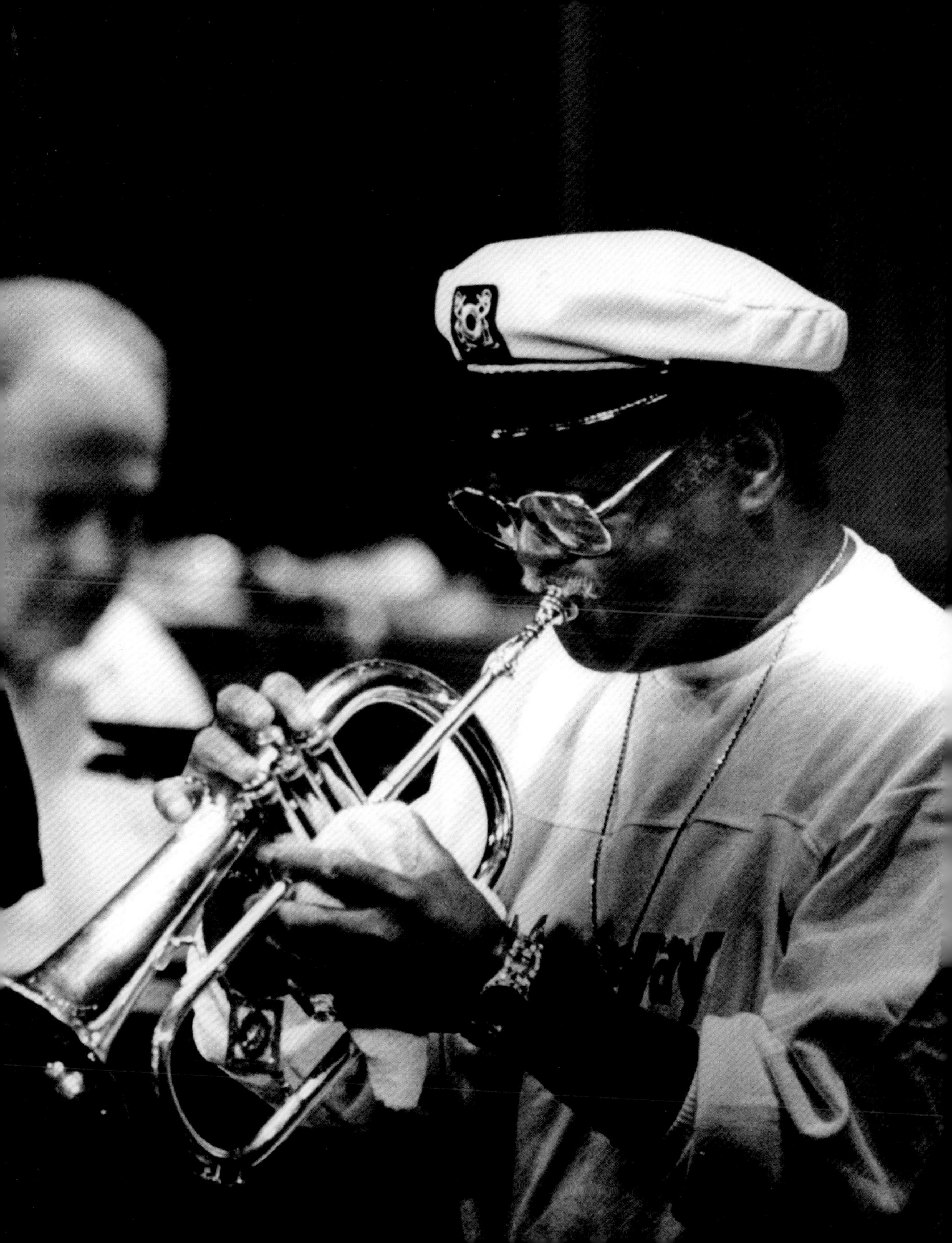

"Dizzy Gillespie was always "cooler" than everyone else. He was a ladies' man–very charming and stylish and fun to be around. On the SS Norway he was very interested in the models I brought with me–he told Jeny Howorth that she should come with him to the casino to be his lucky charm."

Dizzy Gillespie
1988, SS Norway

(following pages)
Christian Mcades
1998, New York City

Ron Carter
1988, New York City

Clark Terry
1988, SS Norway

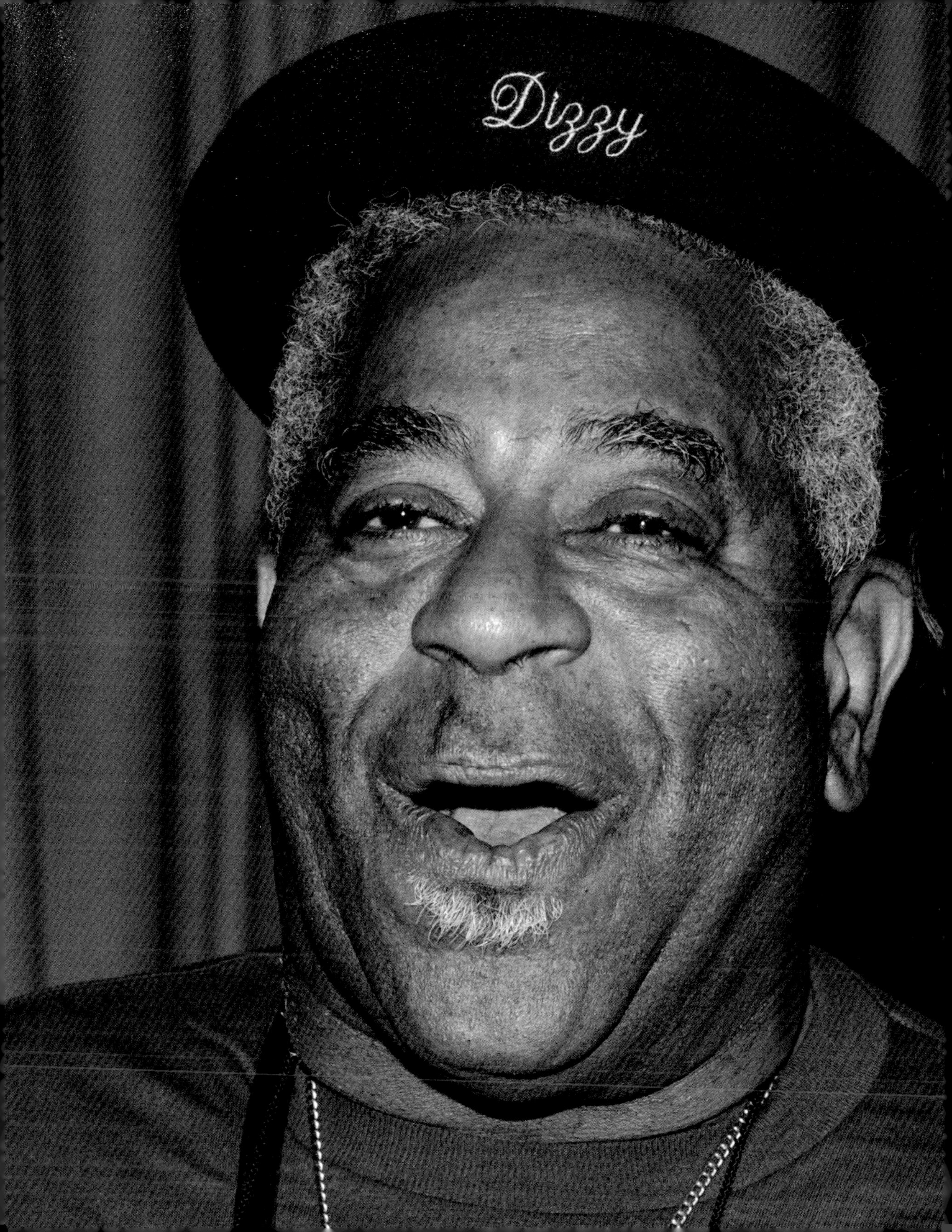
Dizzy

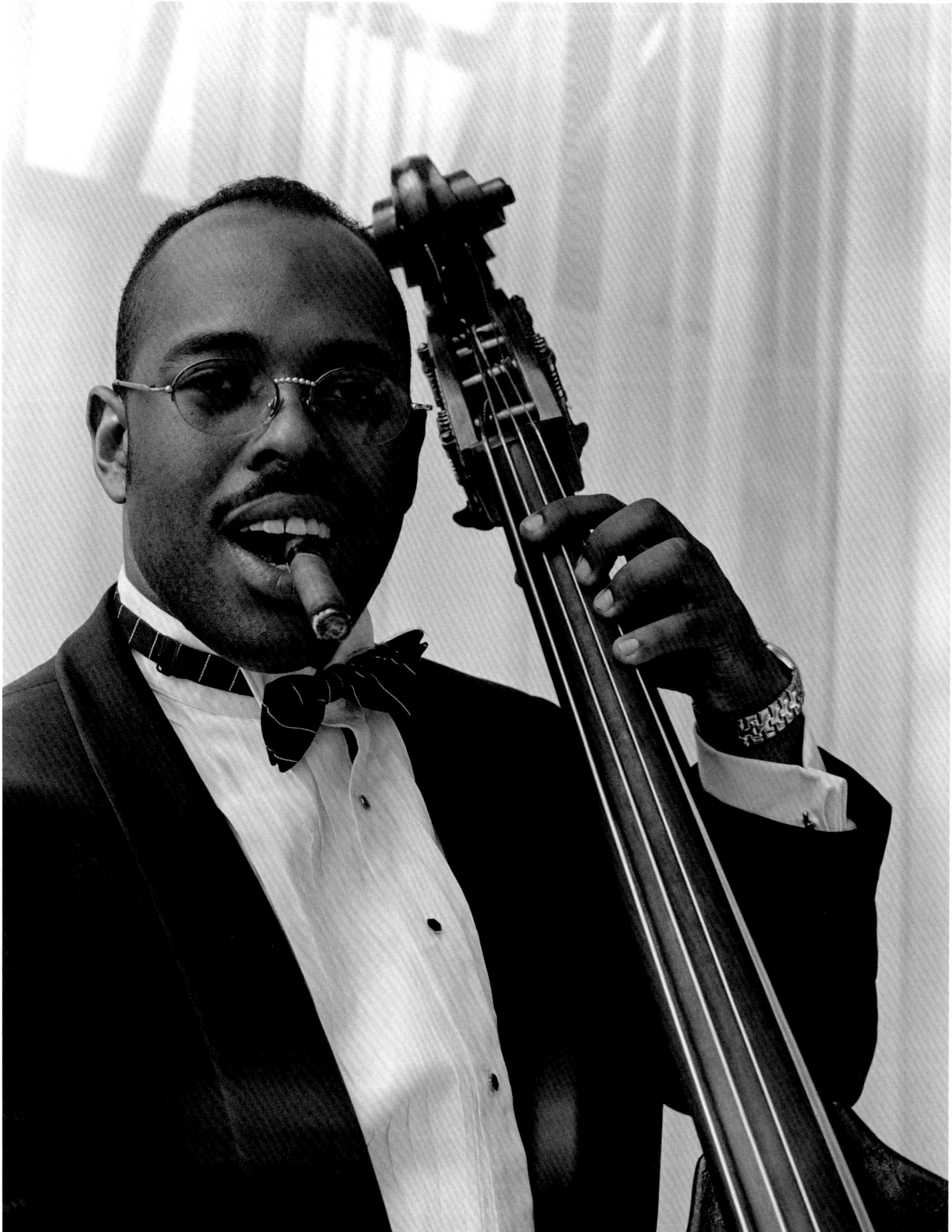

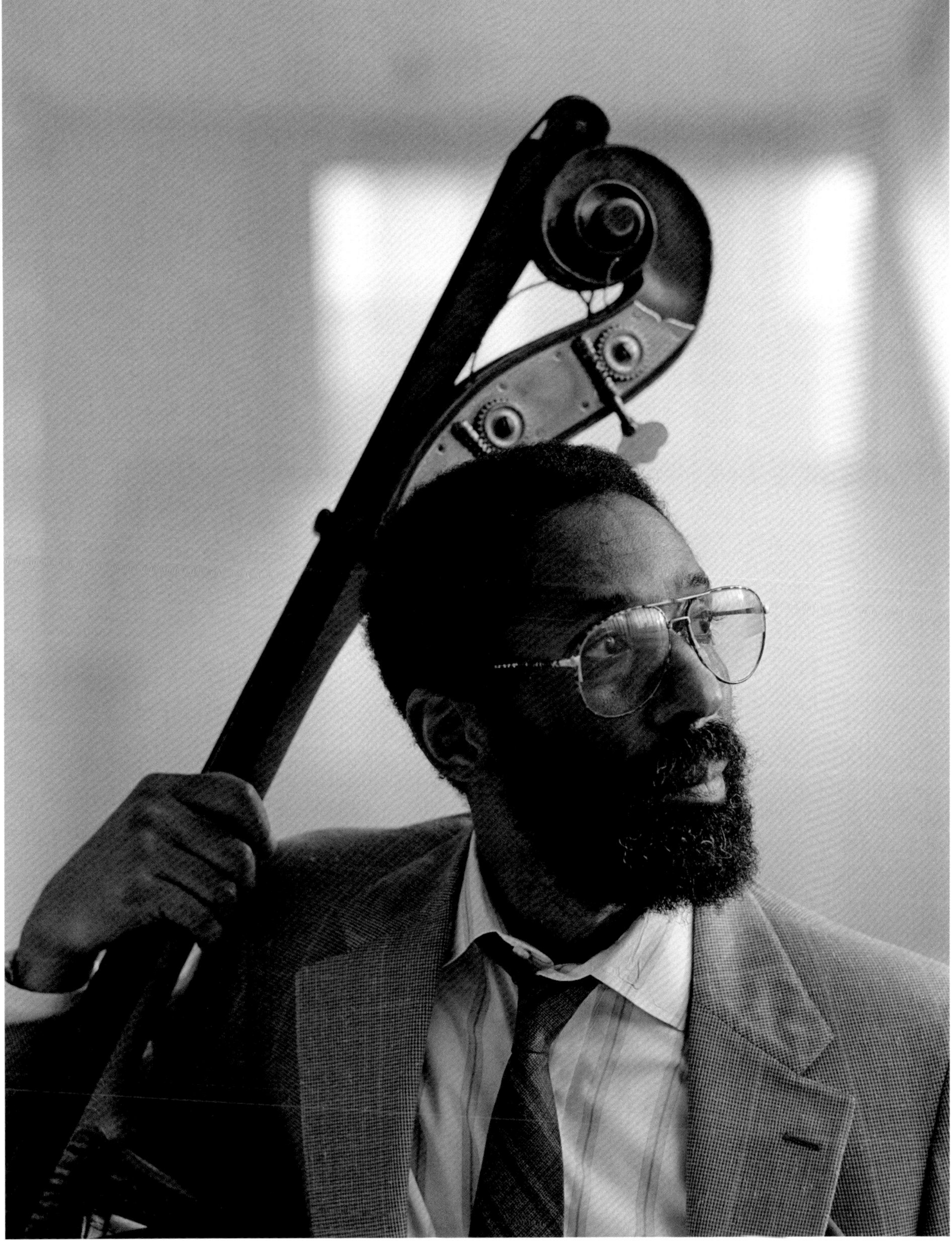

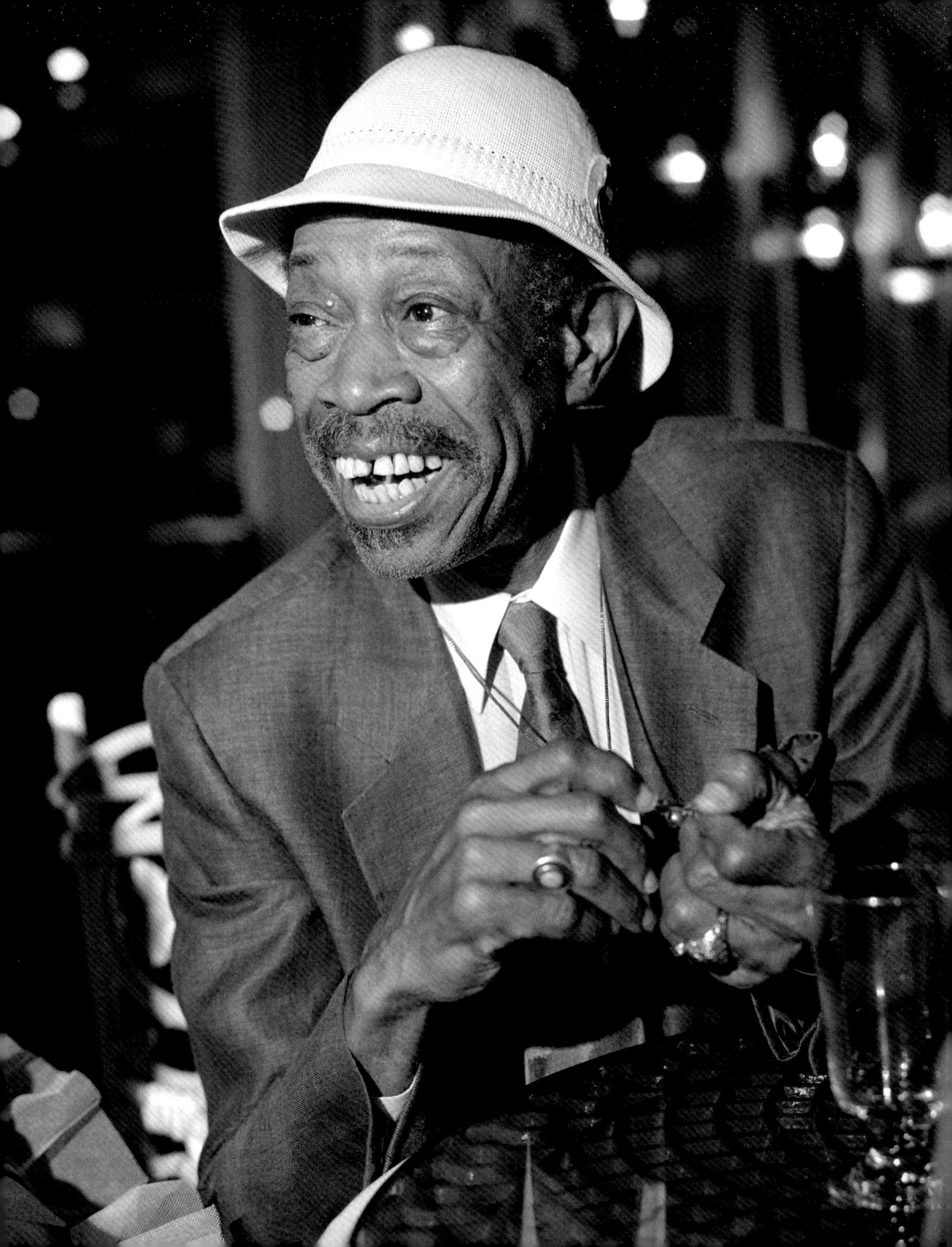

Al Grey
1990, New York City

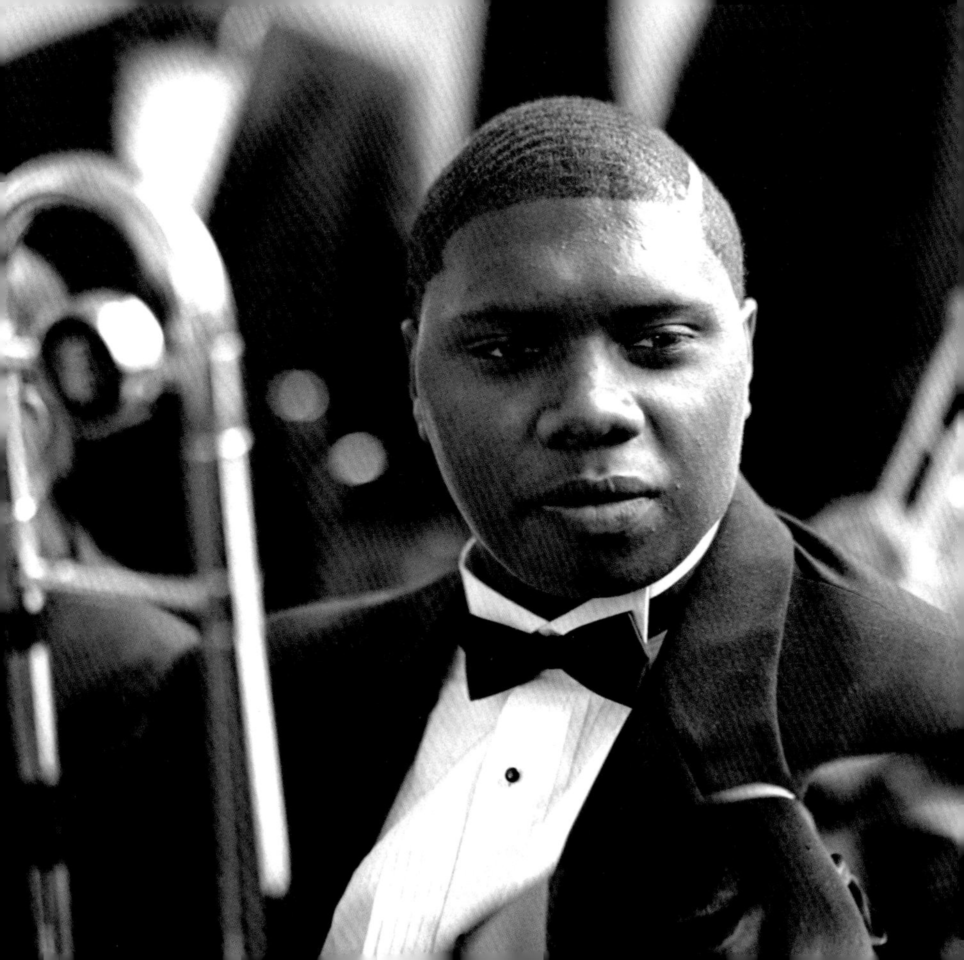

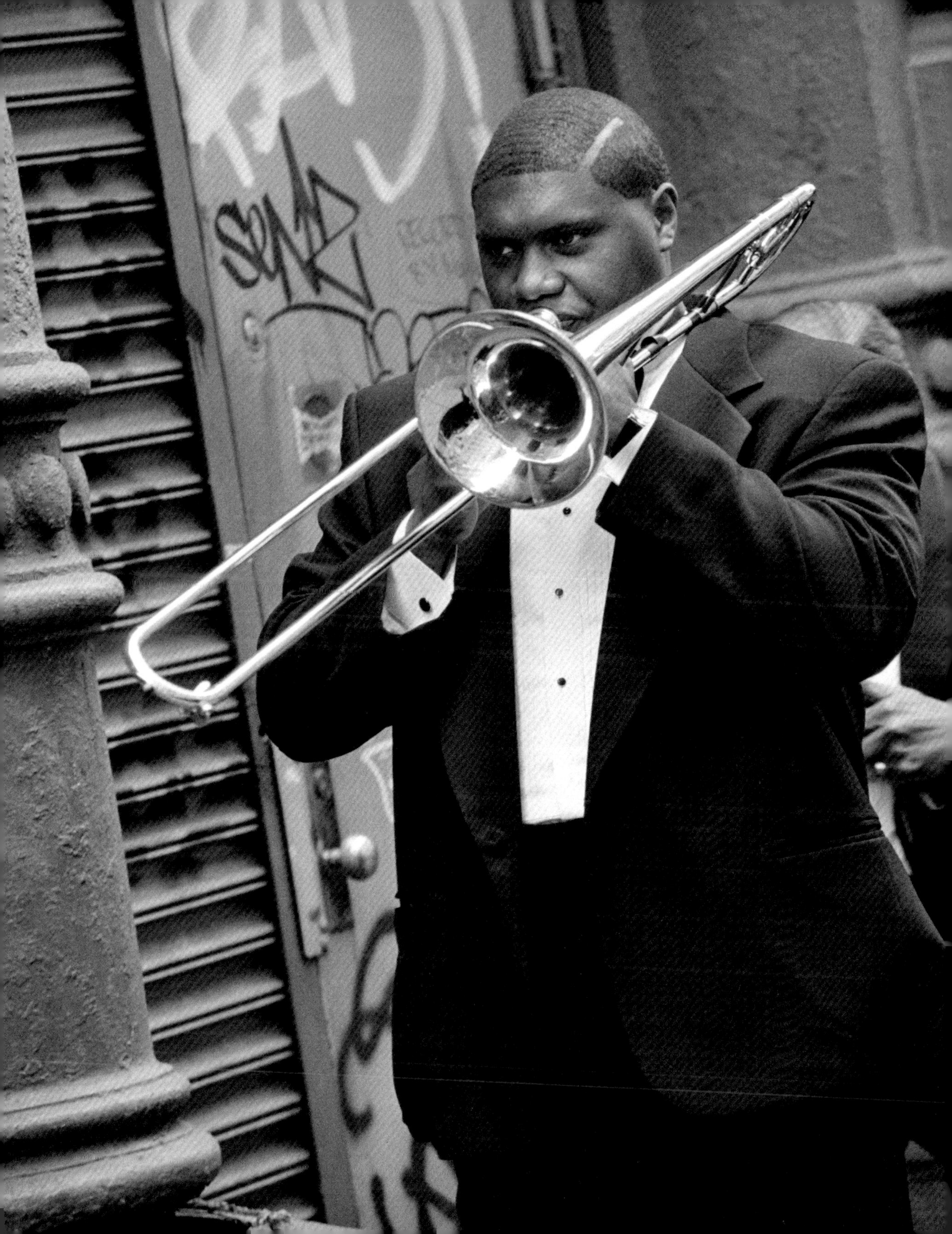

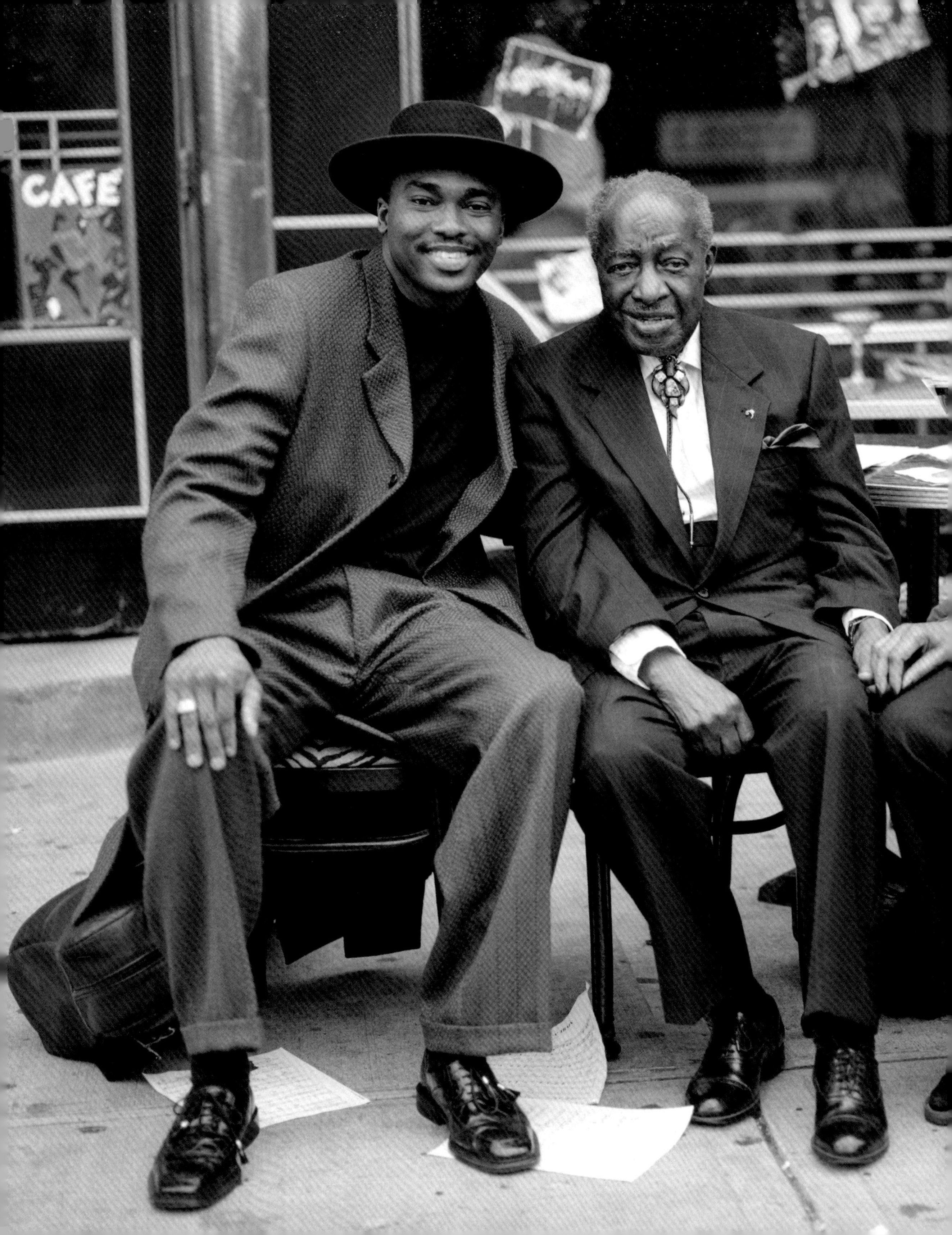
CAFÉ

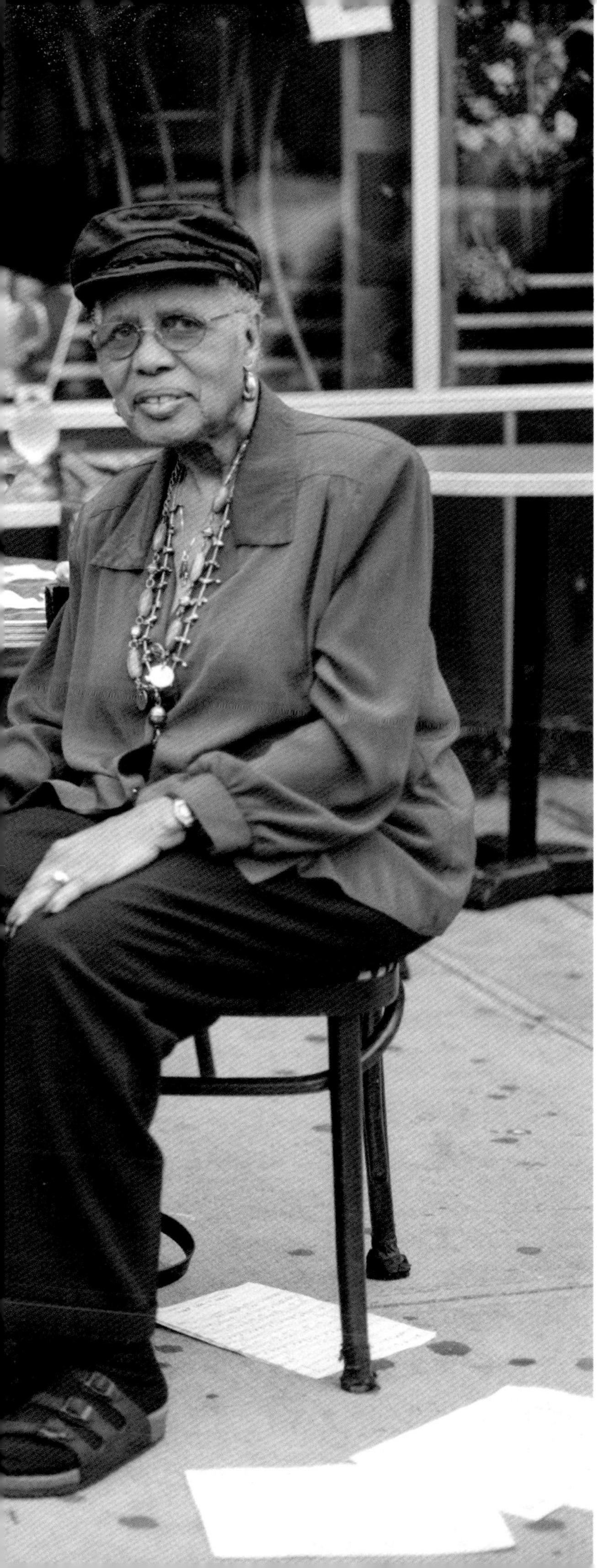

James Carter, Milt Hinton, and Mona Hinton
2000, New York City

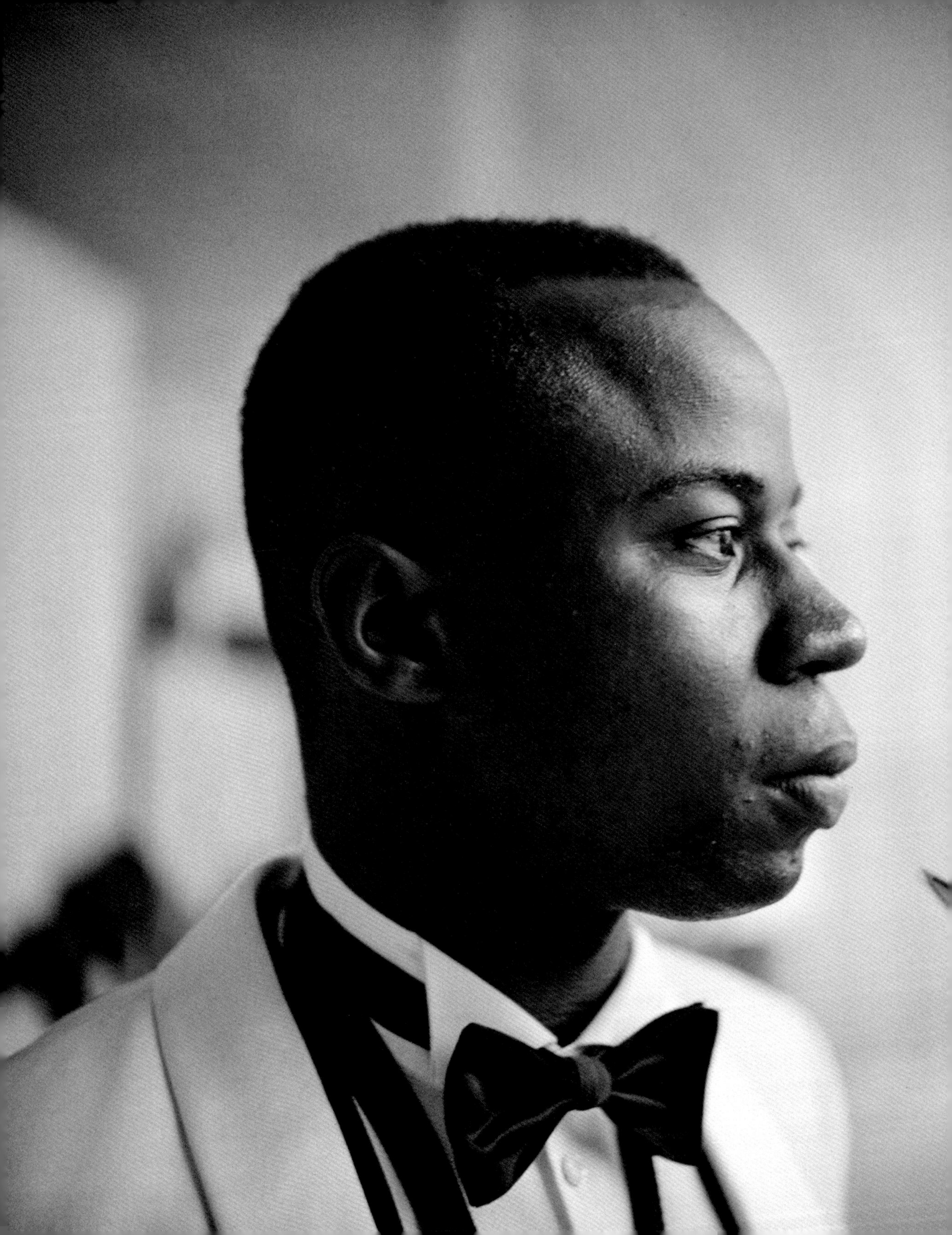

Sam Newsome
1992, New York City

Milt Hinton, Jon Faddis, Roy Hargrove, James Carter
2000, New York City

(following pages)
Roy Hargrove
2000, New York City

John Faddis
2000, New York City

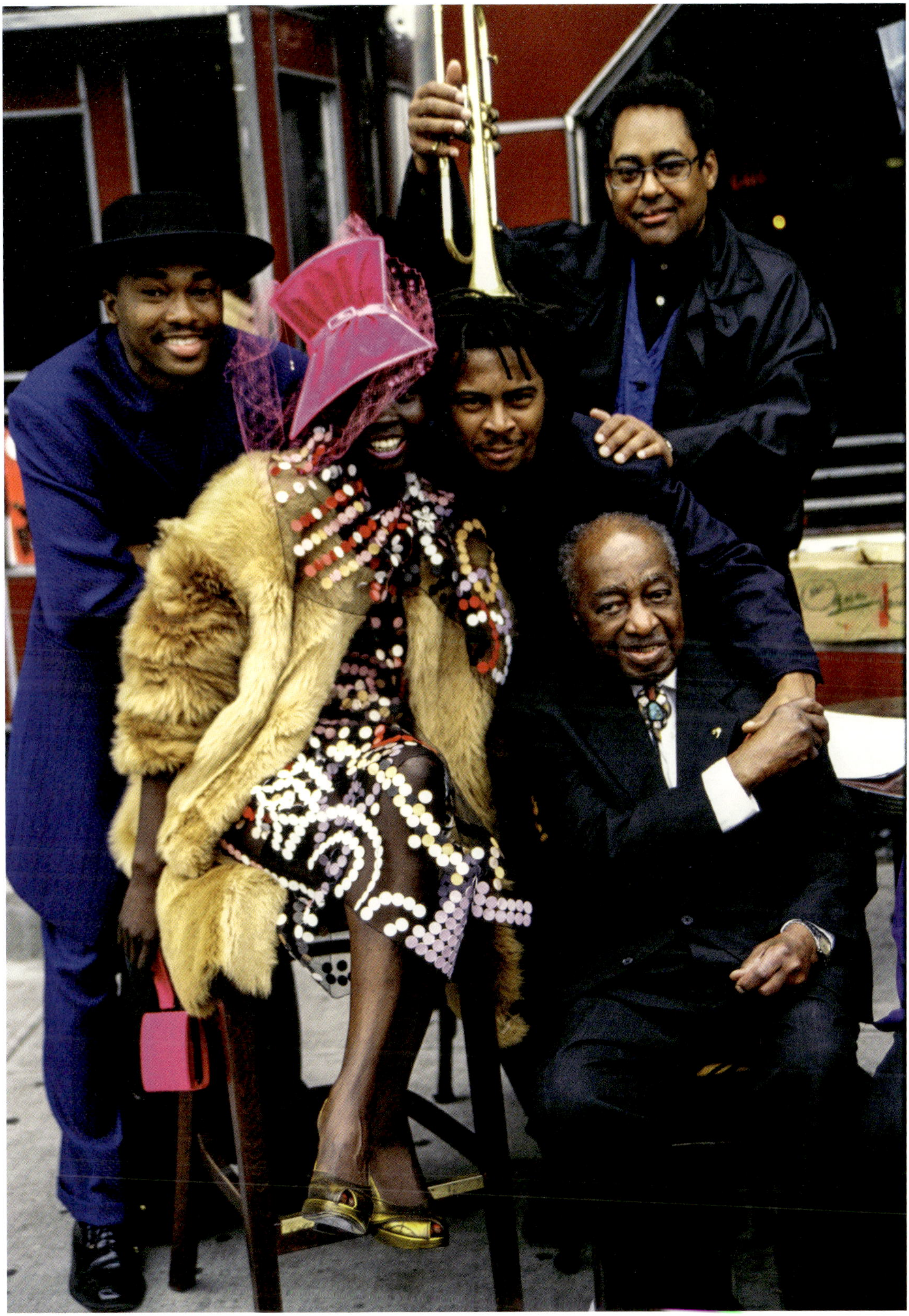

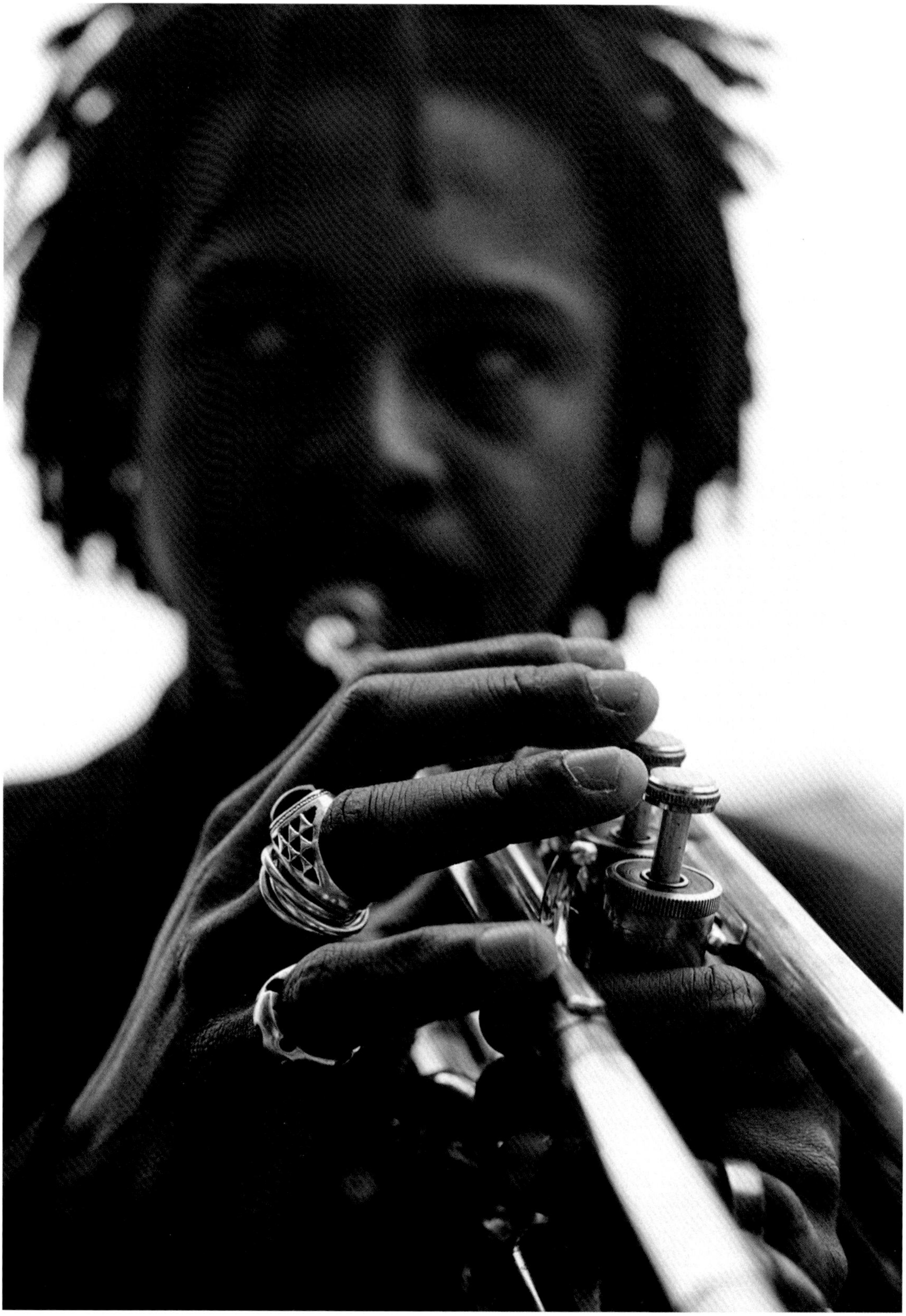

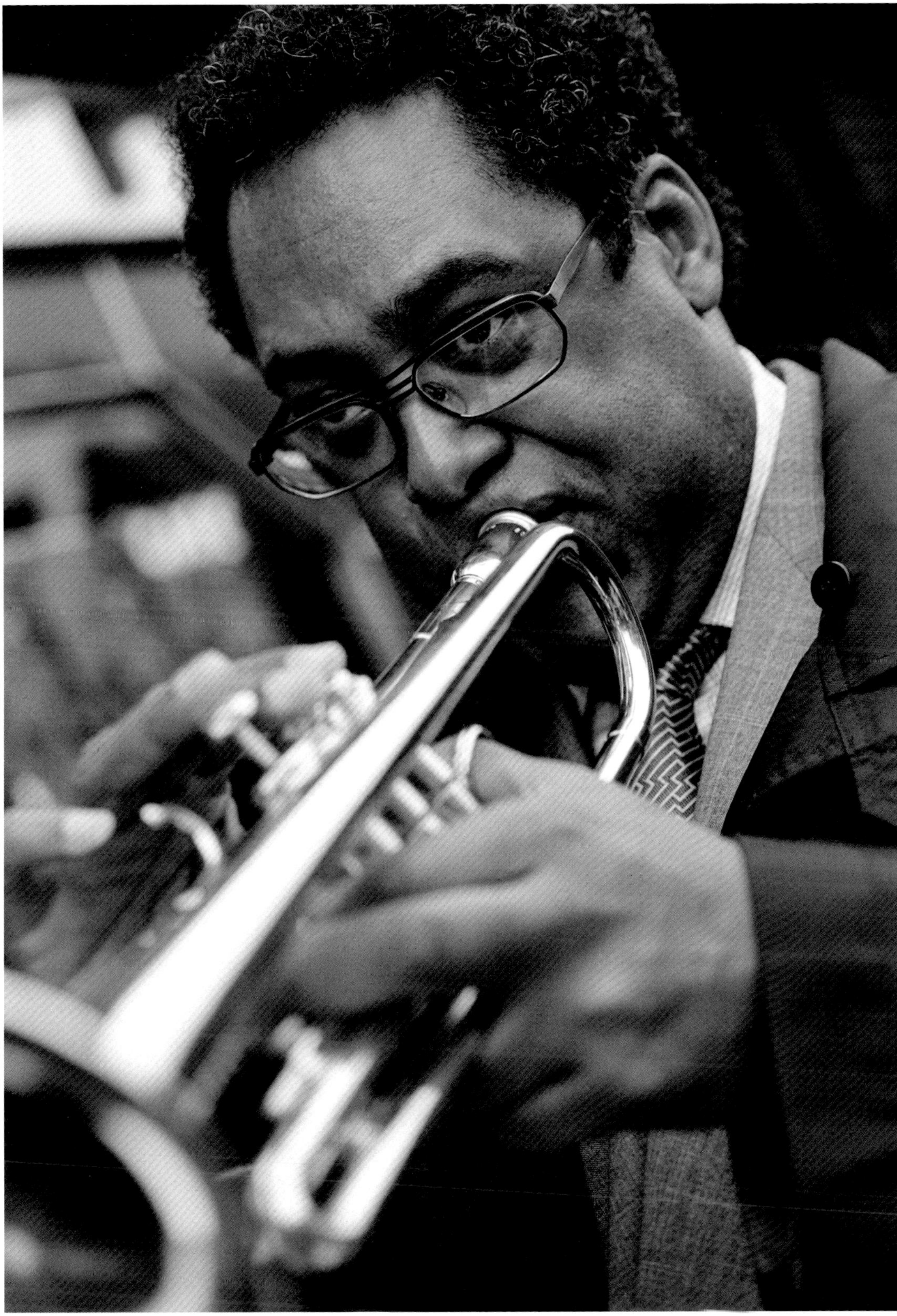

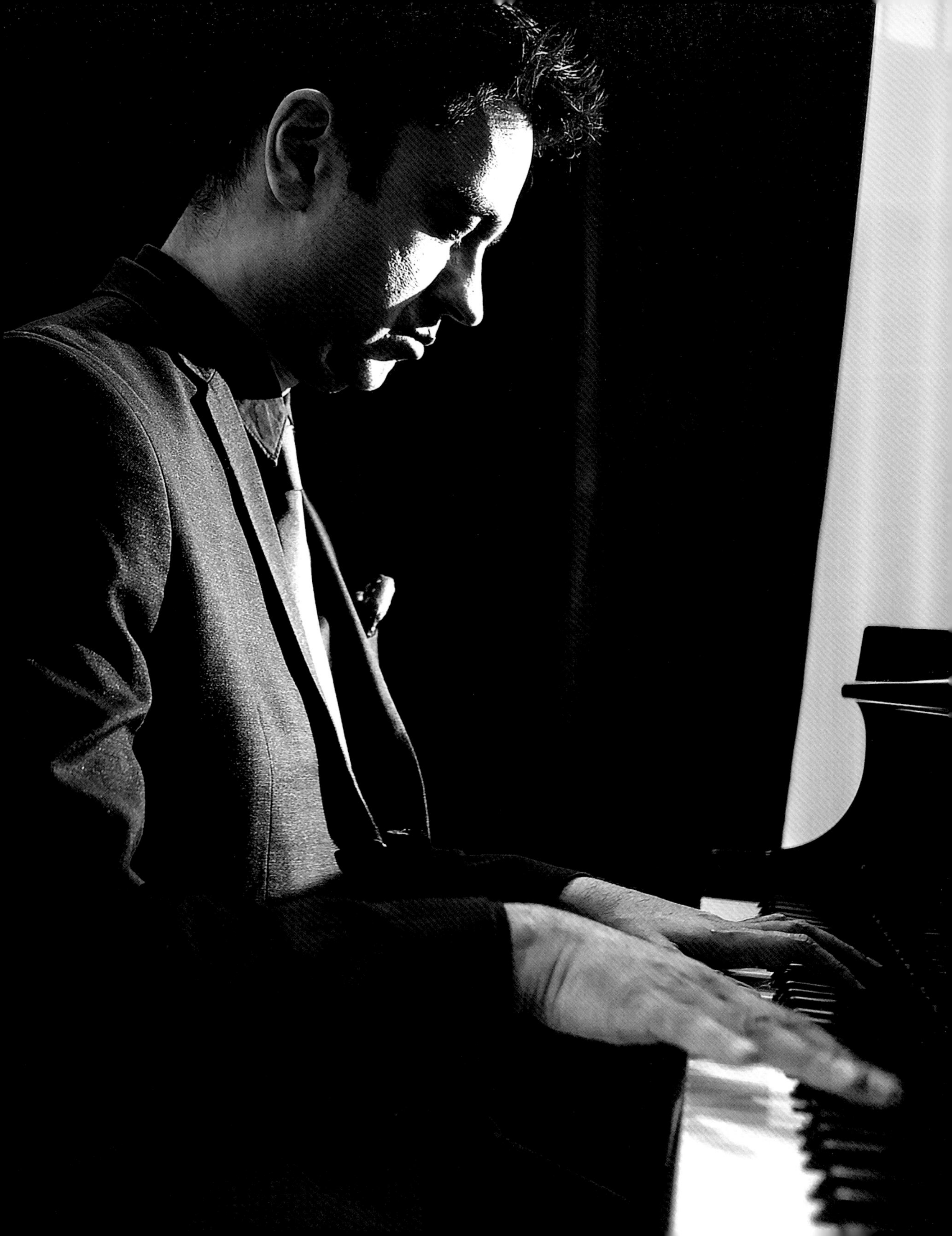

Vijay Iyler
2018, New York City

(following pages)
Max Roach
1998, New York City

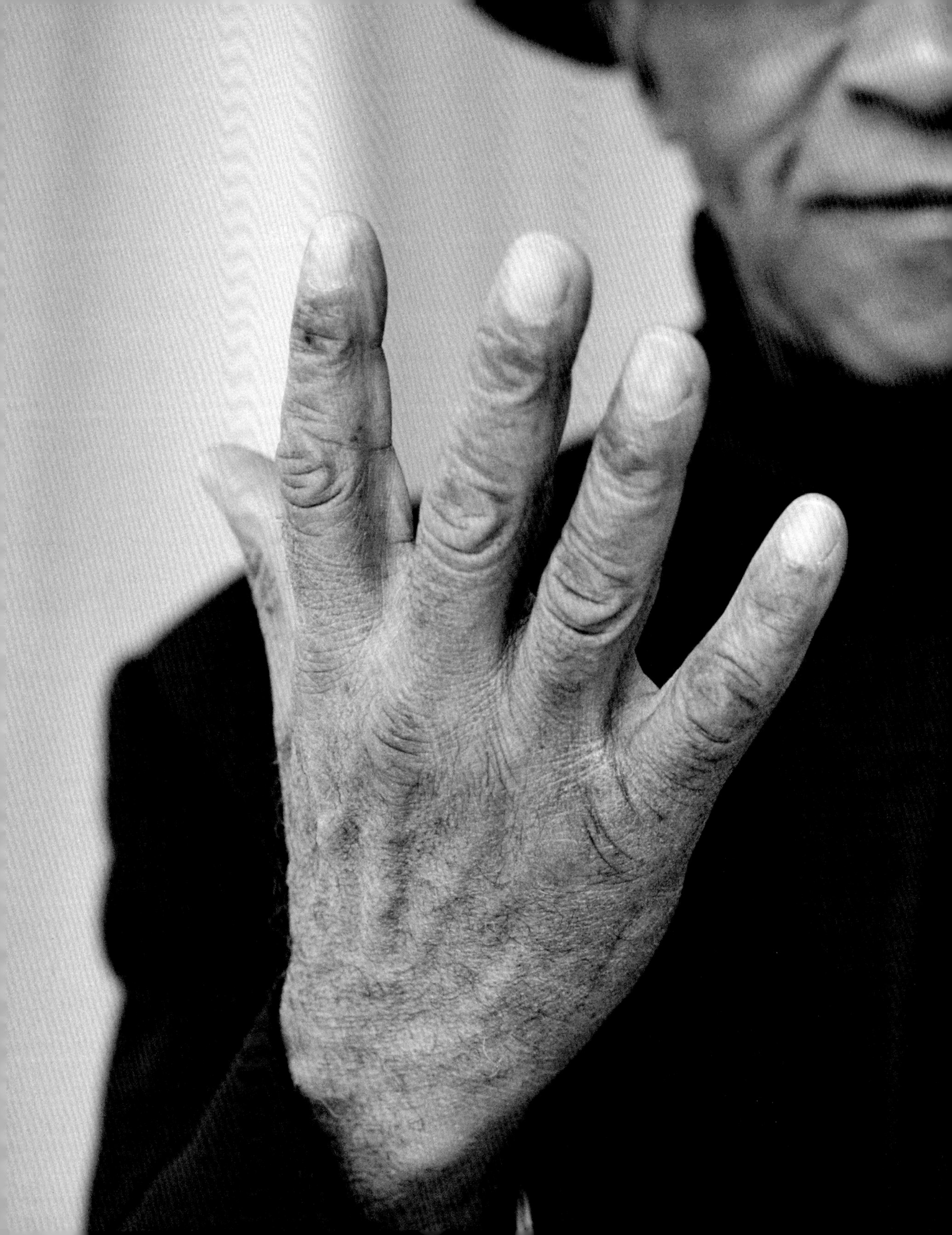

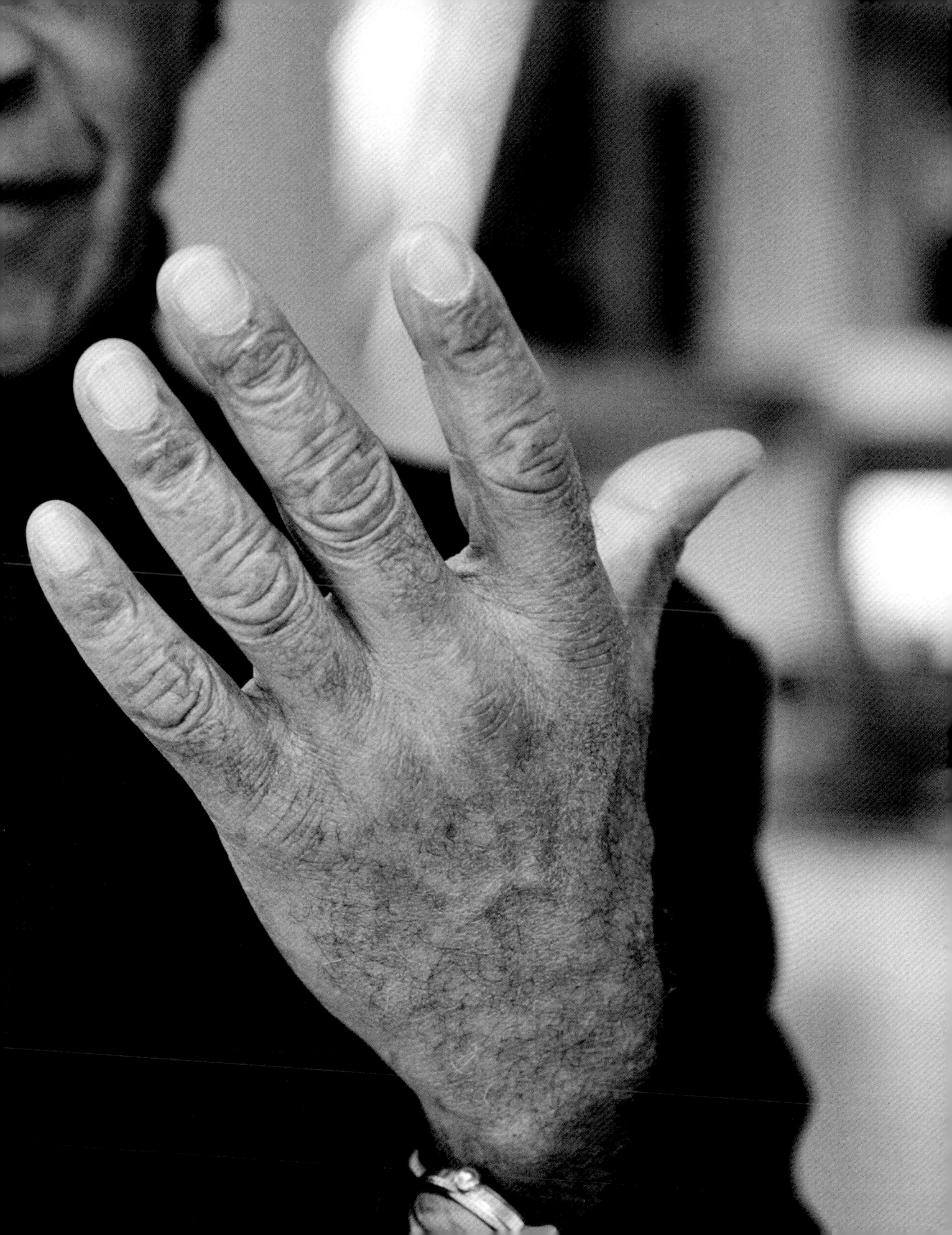

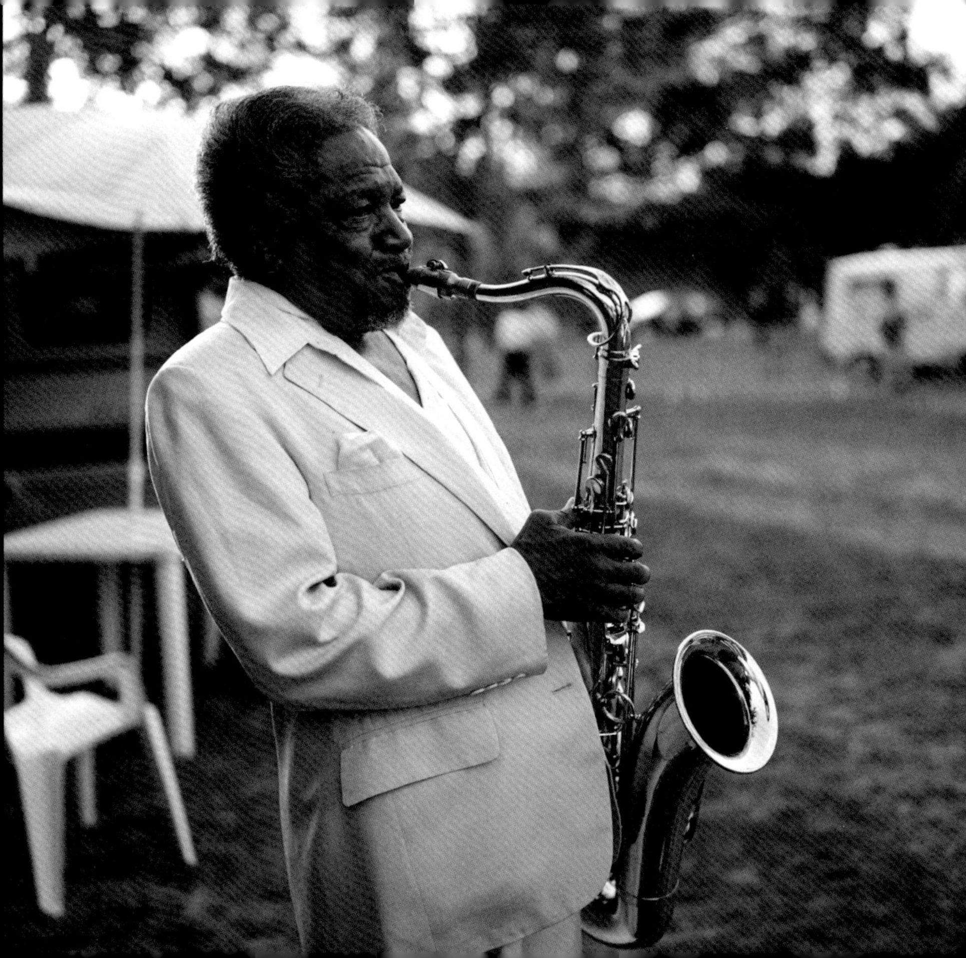

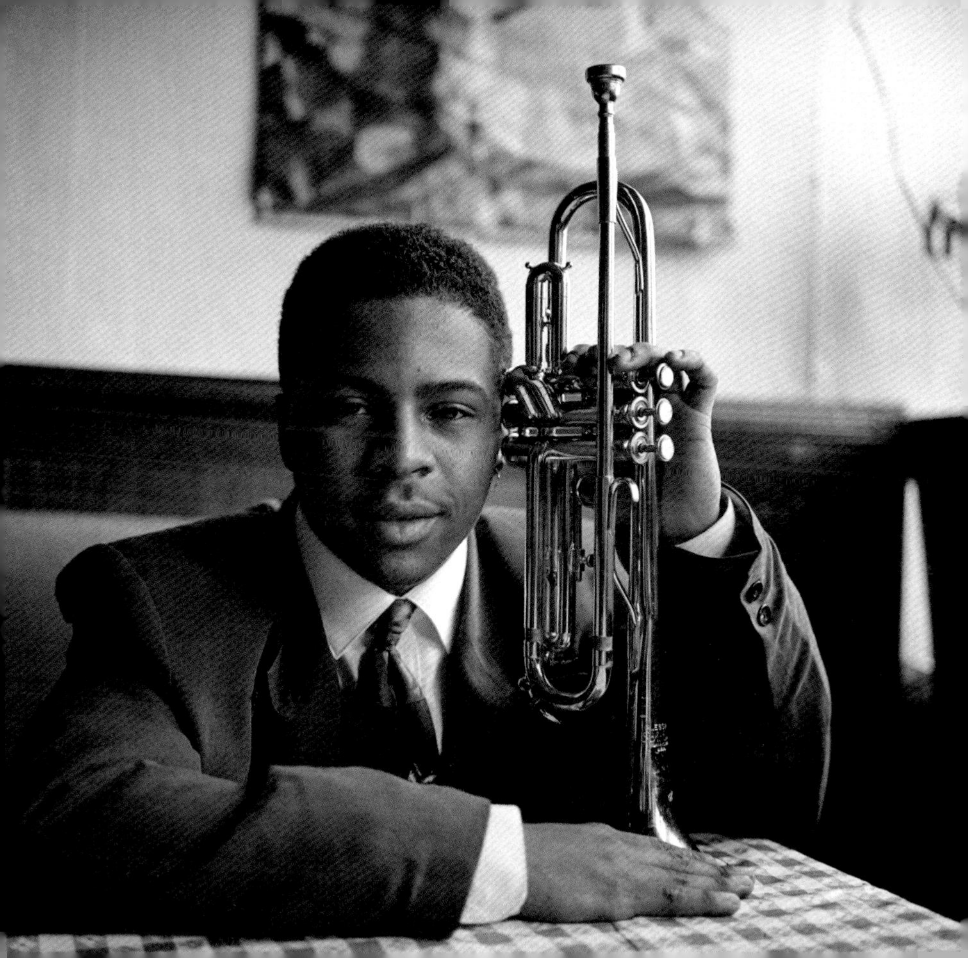

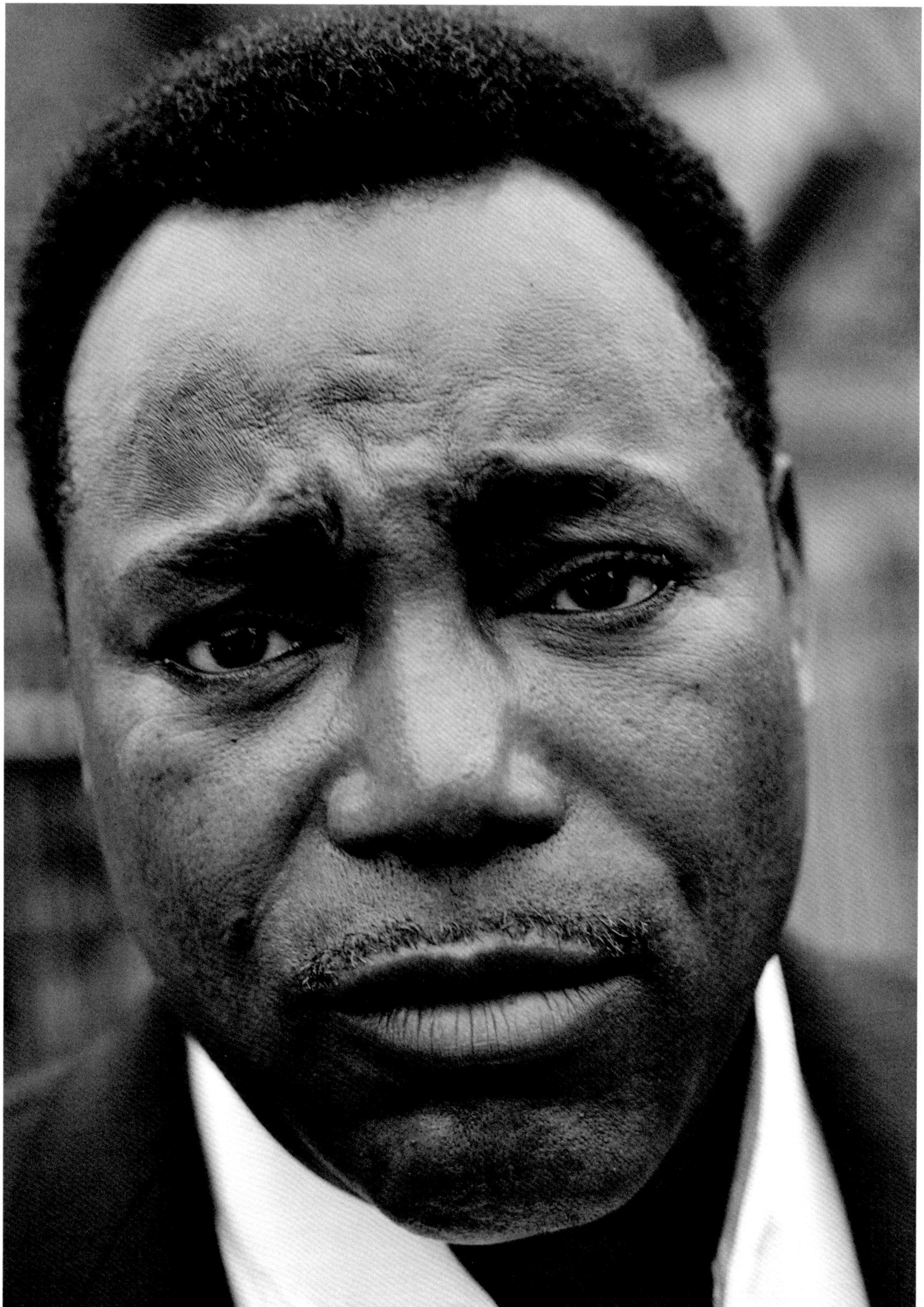

George Benson
2000, New York City

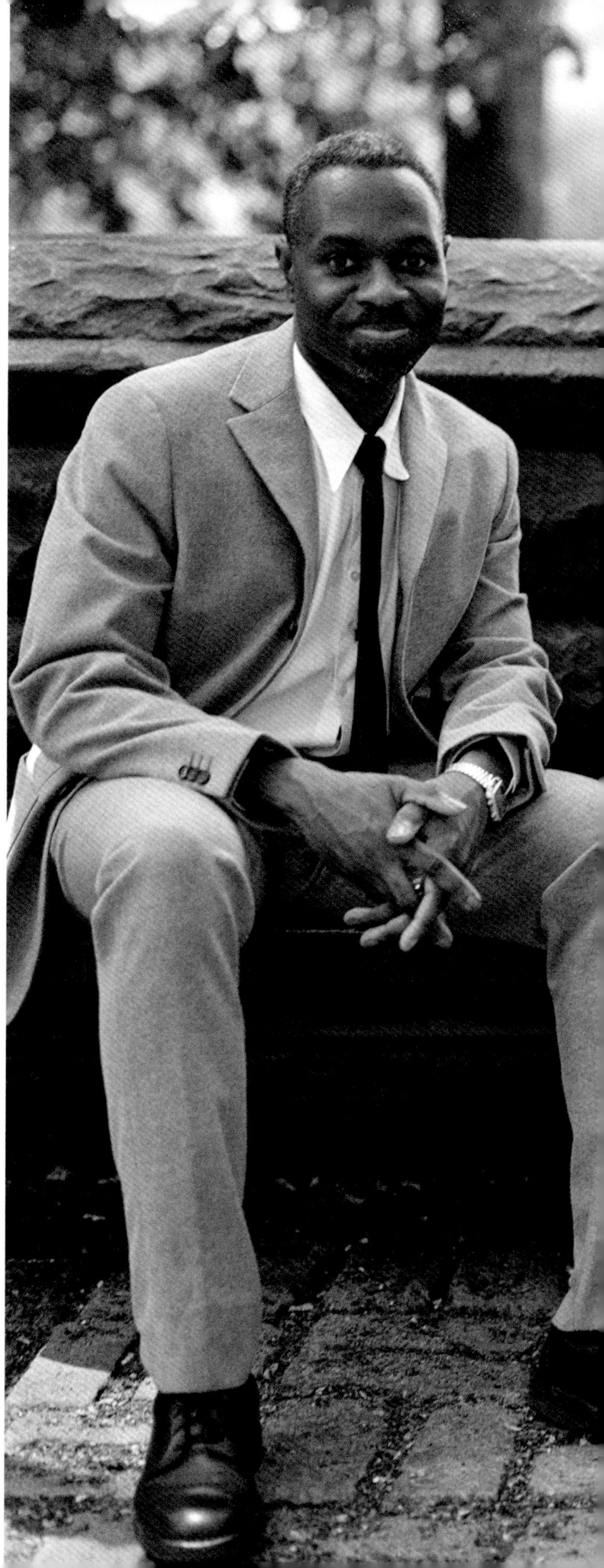

Jerome Harris, Jack DeJohnette, and Michael Cain
1998, New York City

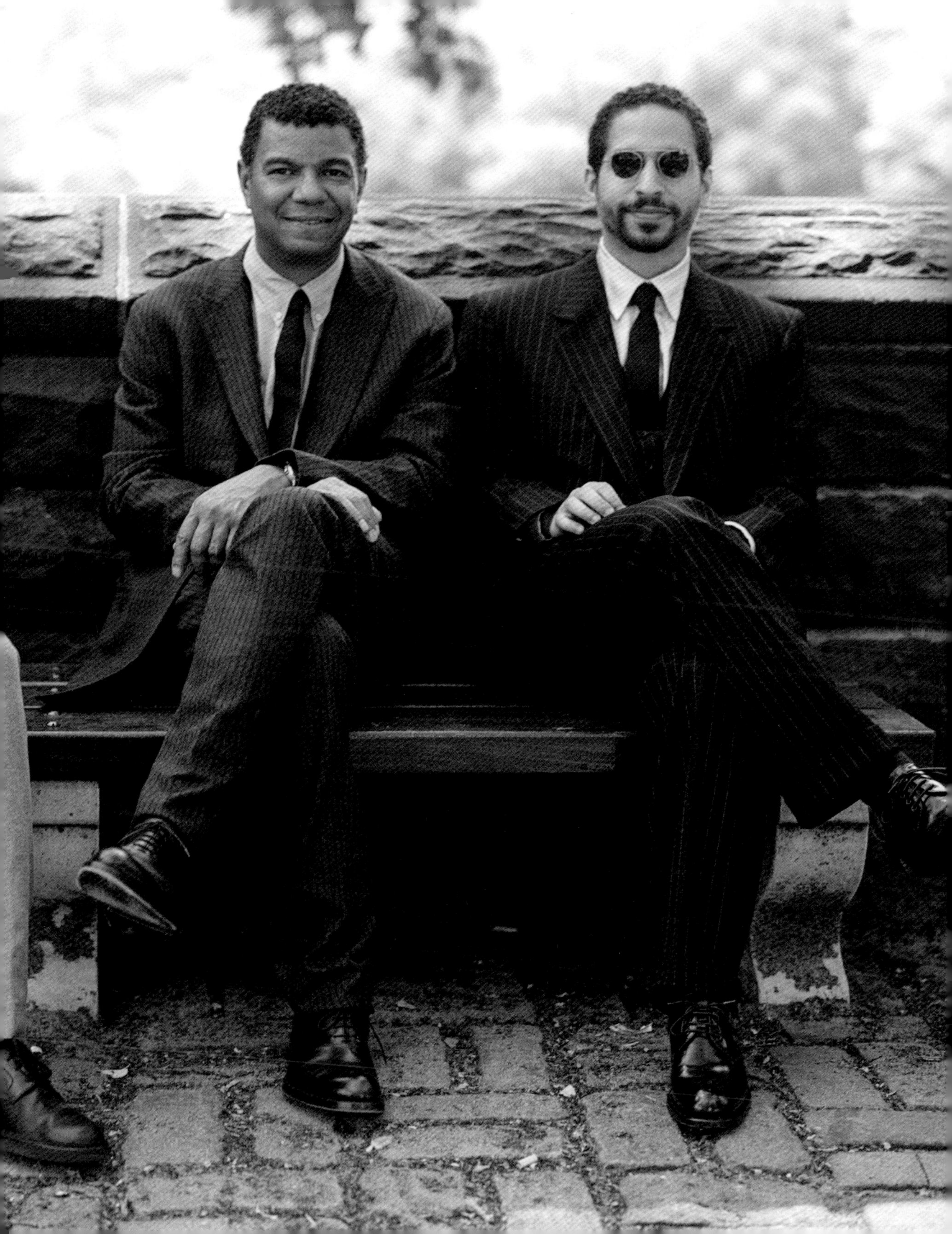

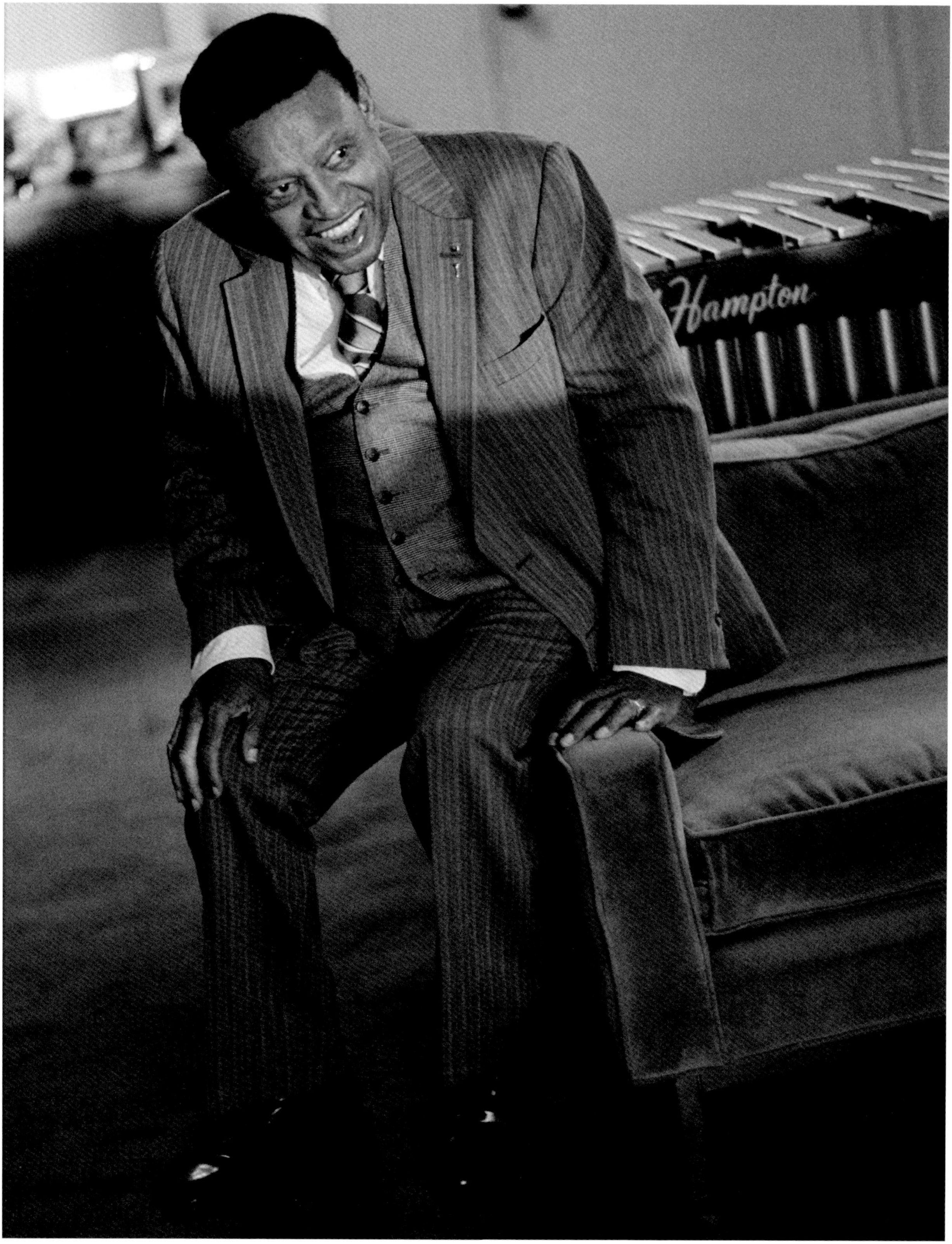
Hampton

“When Lionel Hampton started his own band he hired Illinois Jacquet and Dexter Gordon. That’s how I first started listening to Illinois and Dexter when they were young. Lionel knew how to pick the best musicians. In fact, it was he who told Illinois that he had to learn the tenor sax cause he just didn’t need an alto in his band.”

Lionel Hampton
1991, New York City

(following page)
Sugar Hill in Harlem
1998, New York City

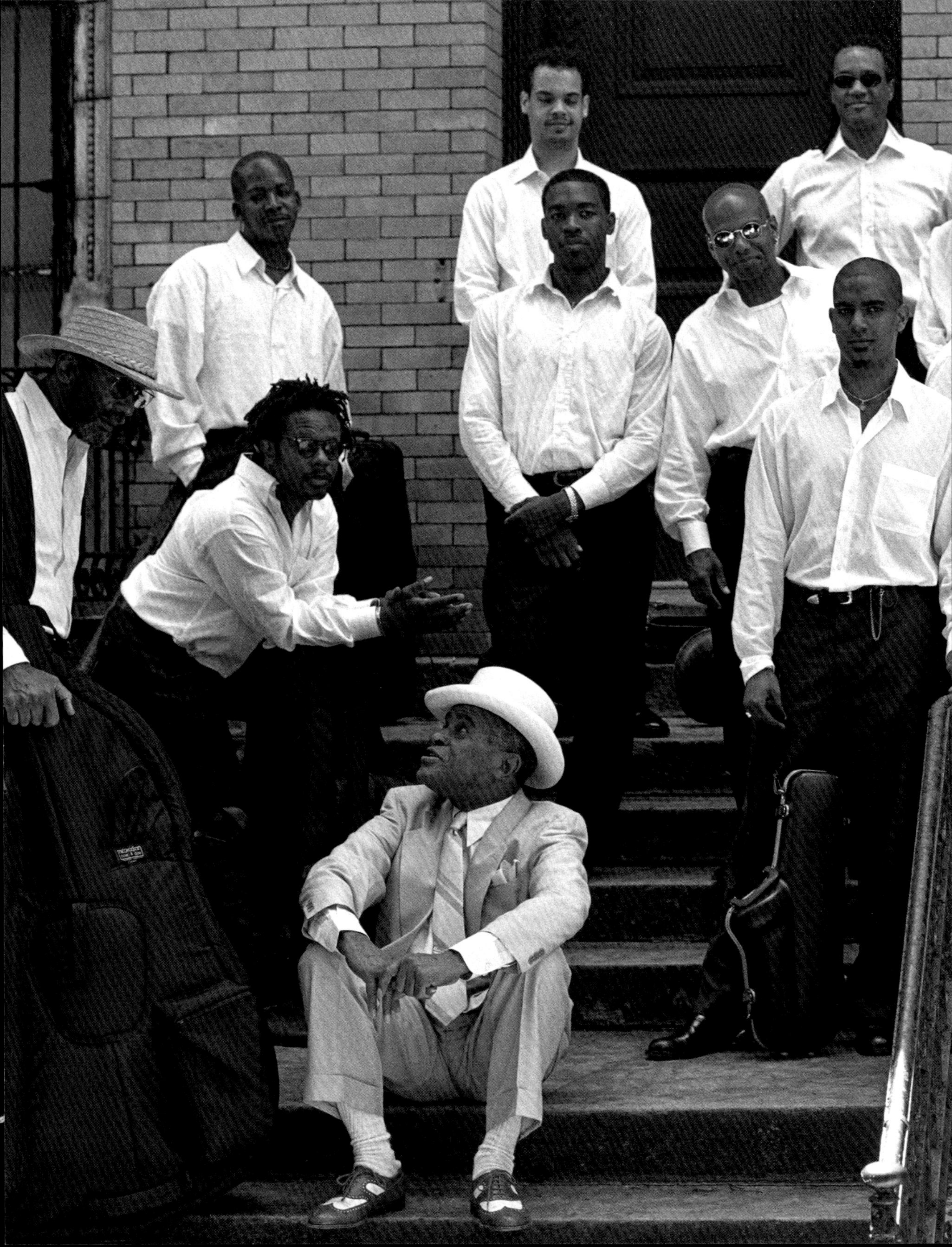

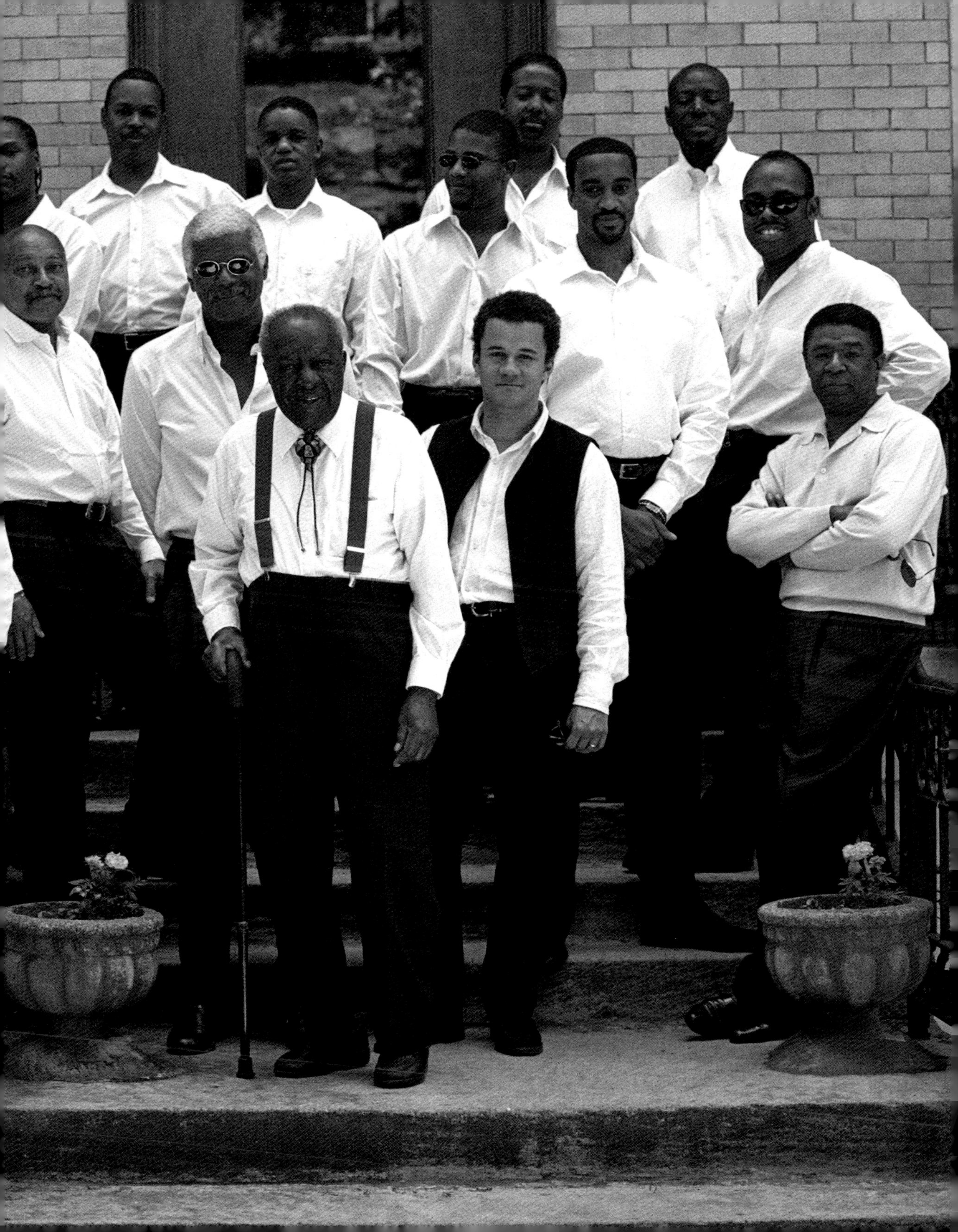

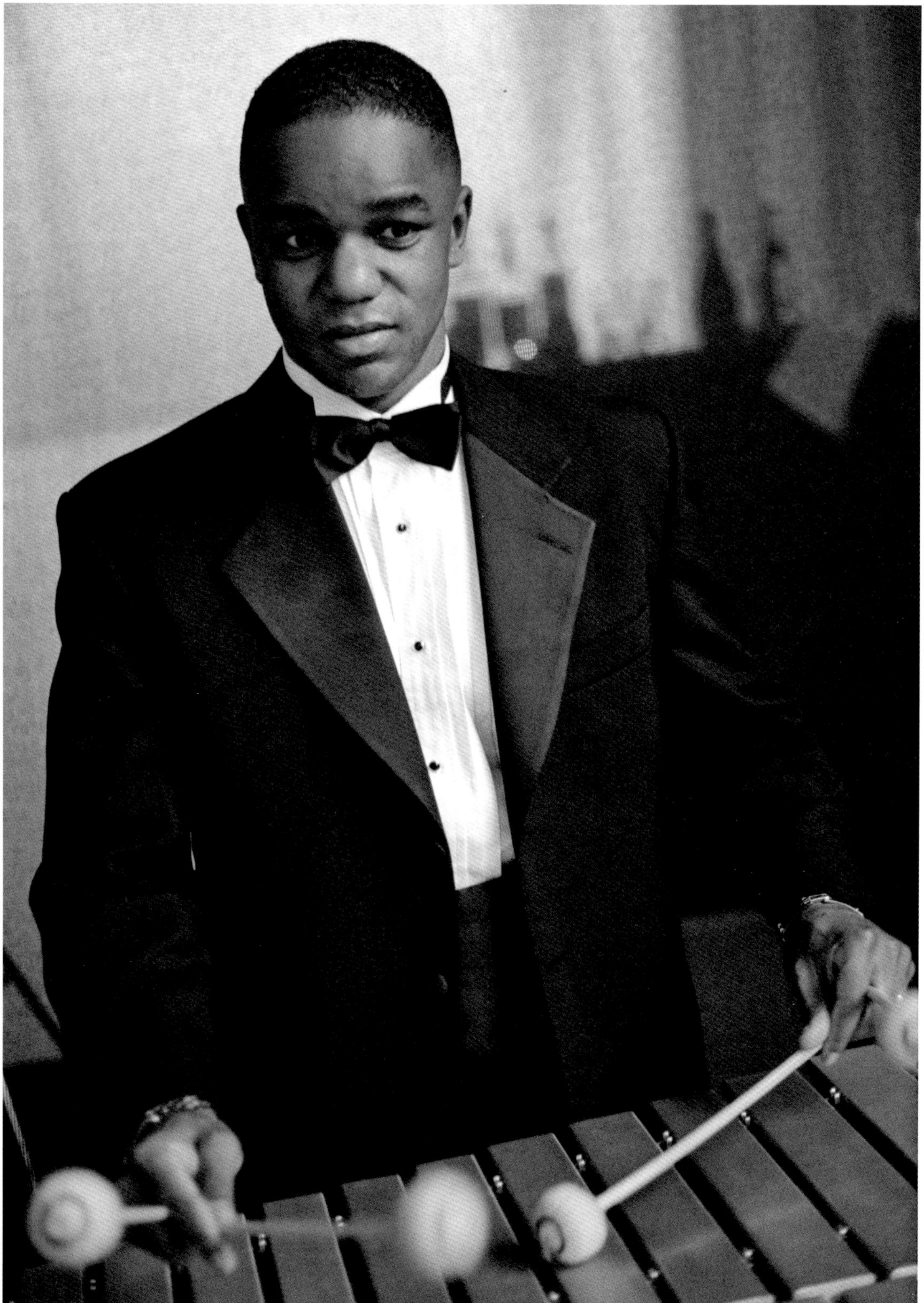

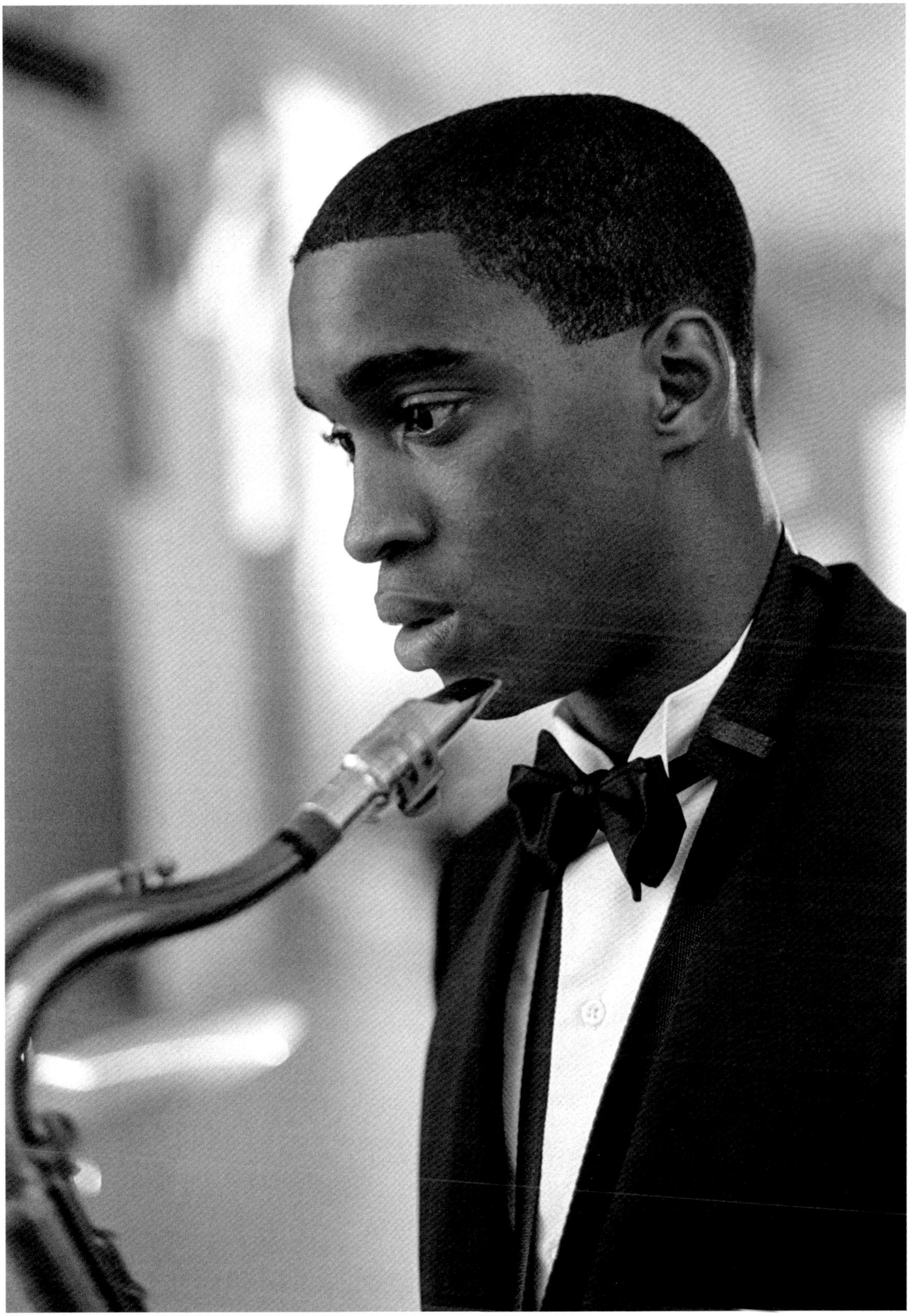

Benny Carter
1988, SS Norway

(preceeding pages)
Stefon Harris
2002, New York City

Javon Jackson
1987, New York City

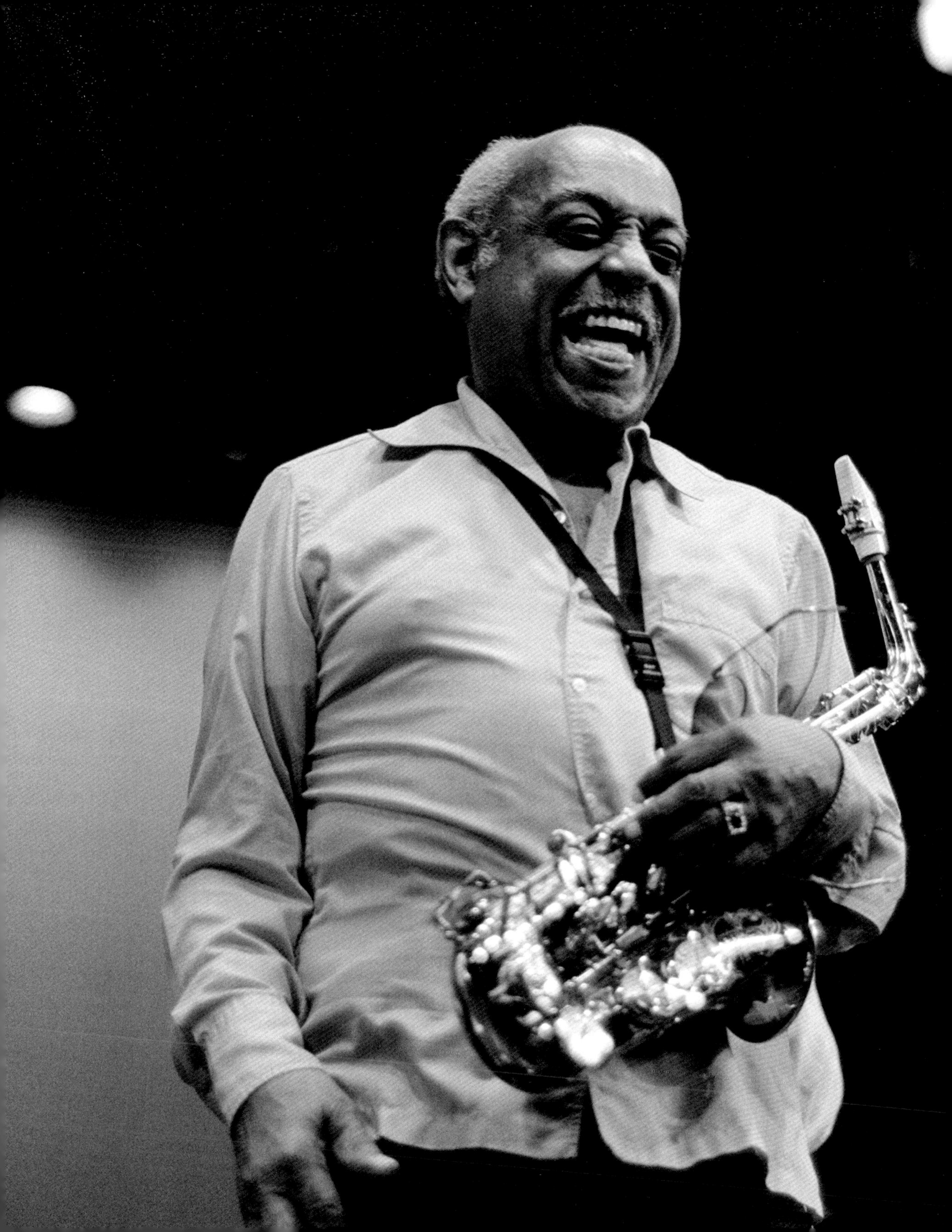

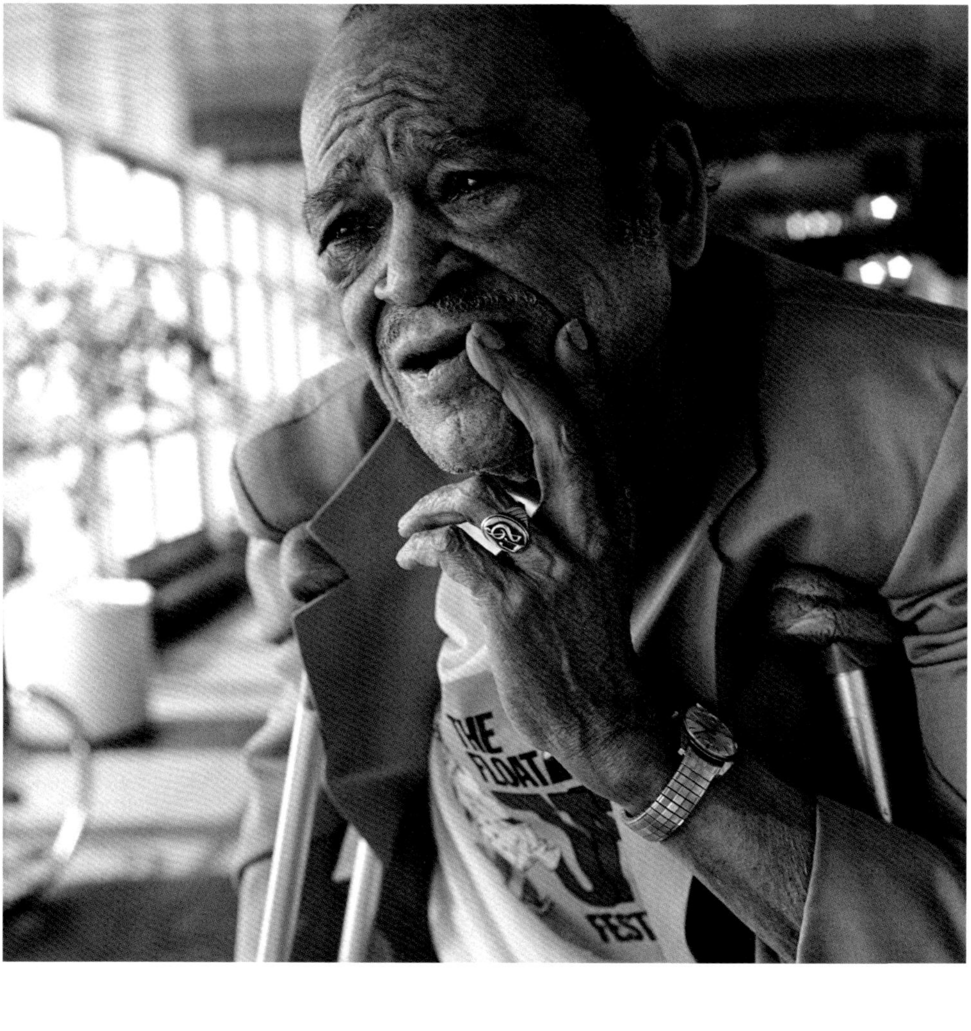

Arnett Cobb
1988, SS Norway

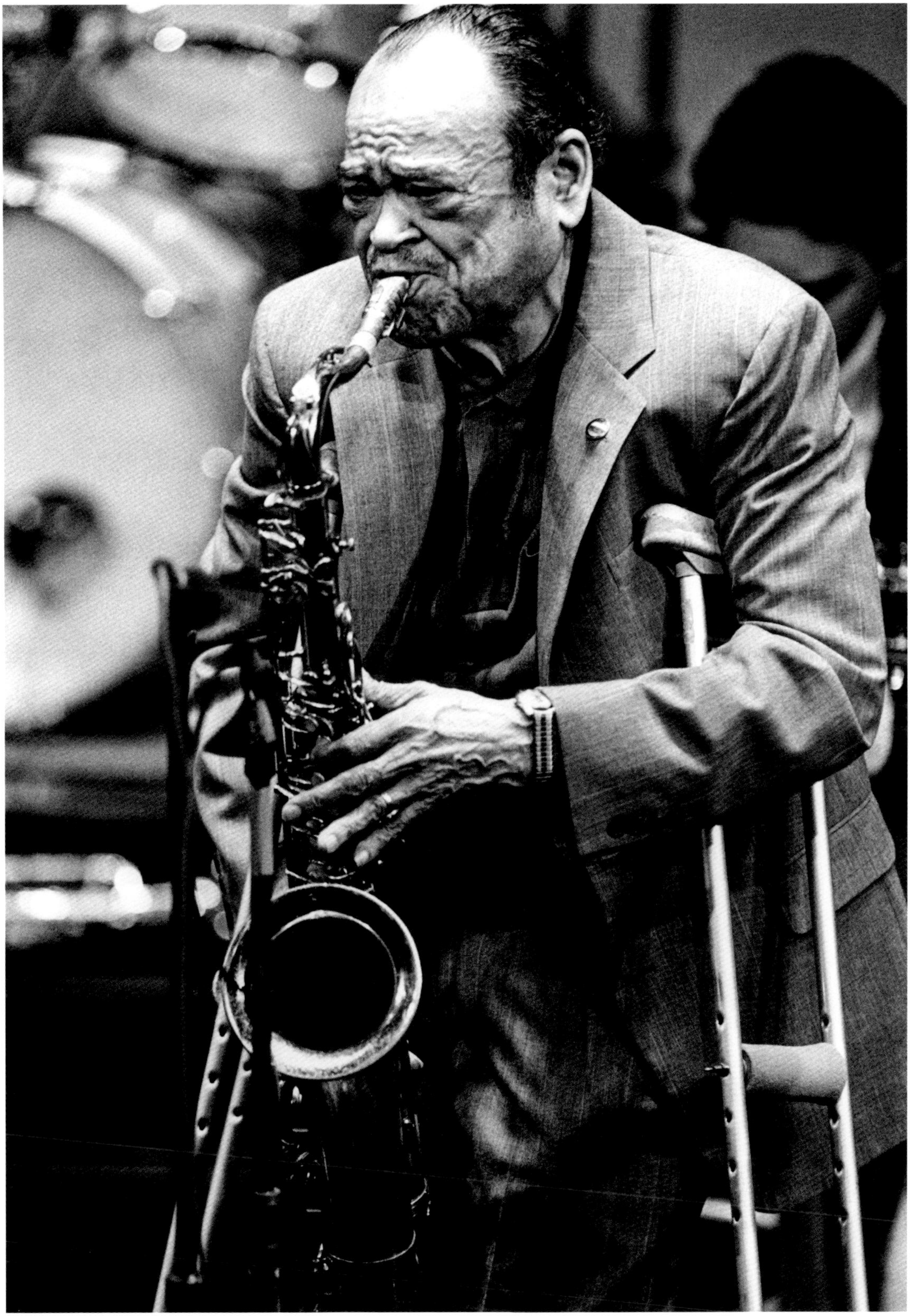

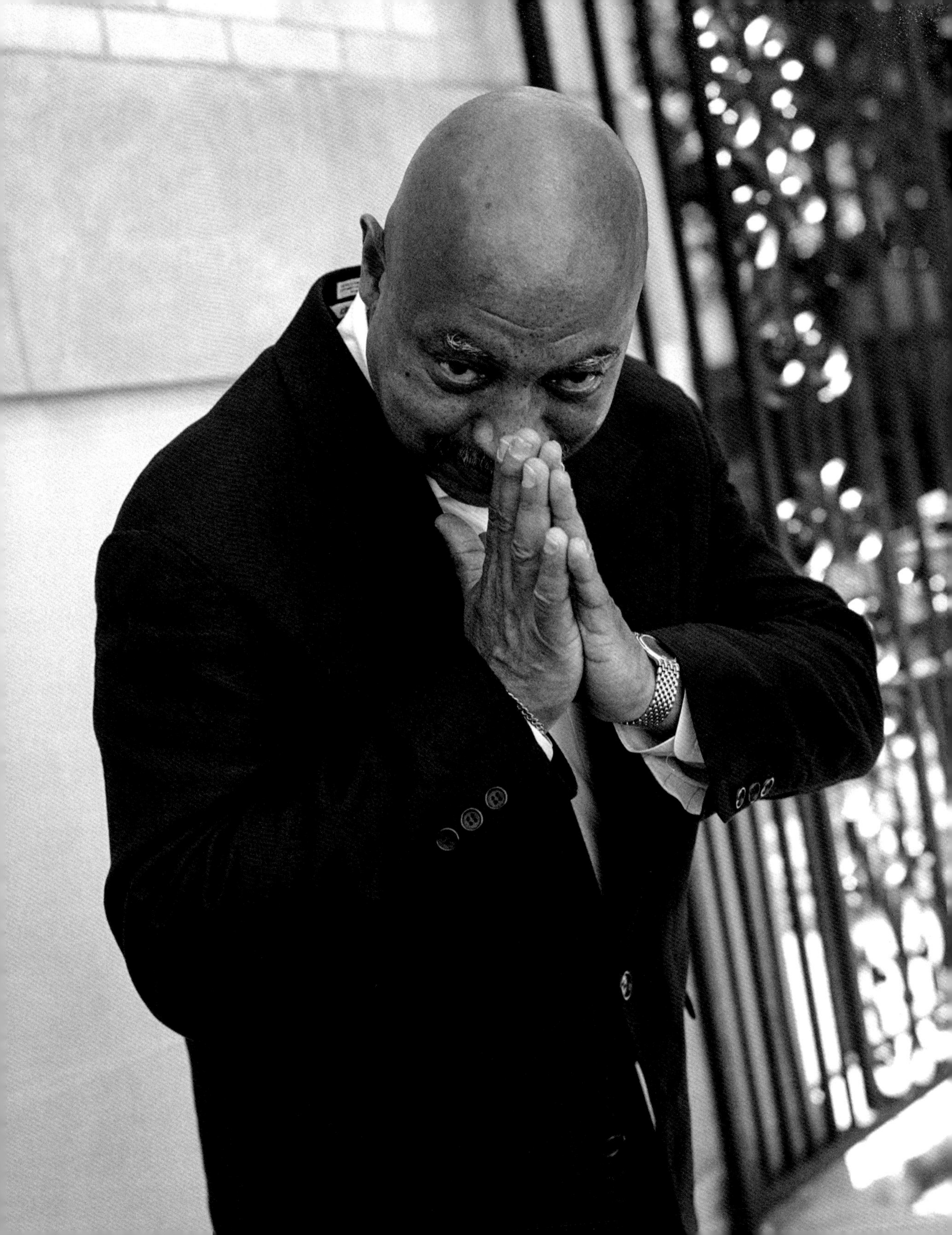

Kenny Barron
1998, New York City

(following pages)
Dexter Gordon and Tommy Flanagan
1988, SS Norway

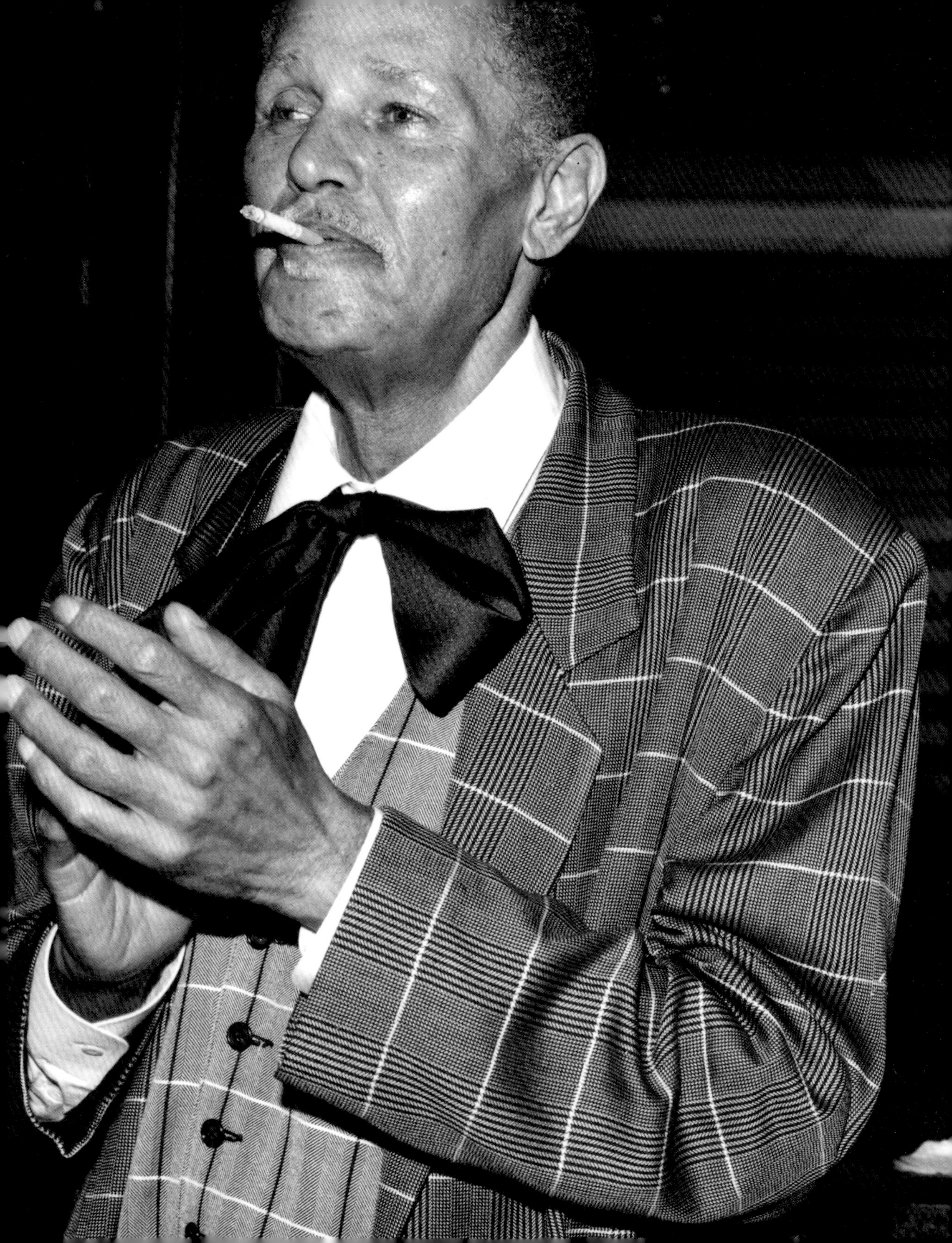

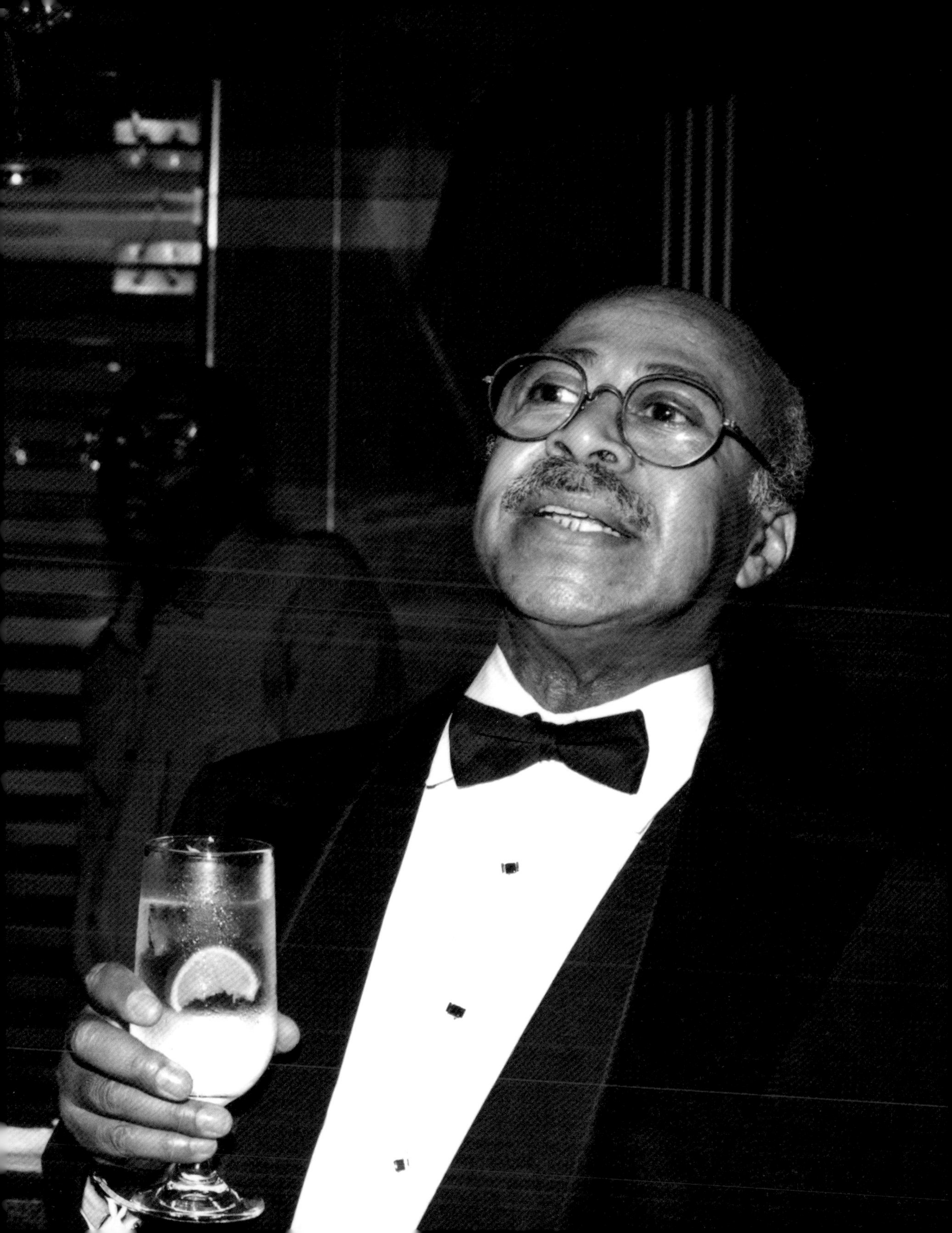

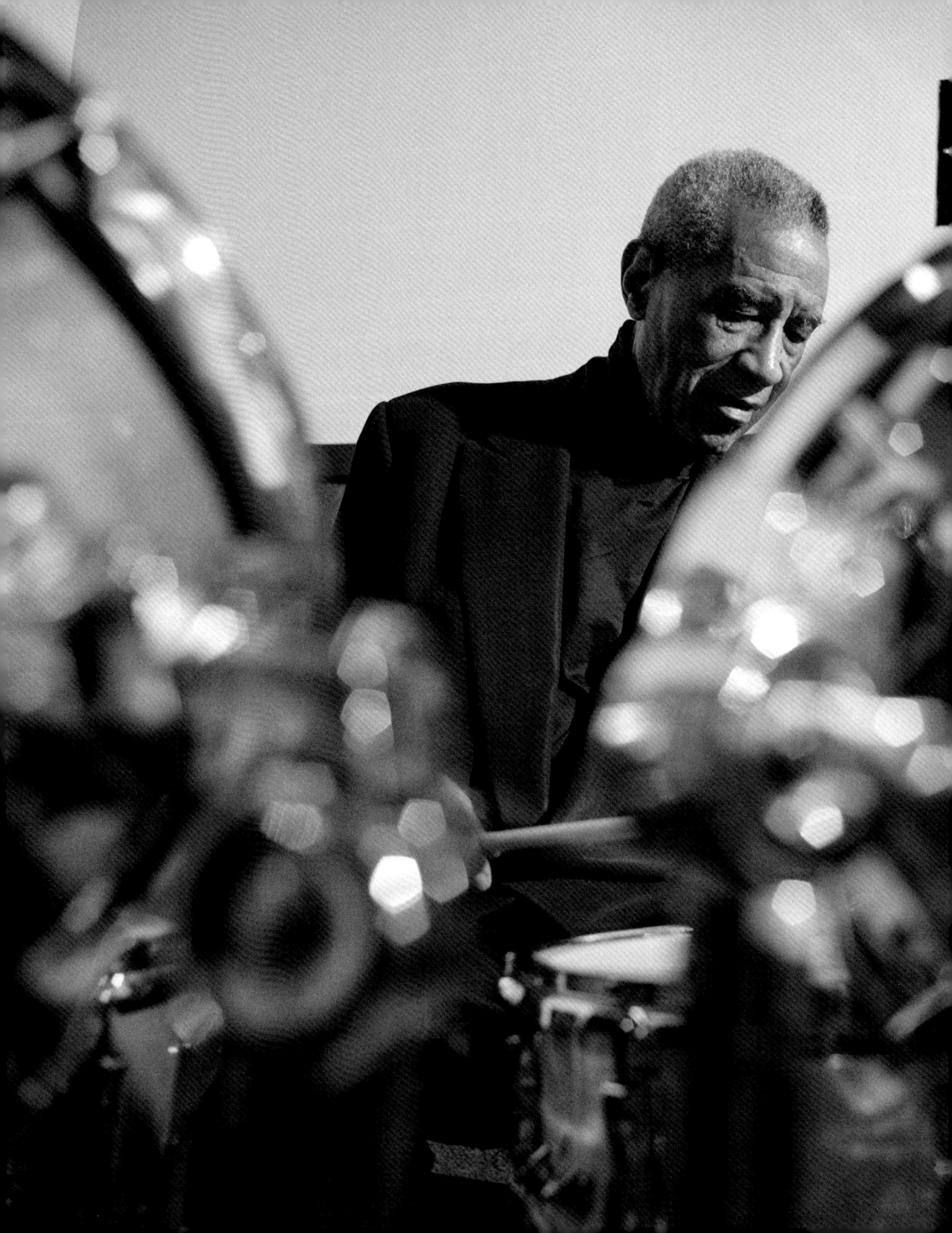

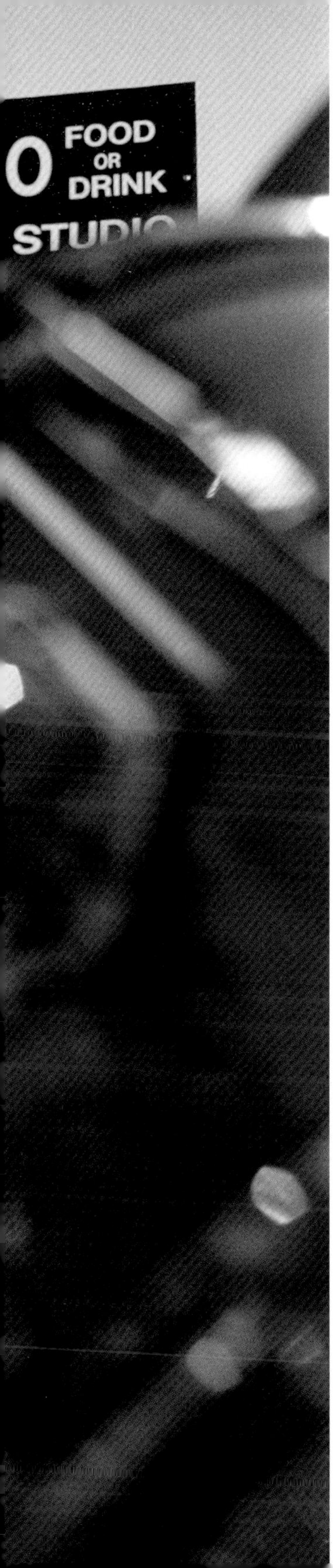

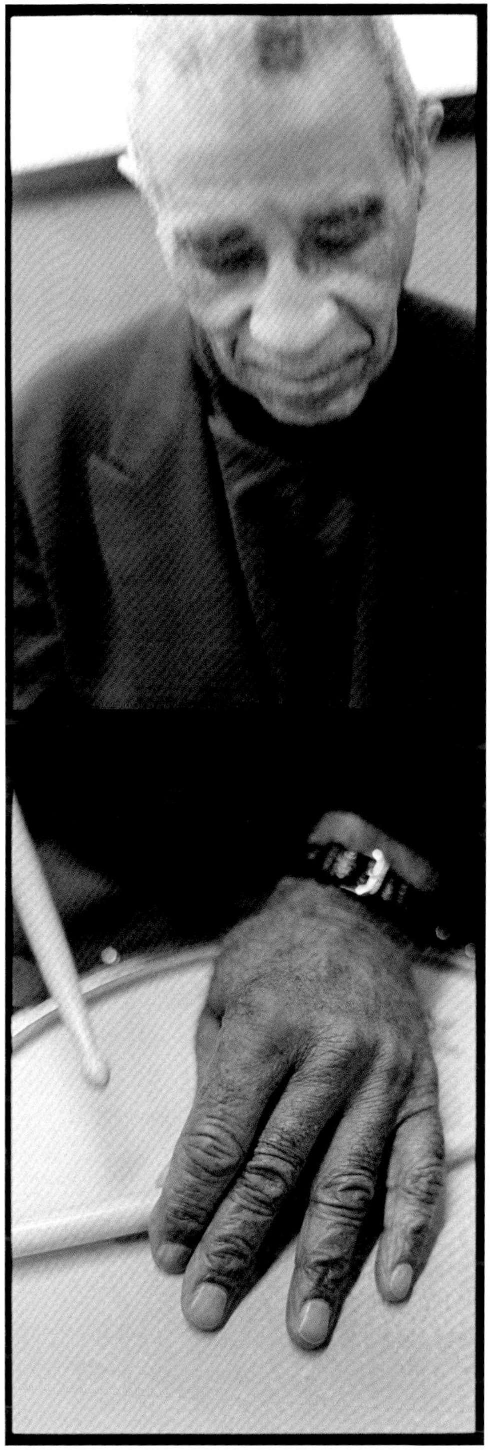

Max Roach
1998, New York City

Dizzy Gillespie
1988, New York City

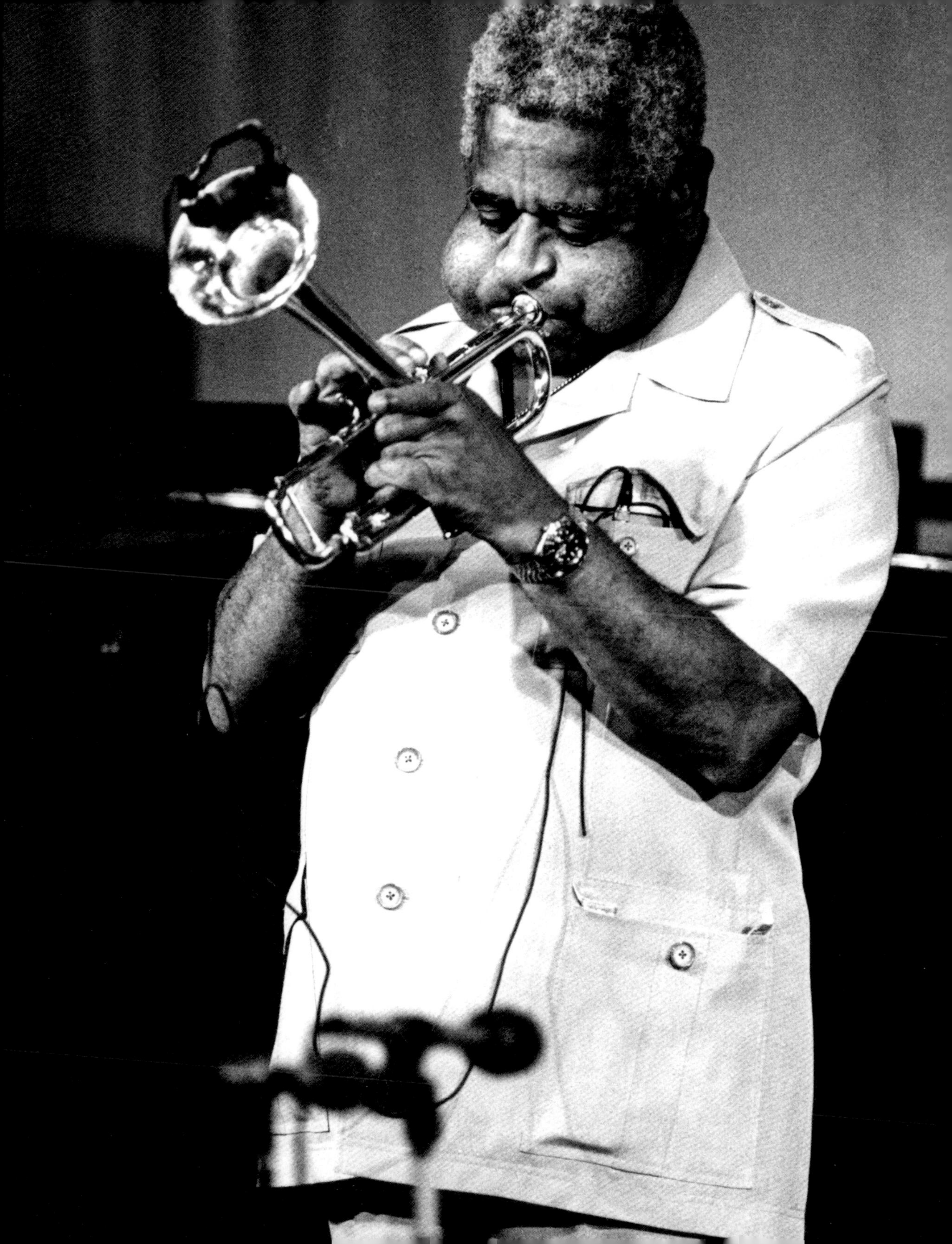

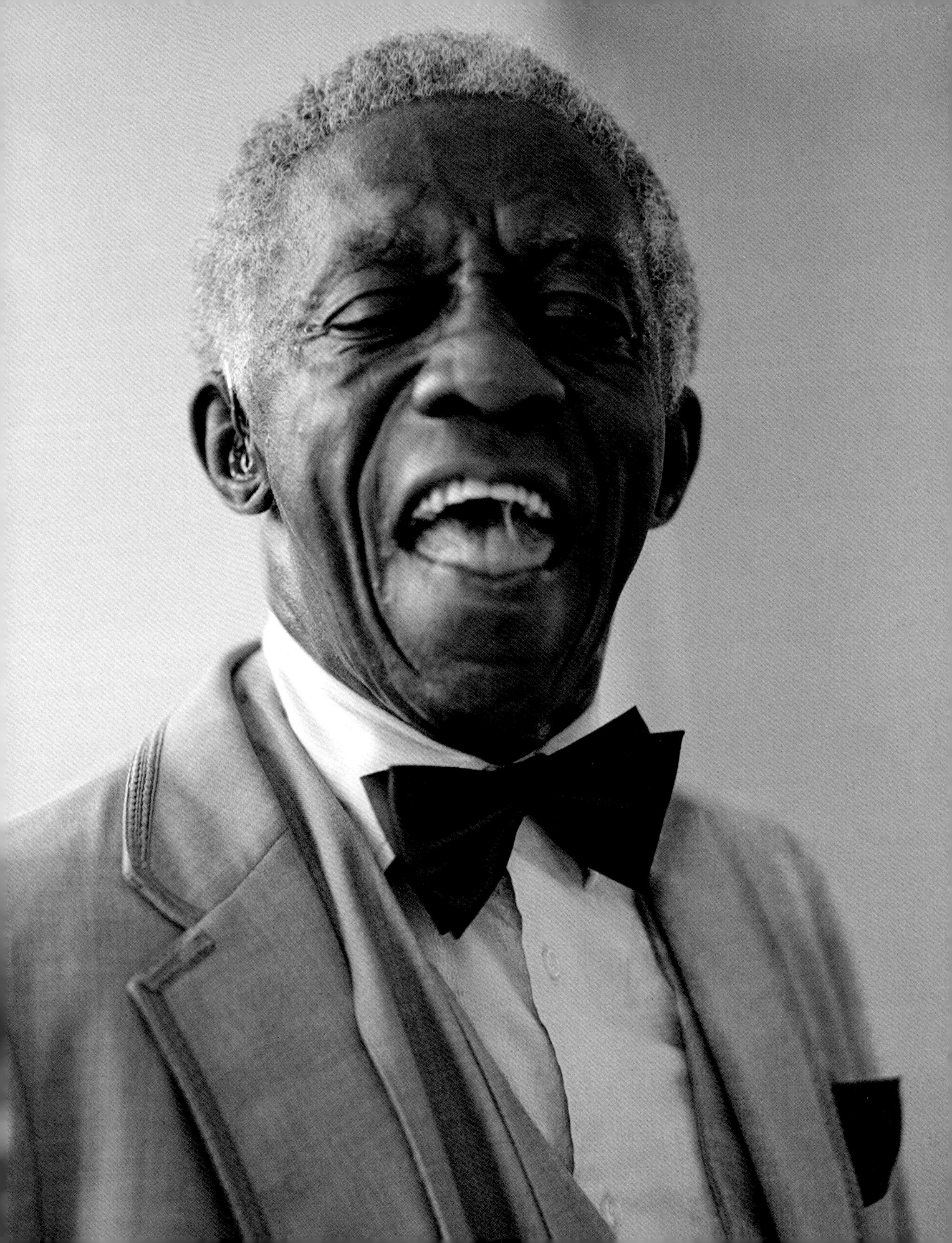

"Art Blakey was the best drummer there was for many years. He was a genius. I think he agreed to be photographed at my studio for French Vogue because he liked the idea of hanging out with beautiful models."

Art Blakey
1987, New York City

(following pages)
Jason Moran and Liya Kebede
2000, New York City

Jesse Davis
2000, New York City

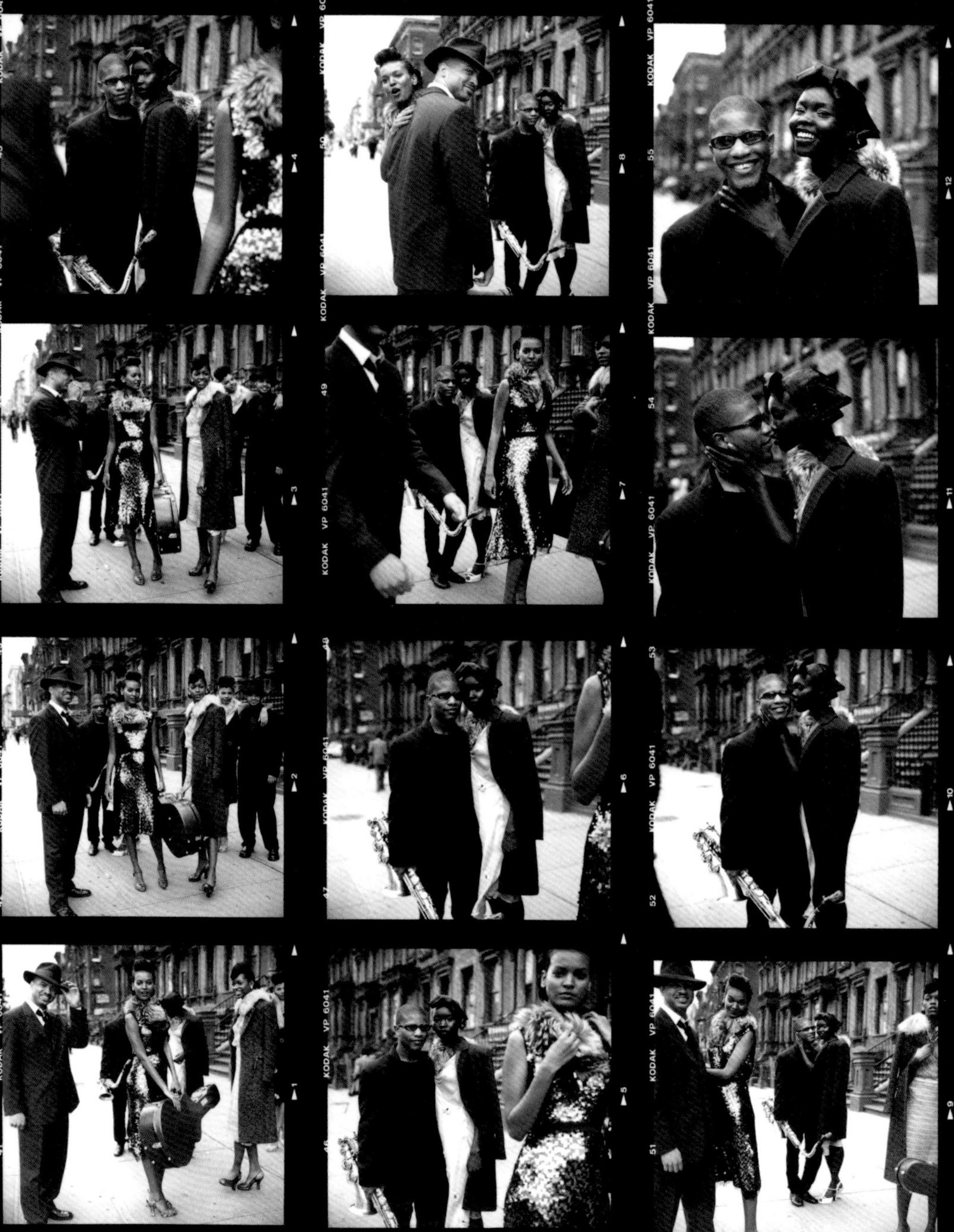

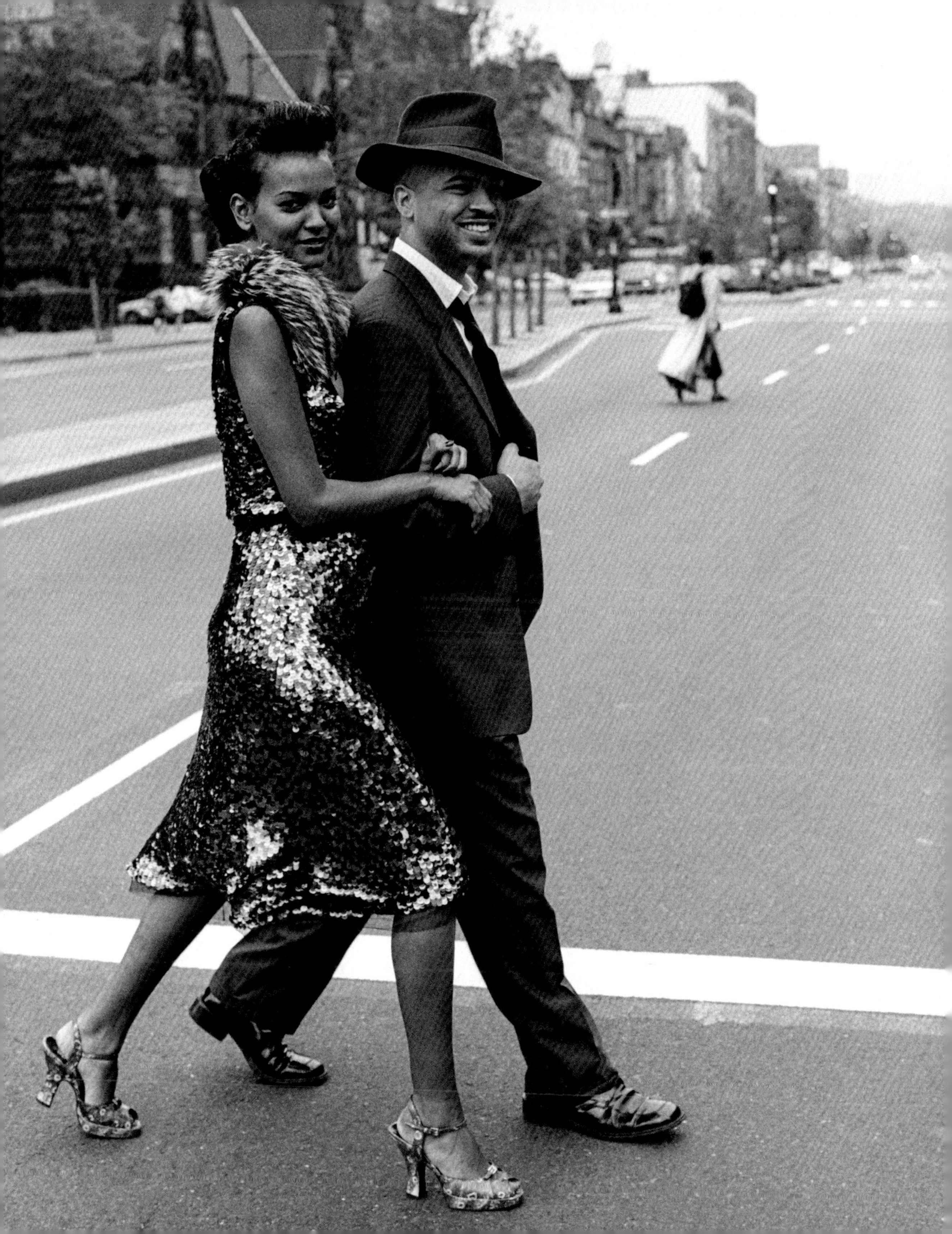

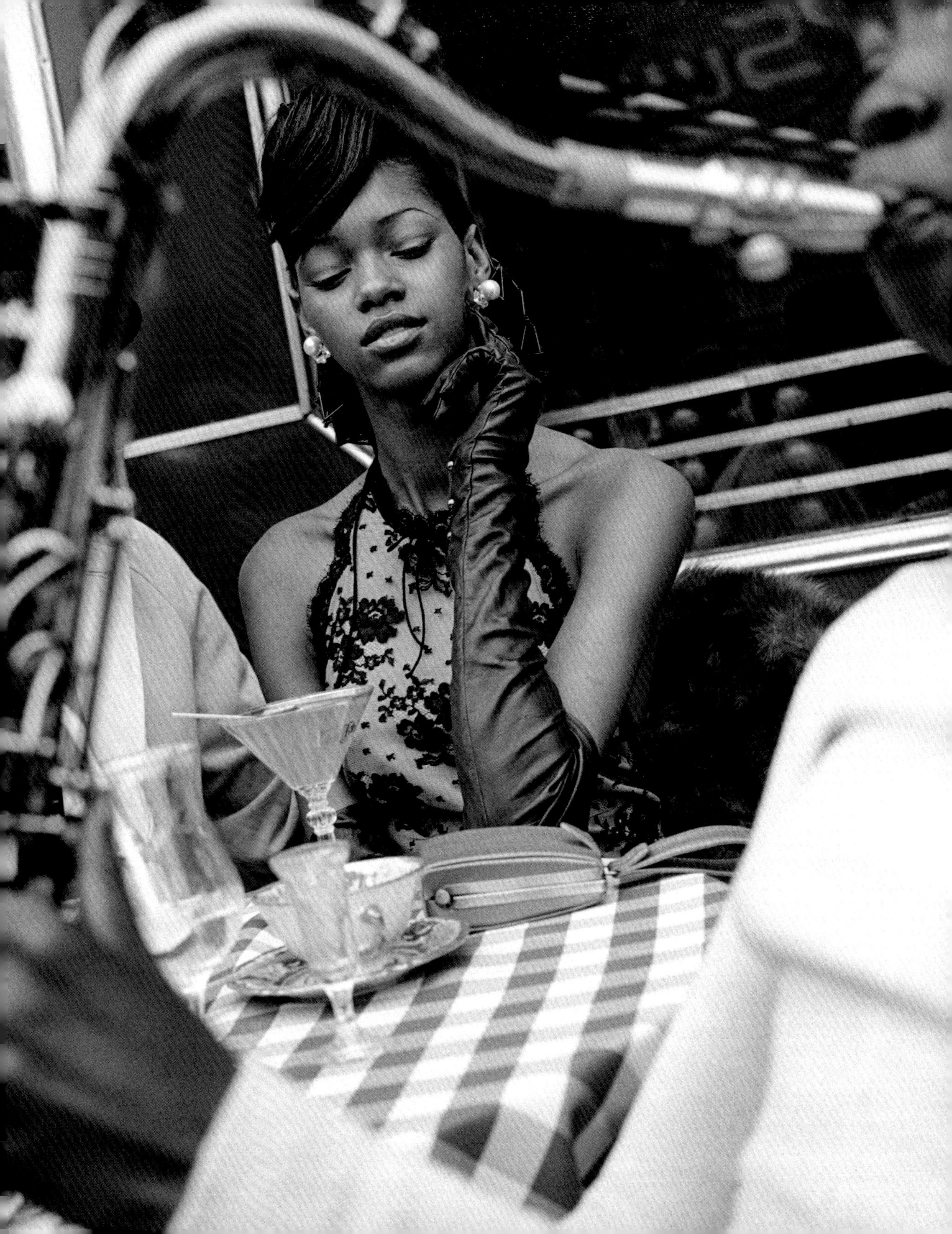

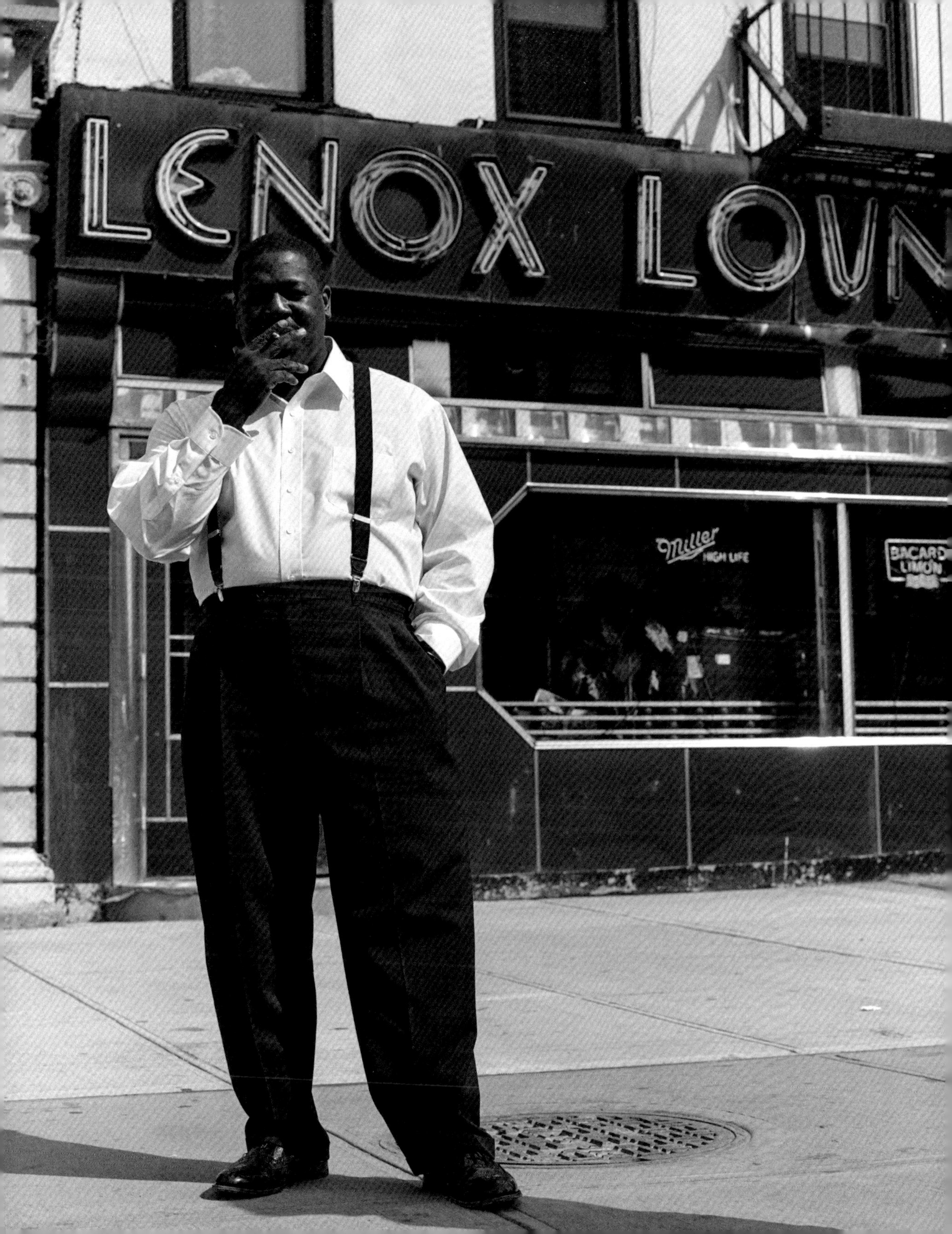
LENOX LOUN
Miller
HIGH LIFE
BACARD
LIMON

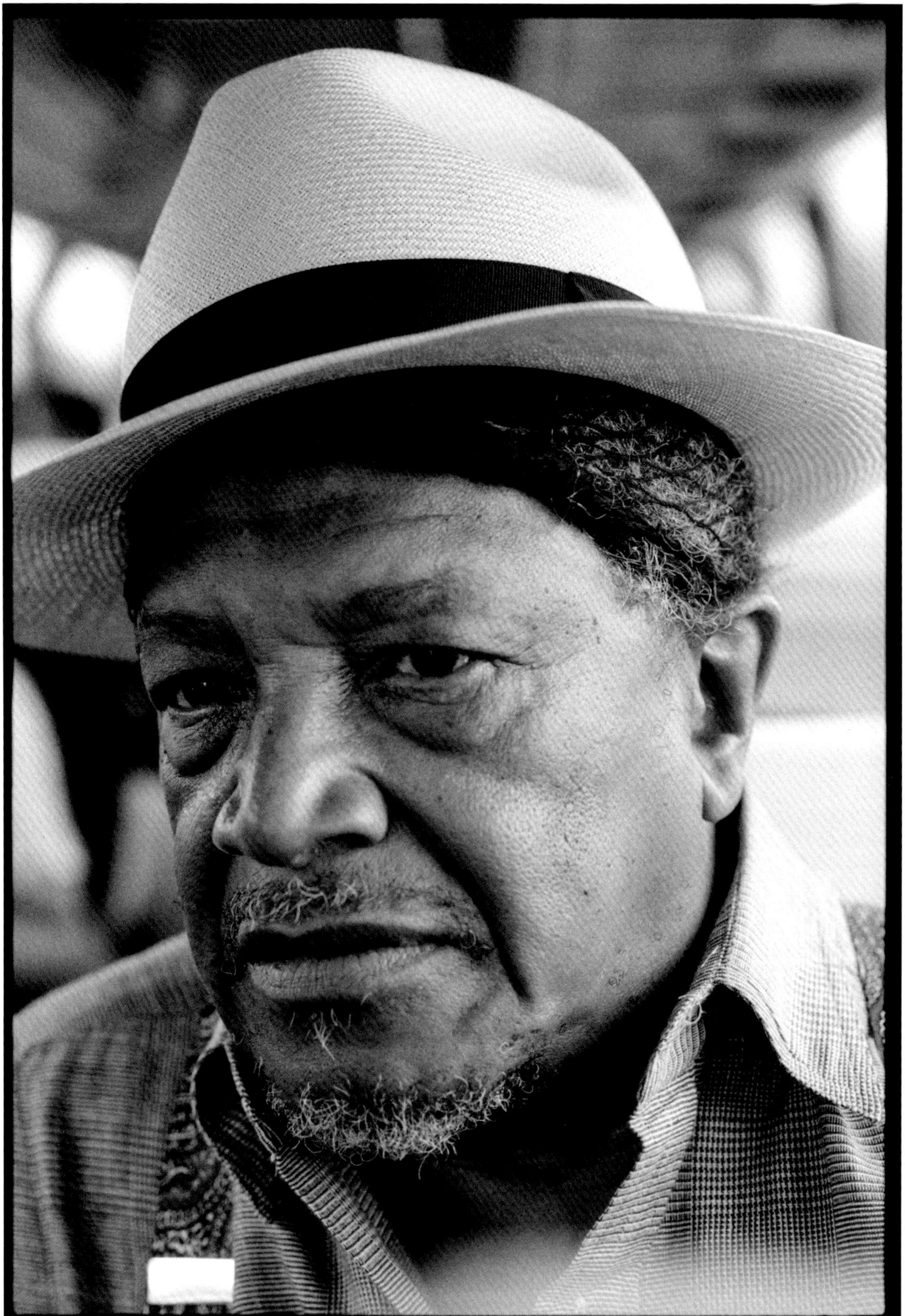

Illinois Jacquet
1988, SS Norway

(following pages)
Milt Hinton
1988, New York City

Illinois Jacquet
1988, New York City

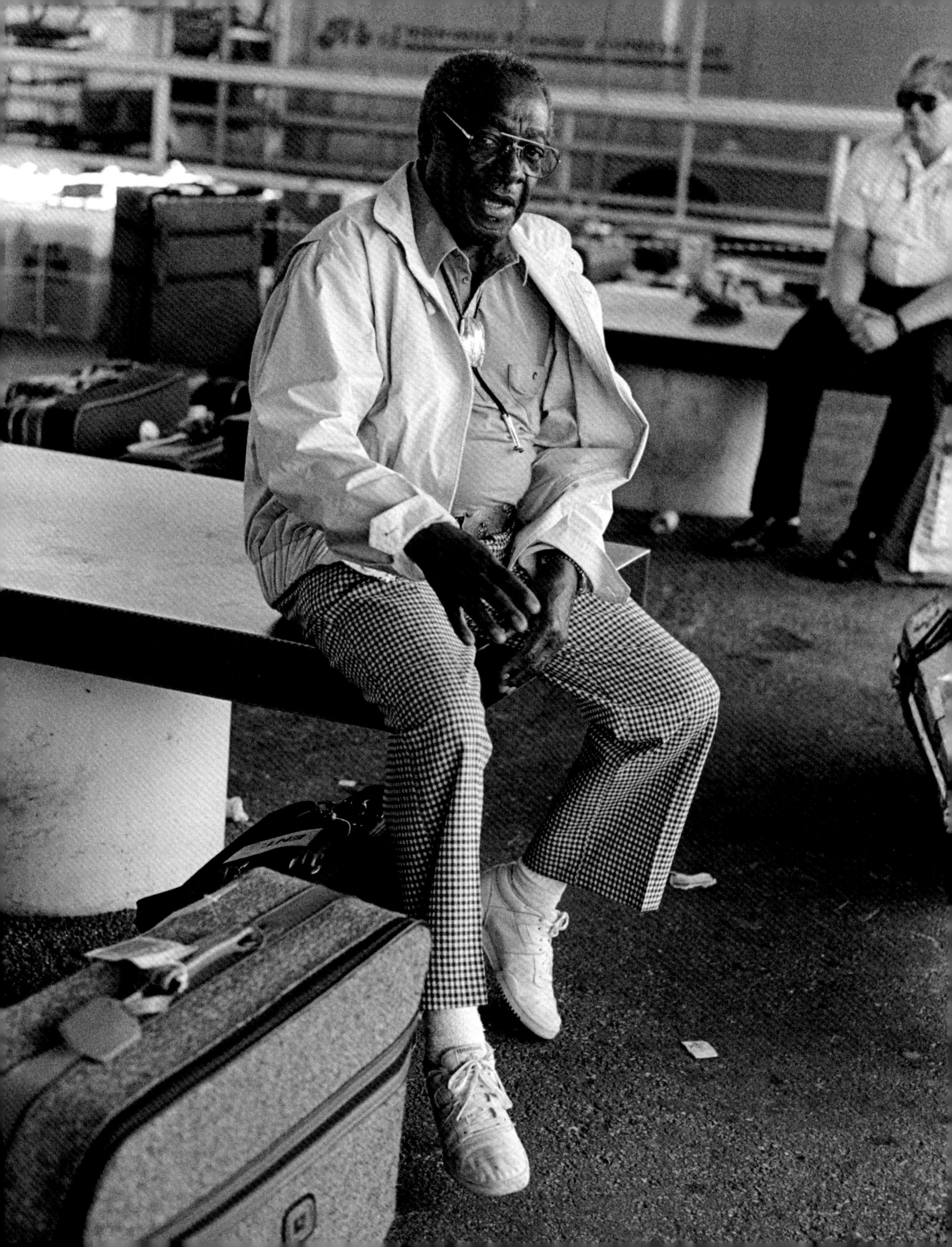

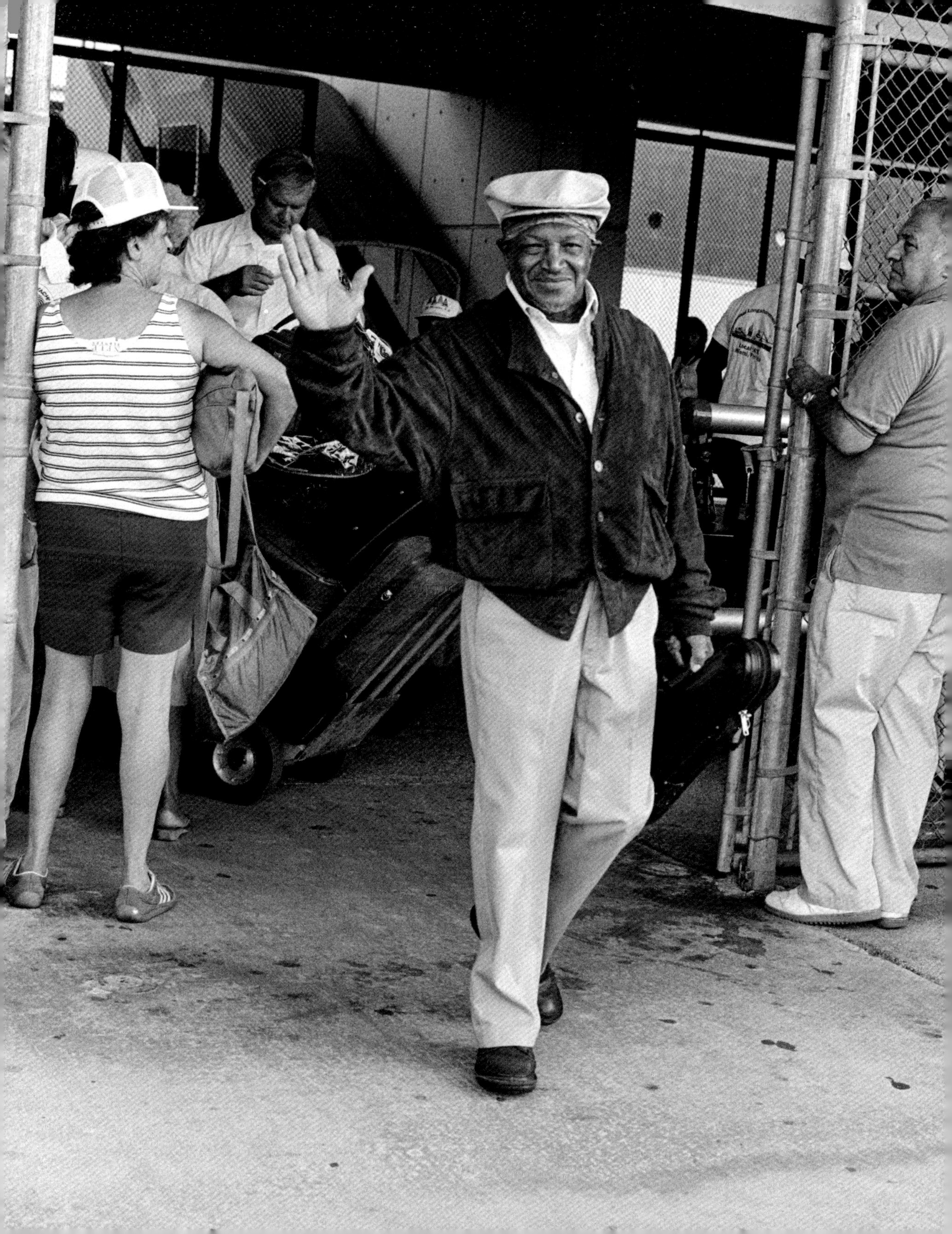

"Illinois was a big personality and
an easy subject for my movie.
There were hundreds of people
at Riverside Church in Morningside
Heights for his funeral.
Illinois and his wife, Carol, had
liked the movie so much that
clips of it were played. It was such
a sad day and yet such an honor."

Illinois Jacquet
1990, Paris

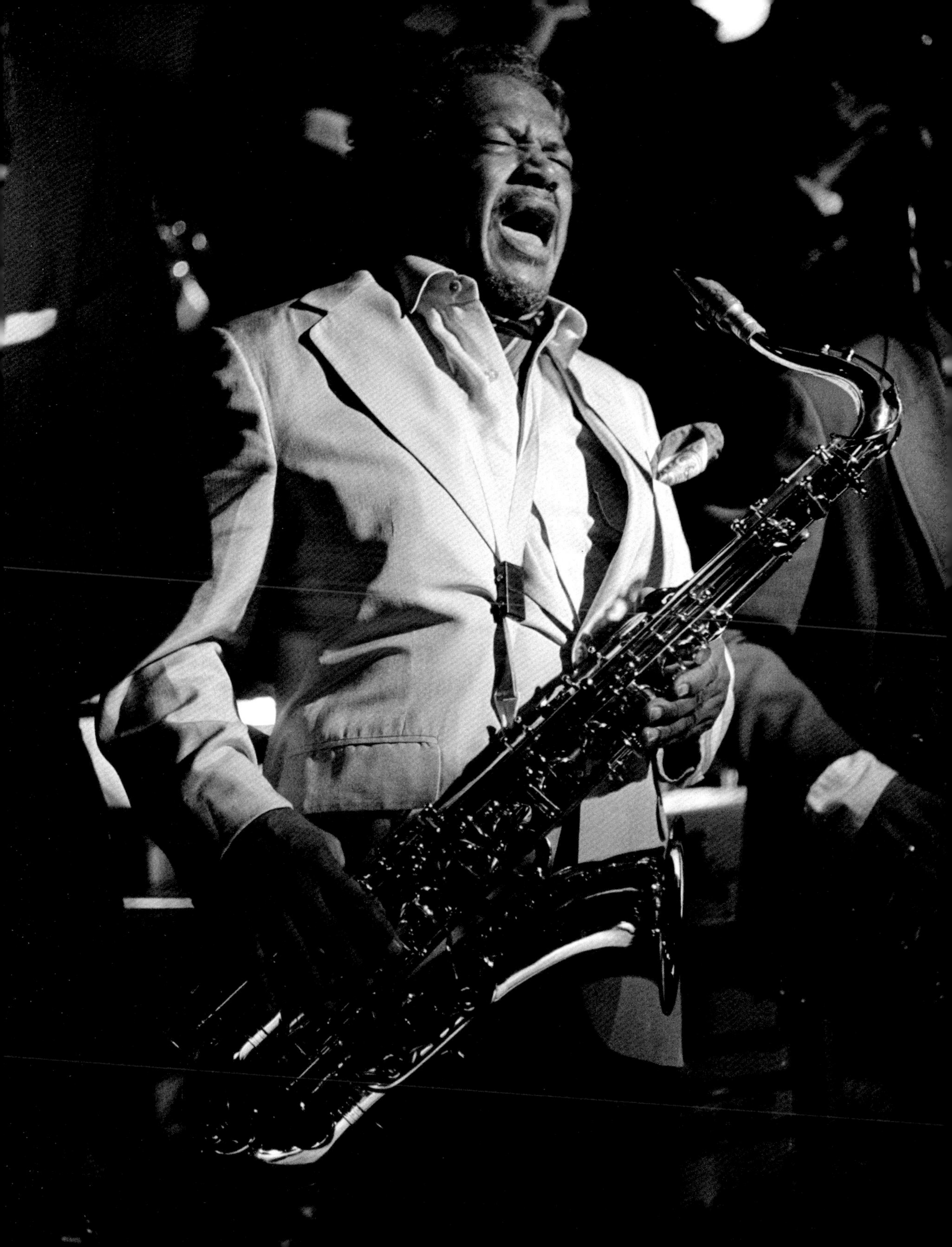

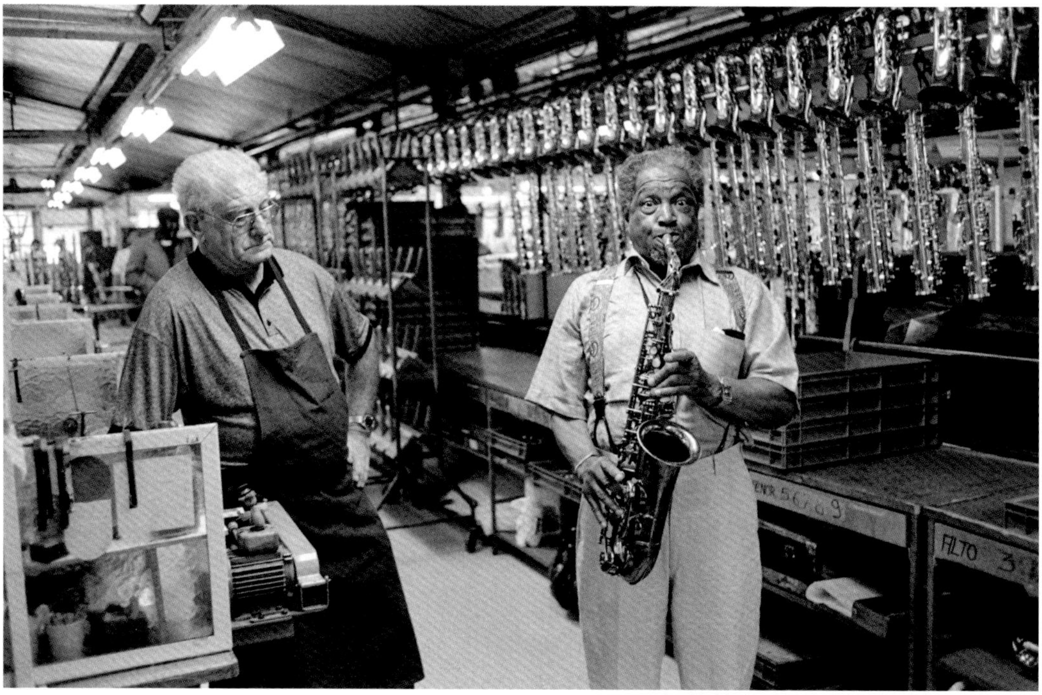
FILTO 3

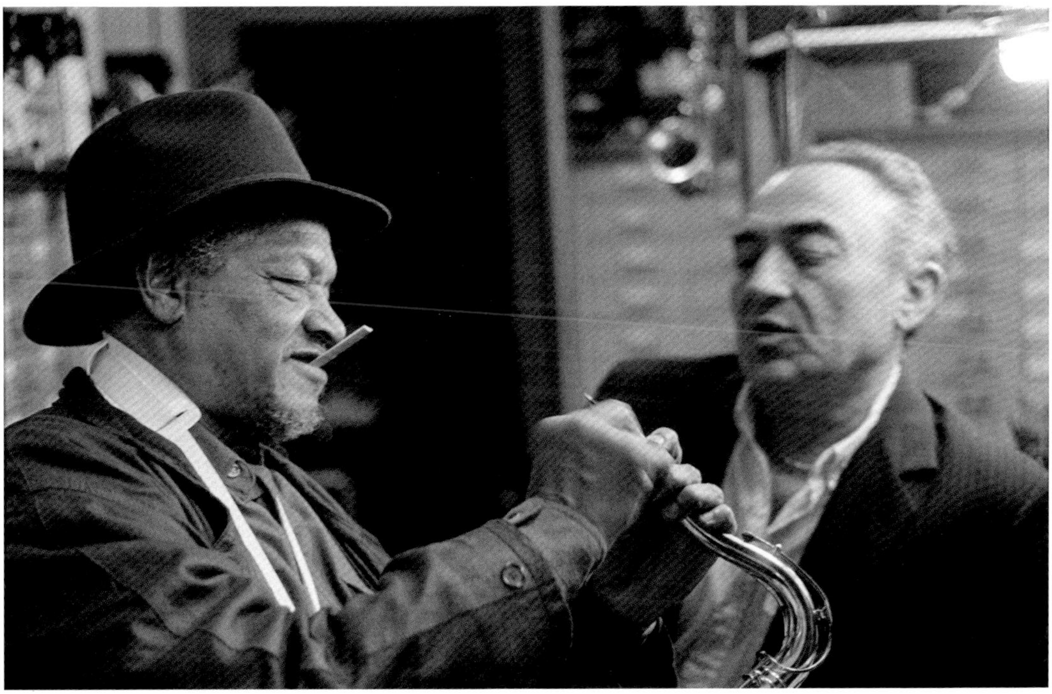

Illinois Jacquet and Emilio Lyons
1990, Boston

Illinois Jacquet at the Selmer Factory
1990, Paris

(following pages)
Jamal Haynes, Stafford Hunter, and Amadou Diallo
1992, SS Norway

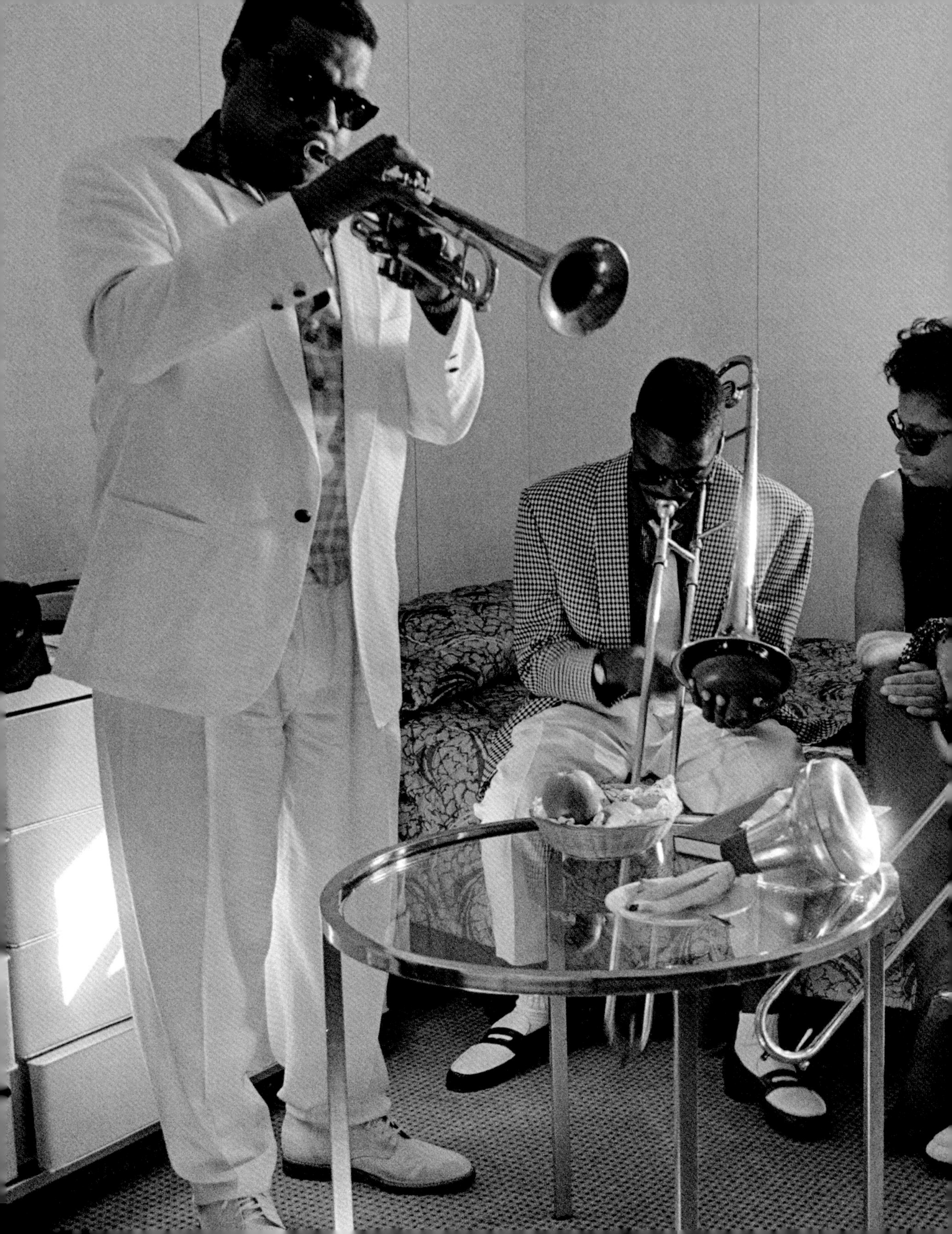

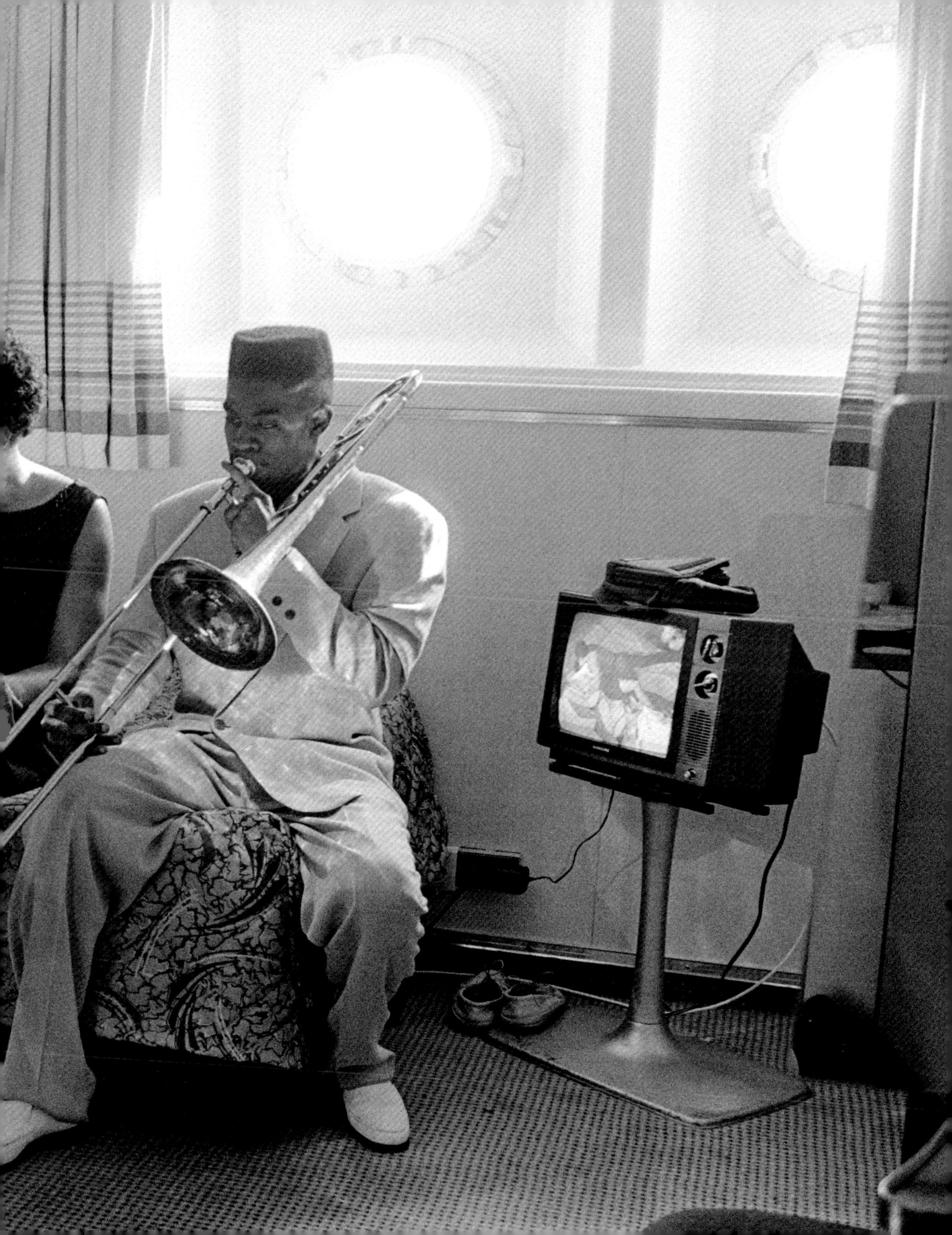

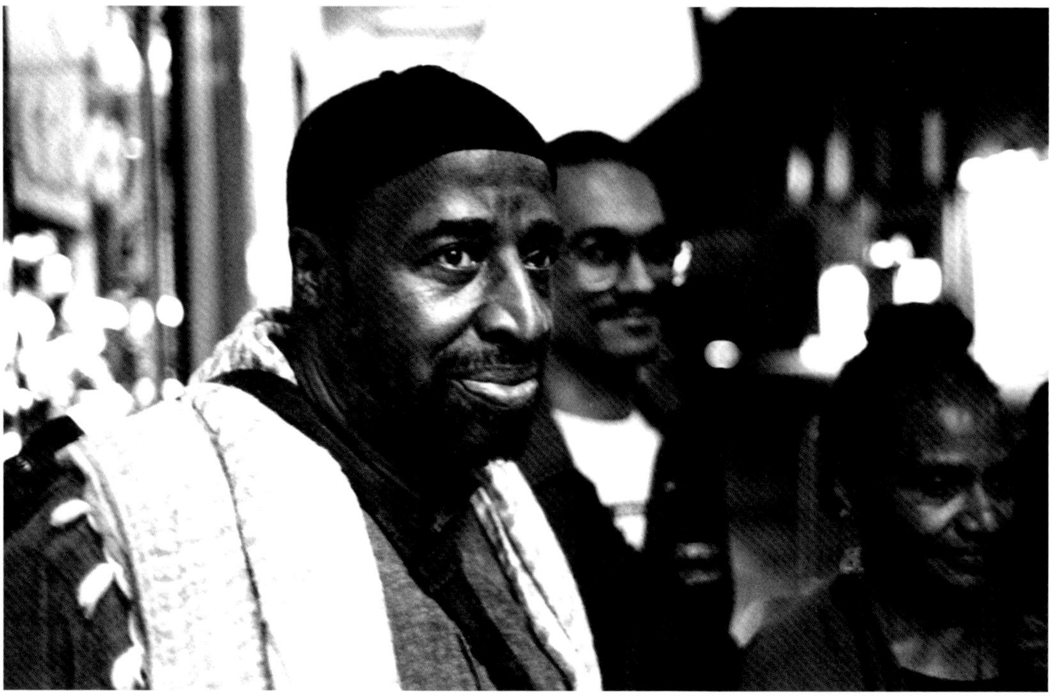

Luther Lafatti
1992, New York City

Courtney Pines and Bradford Marsalis
1990, New York City

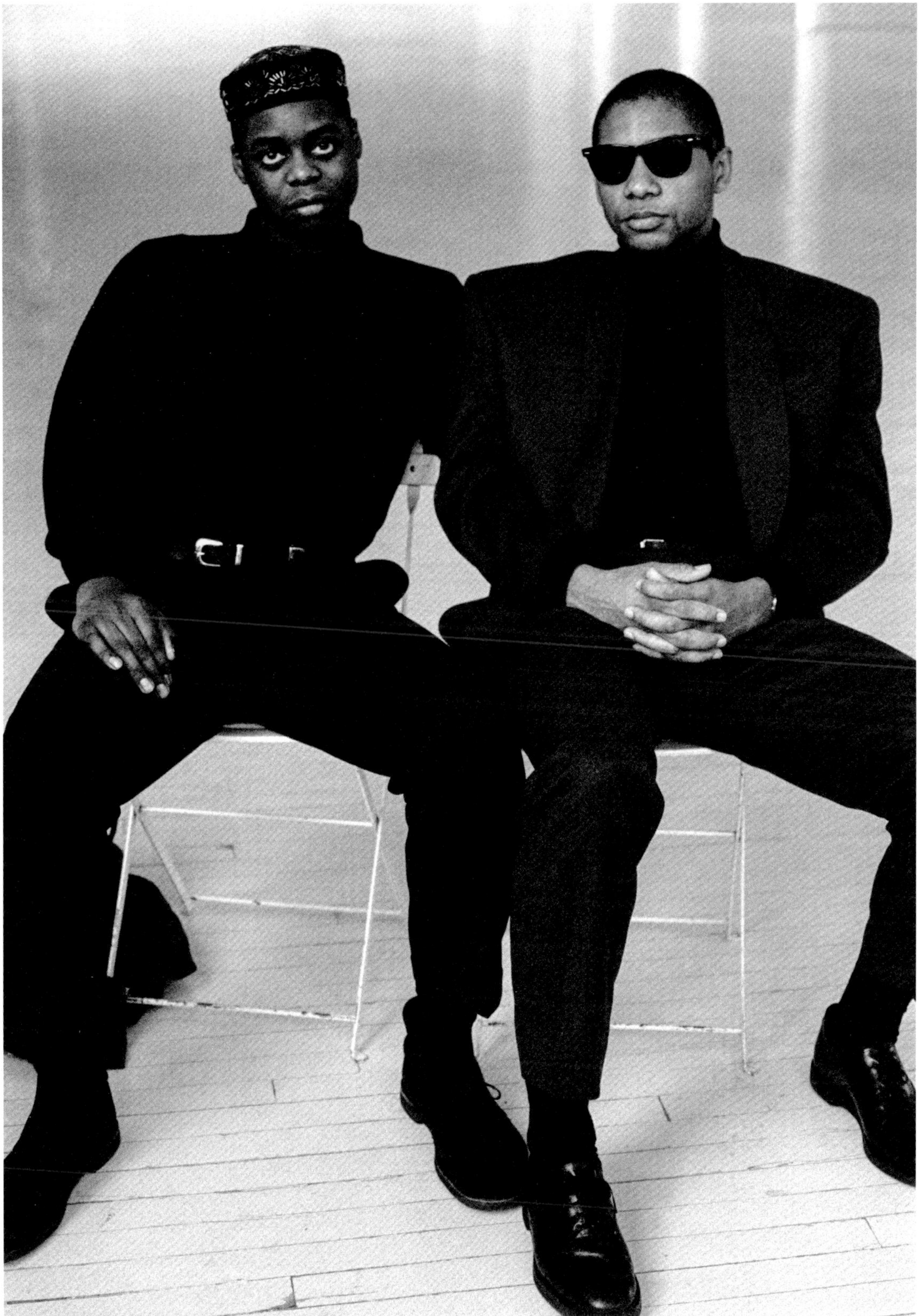

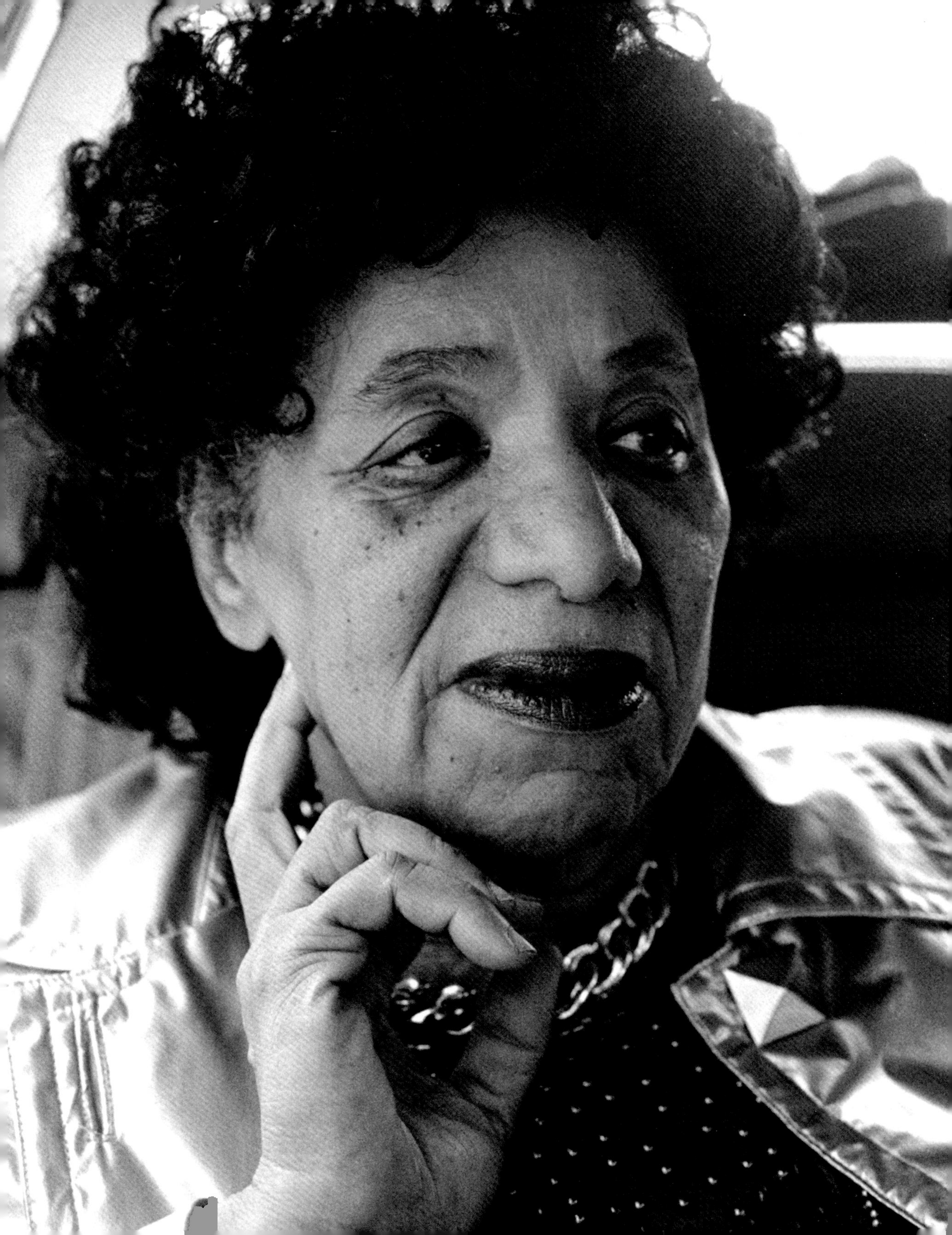

Dorothy Donegan
1991, New York City

(following pages)
Jazz at Lincoln Center Orchestra
1992, New York City

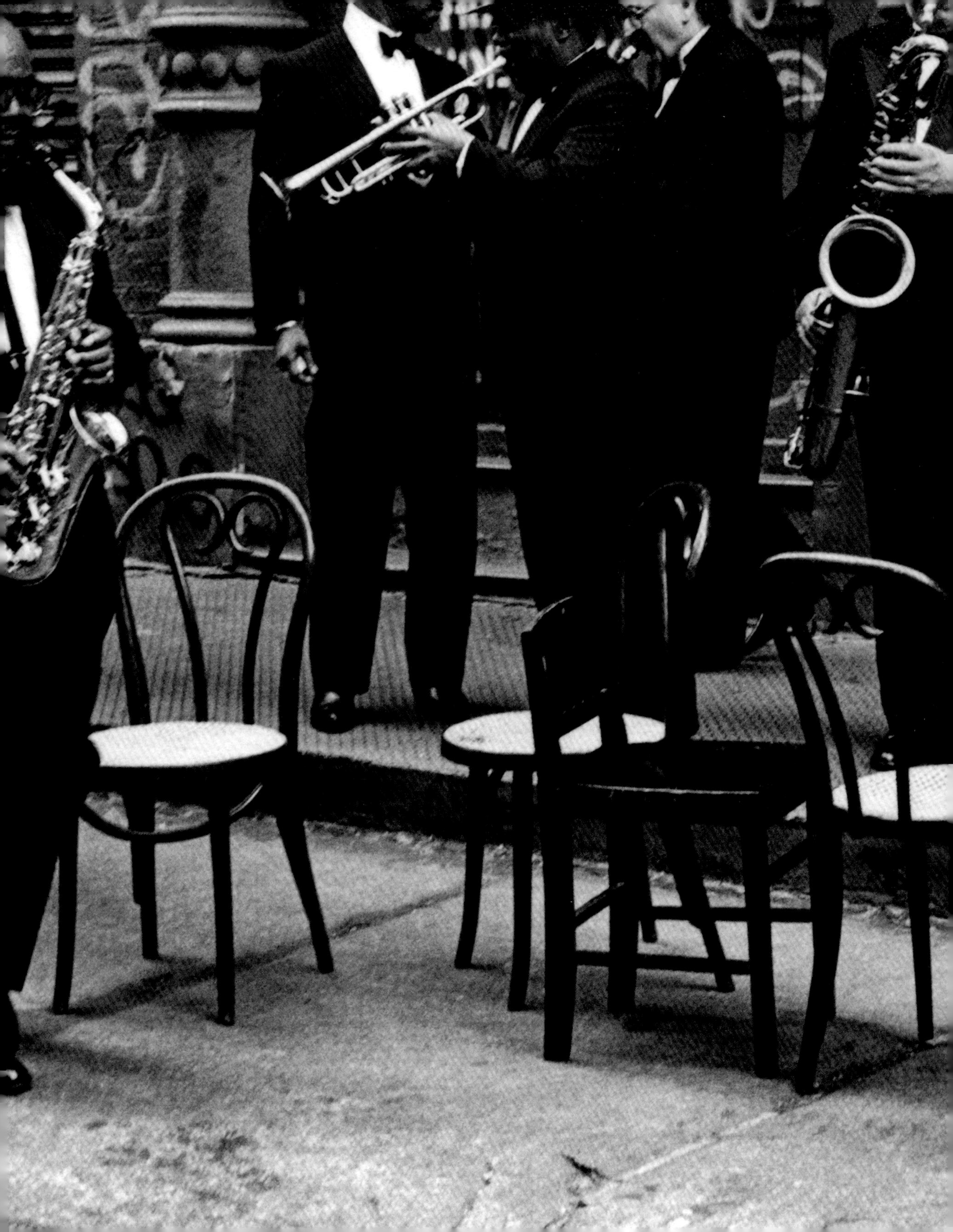

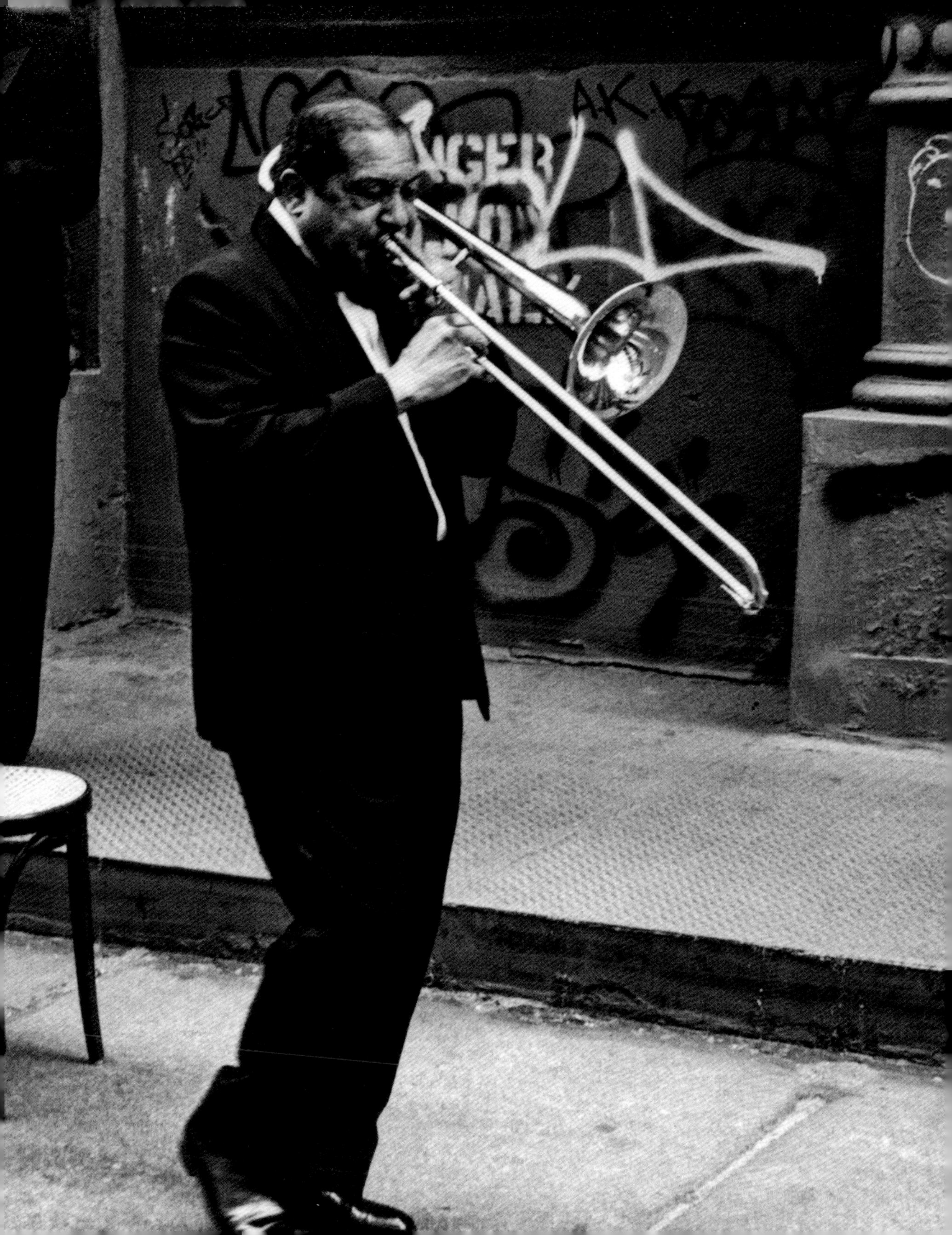

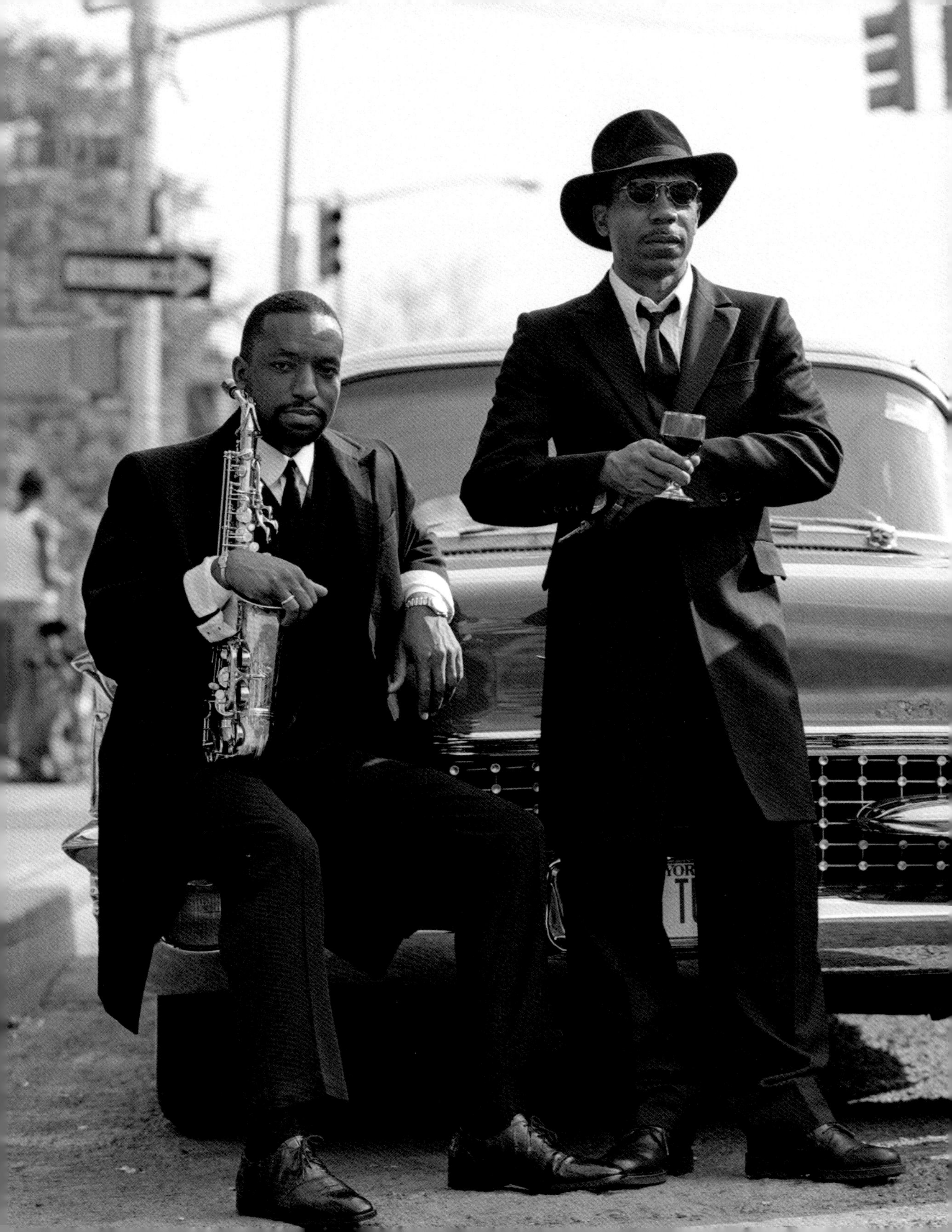

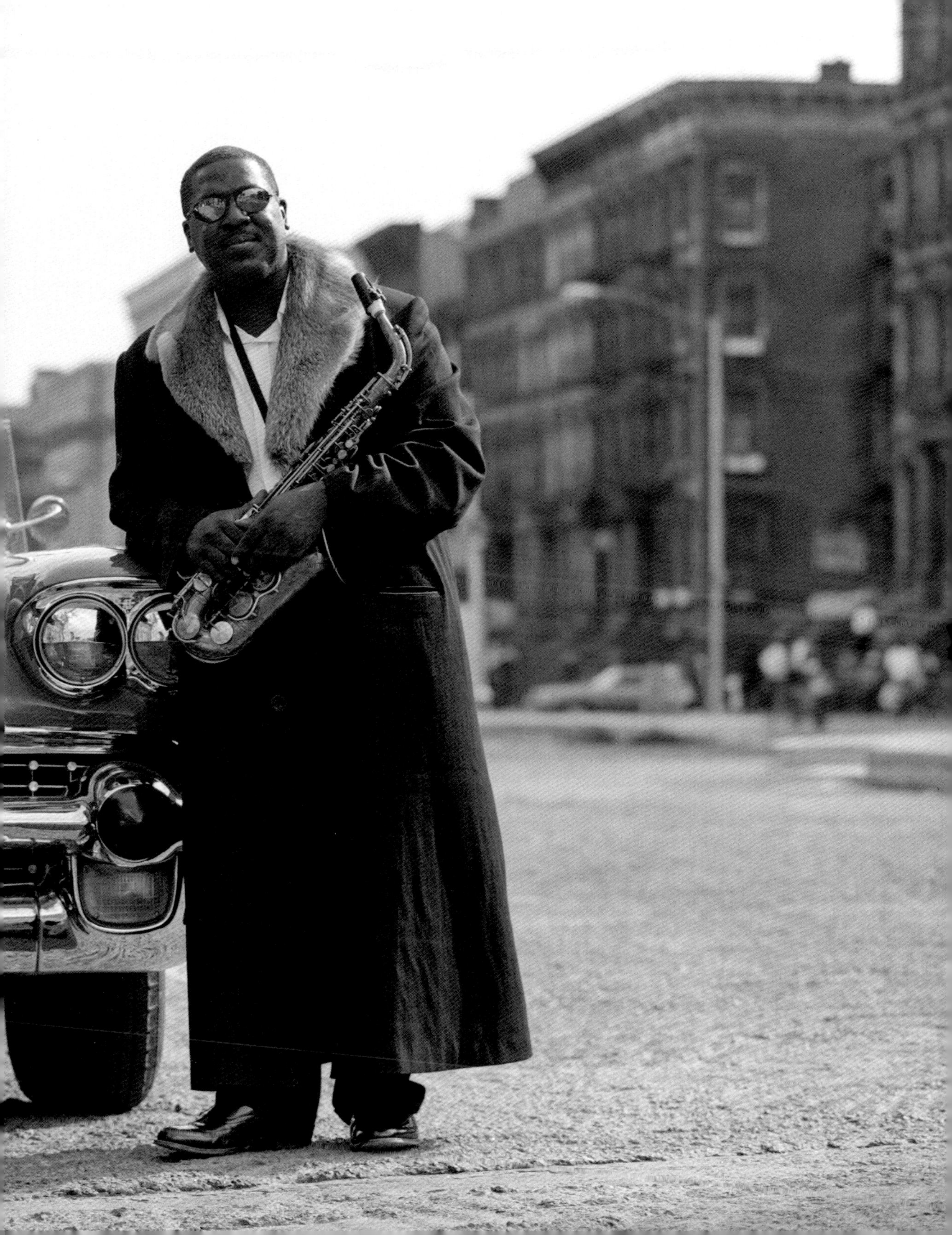

Illinois Jacquet
1988, New York City

(preceding pages)
Donald Harrison, Olu Dara, and Jesse Davis
1998, New York City

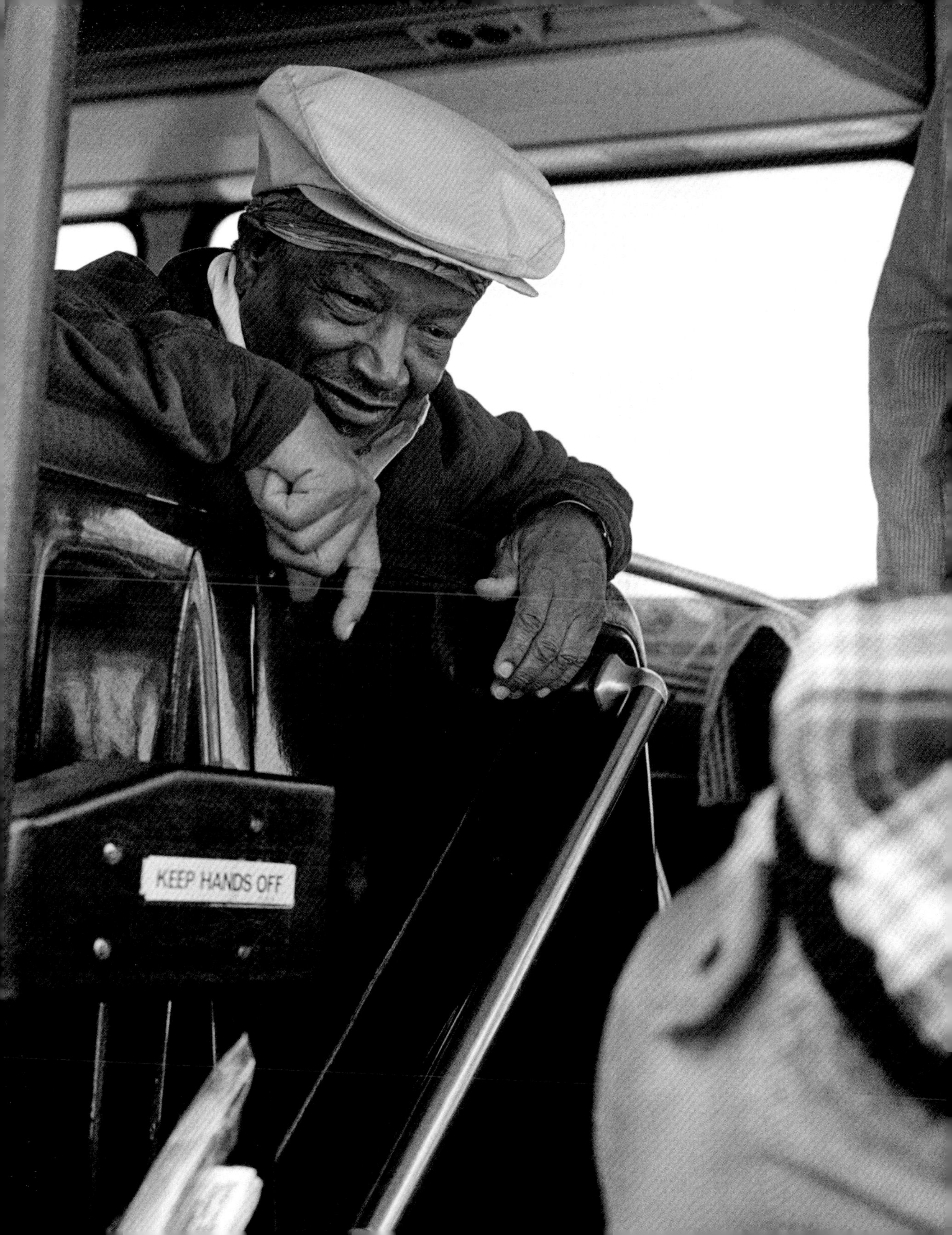
KEEP HANDS OFF

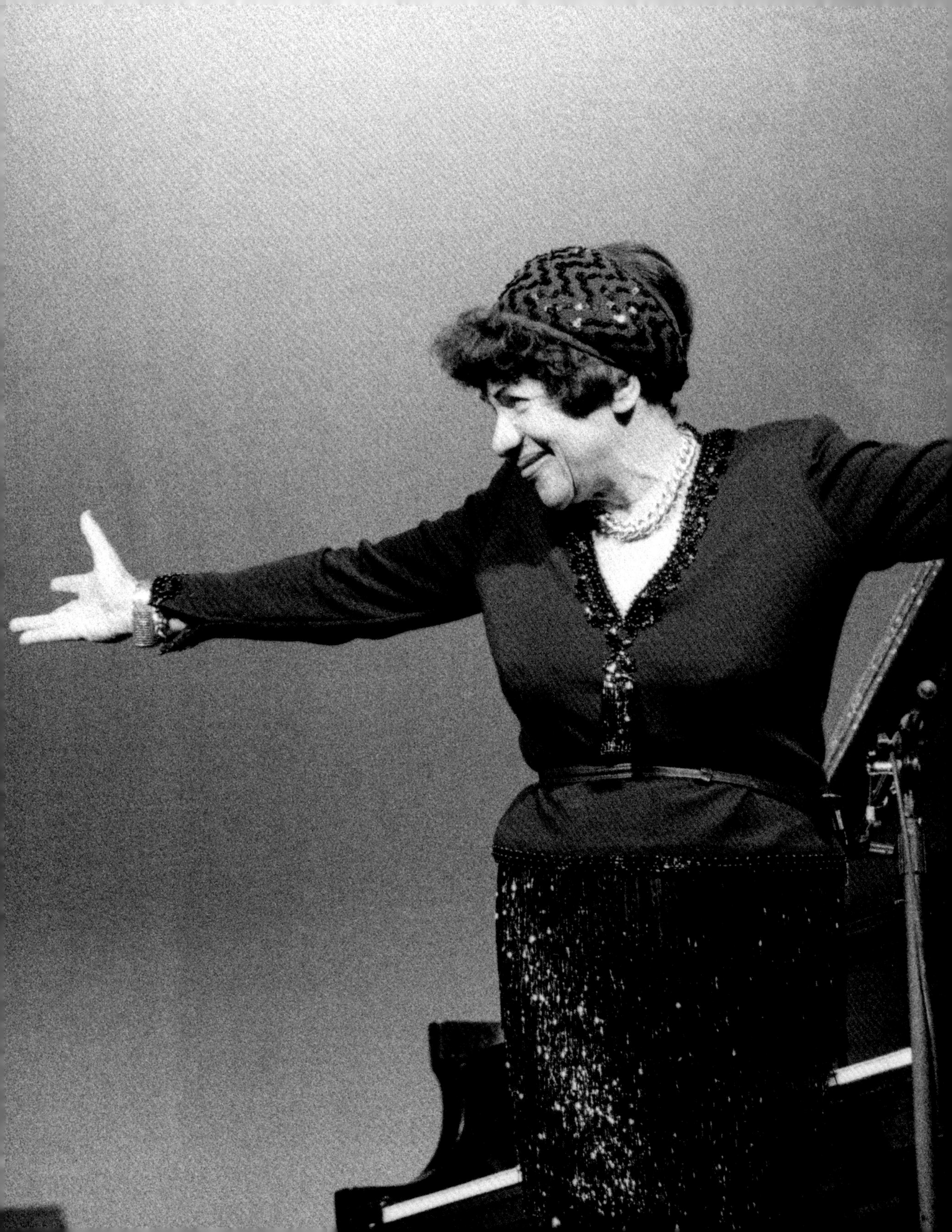

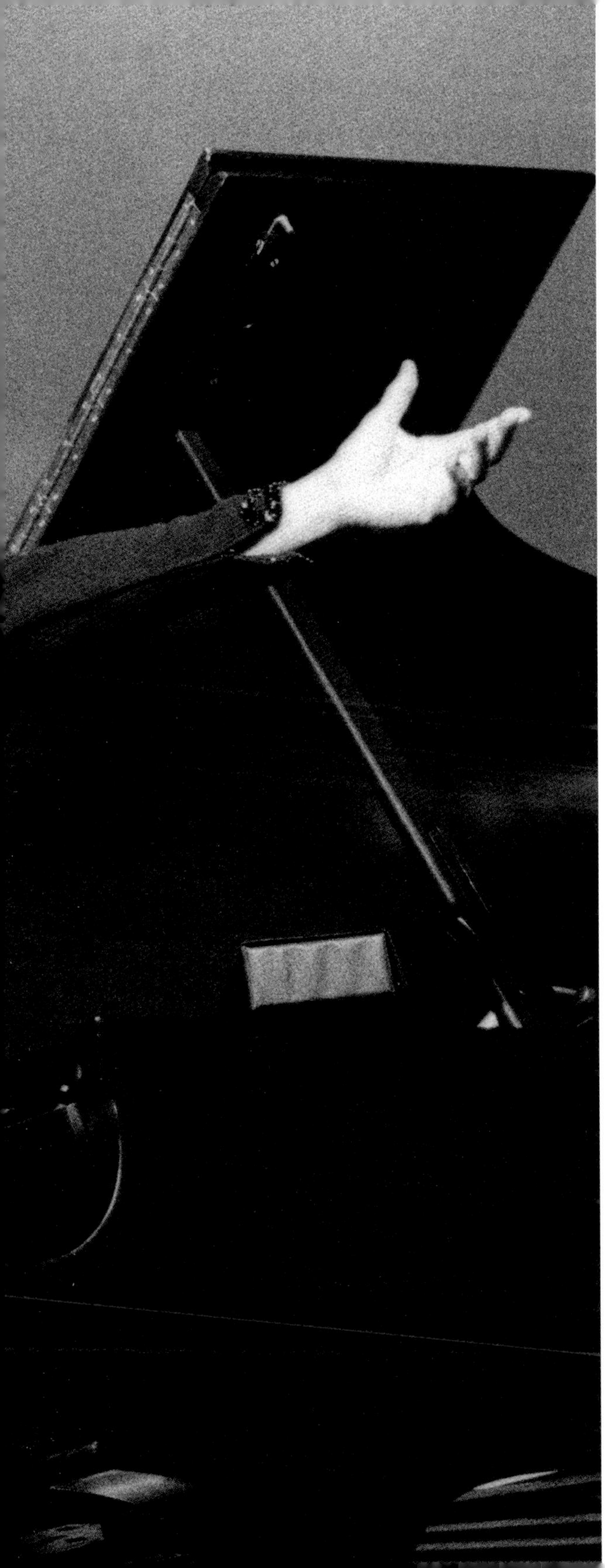

Dorothy Donegan
1990, New York City

(following pages)
Arnett Cobb, Buddy Tate, and Illinois Jacquet
1988, SS Norway

Anton Rooney
1991, New York City

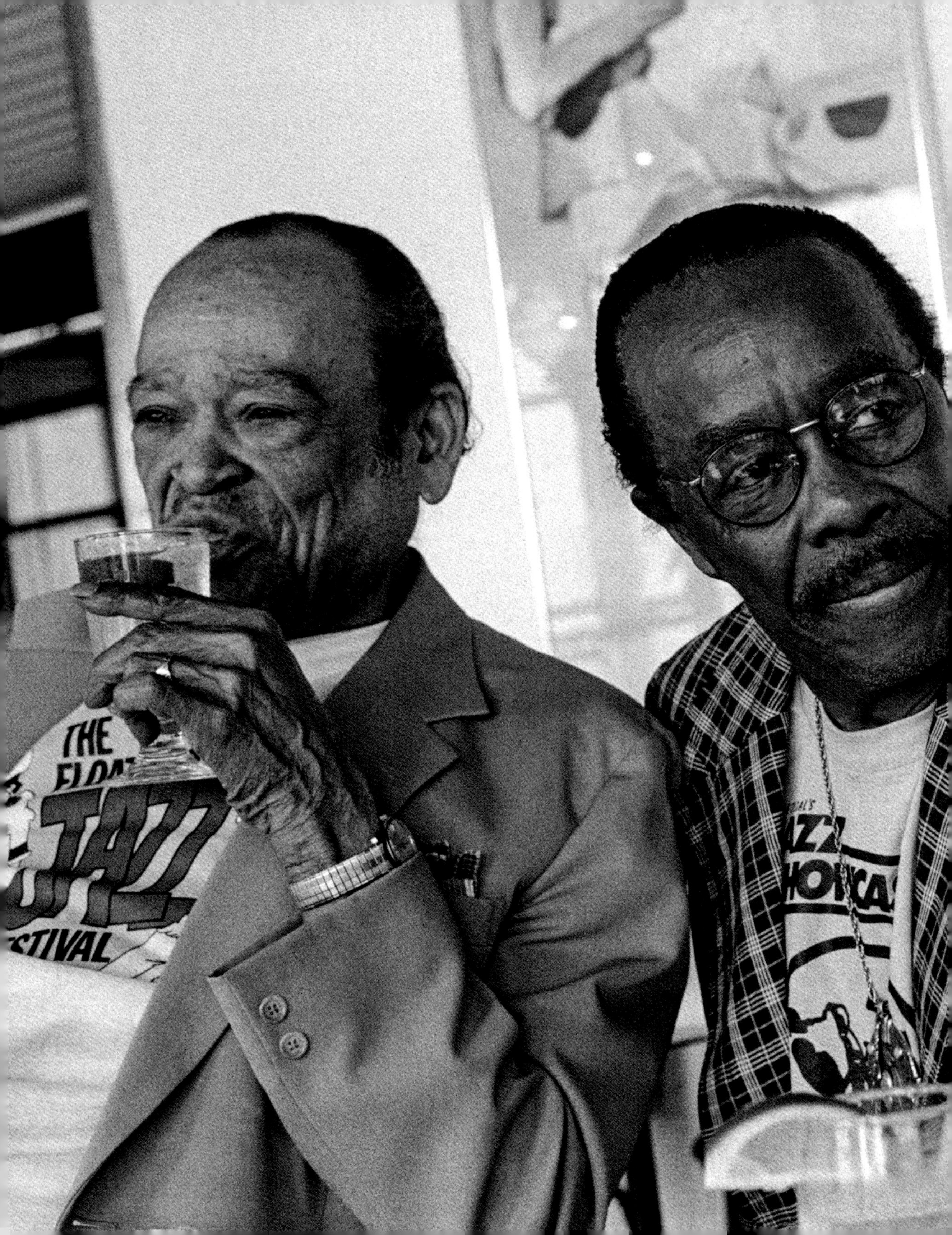
THE
JAZZ

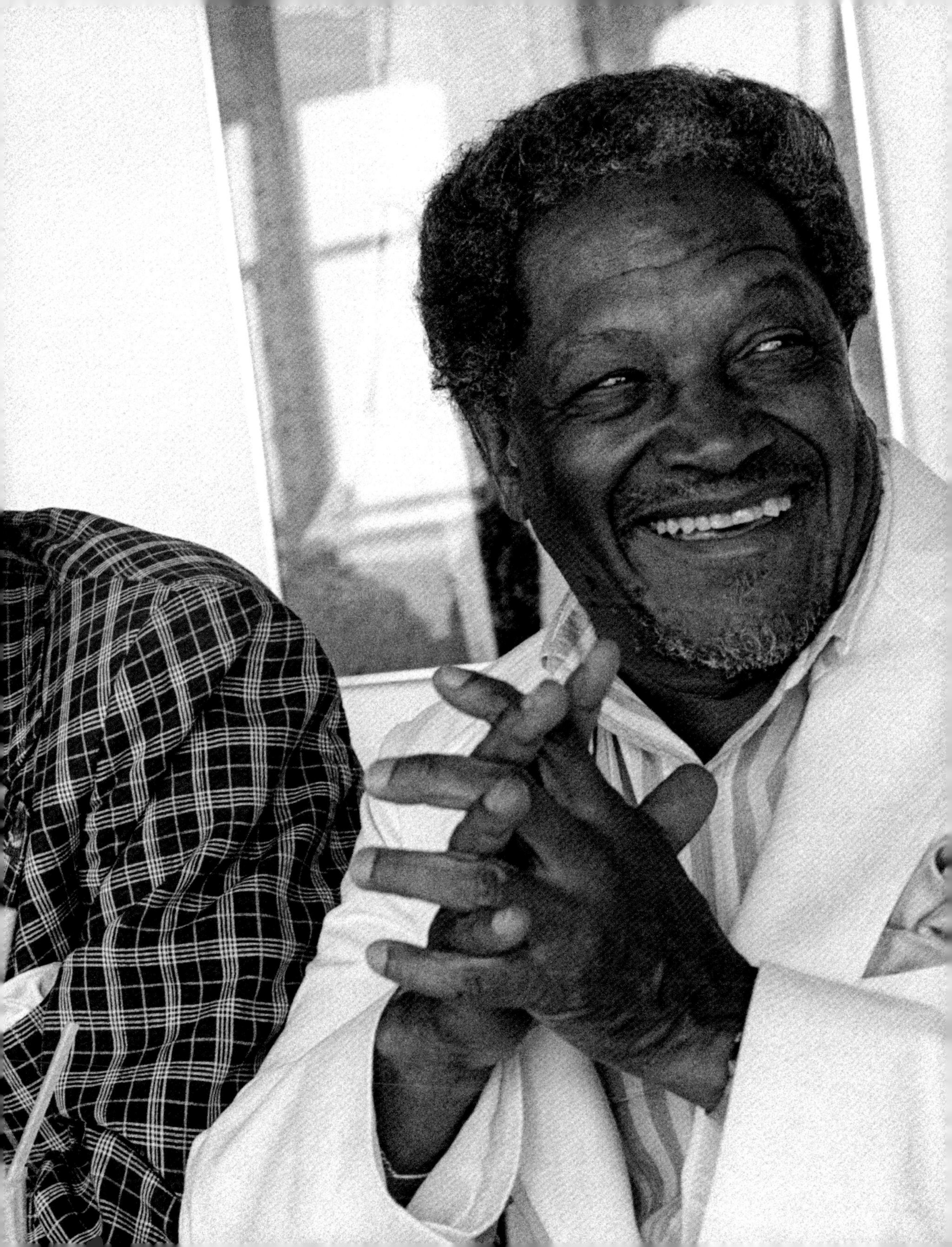

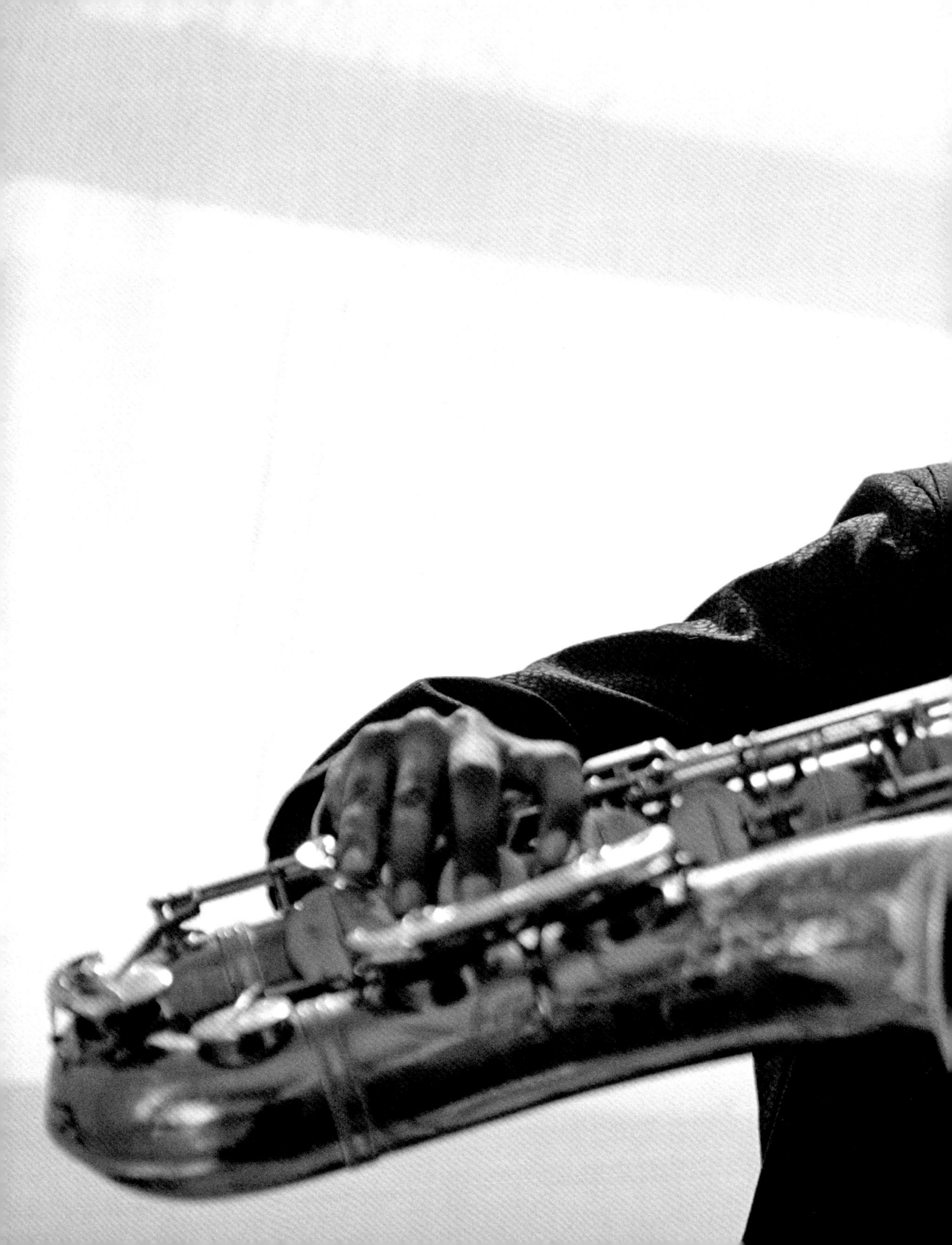

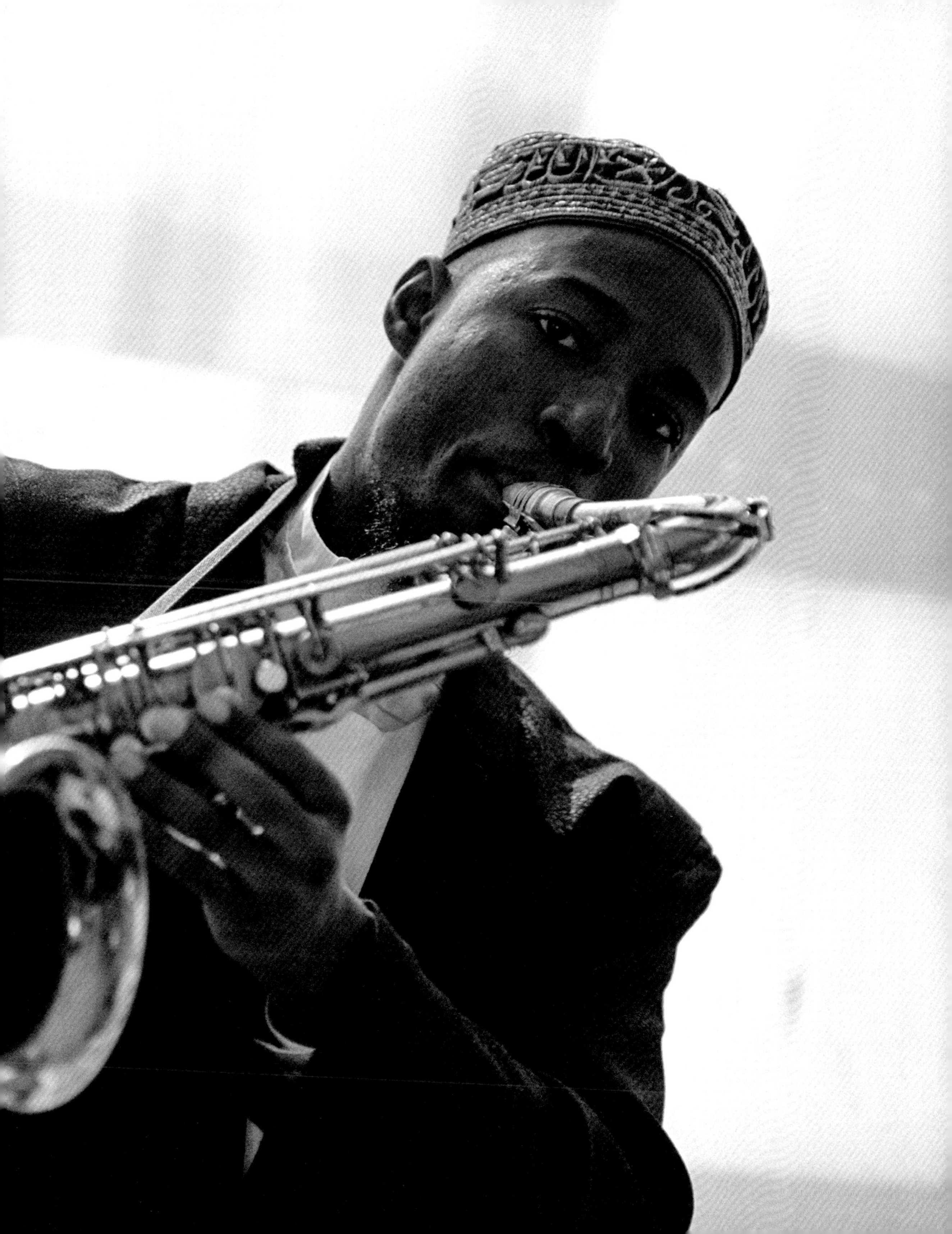

Dexter Gordon and Illinois Jacquet
1988, SS Norway

(following pages)
Flip Phillips
1996, New York City

Sam Rivers
1988, SS Norway

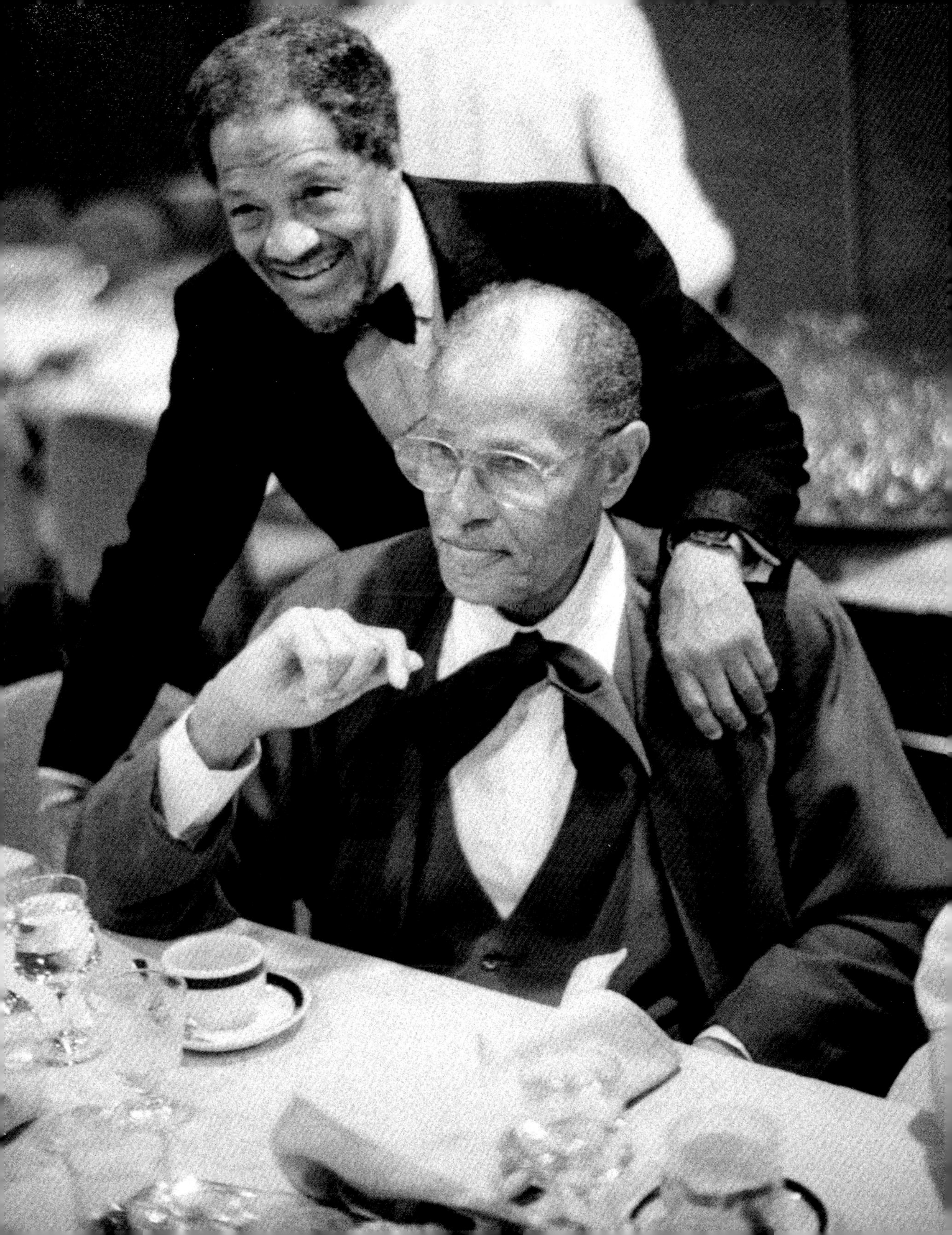

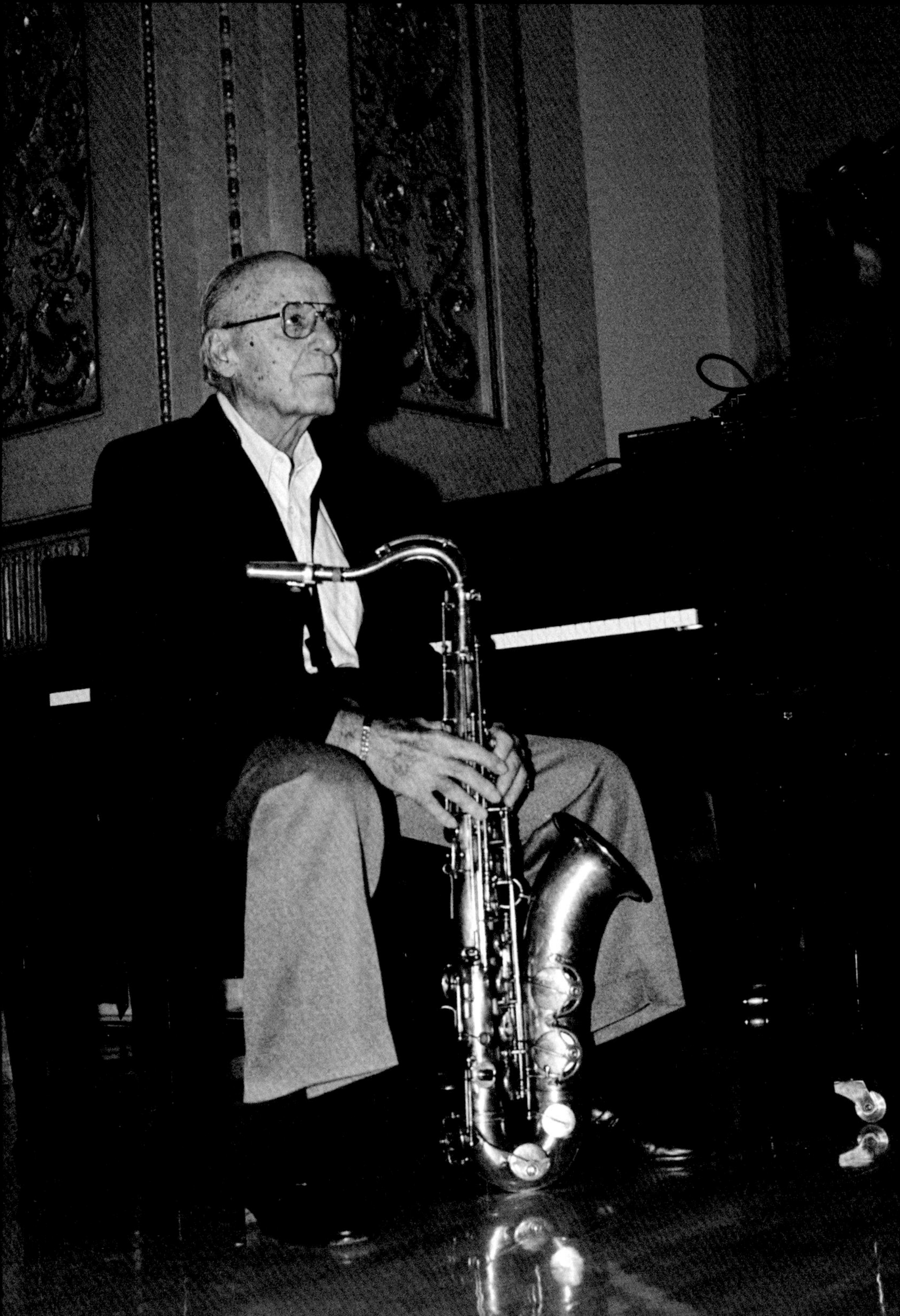

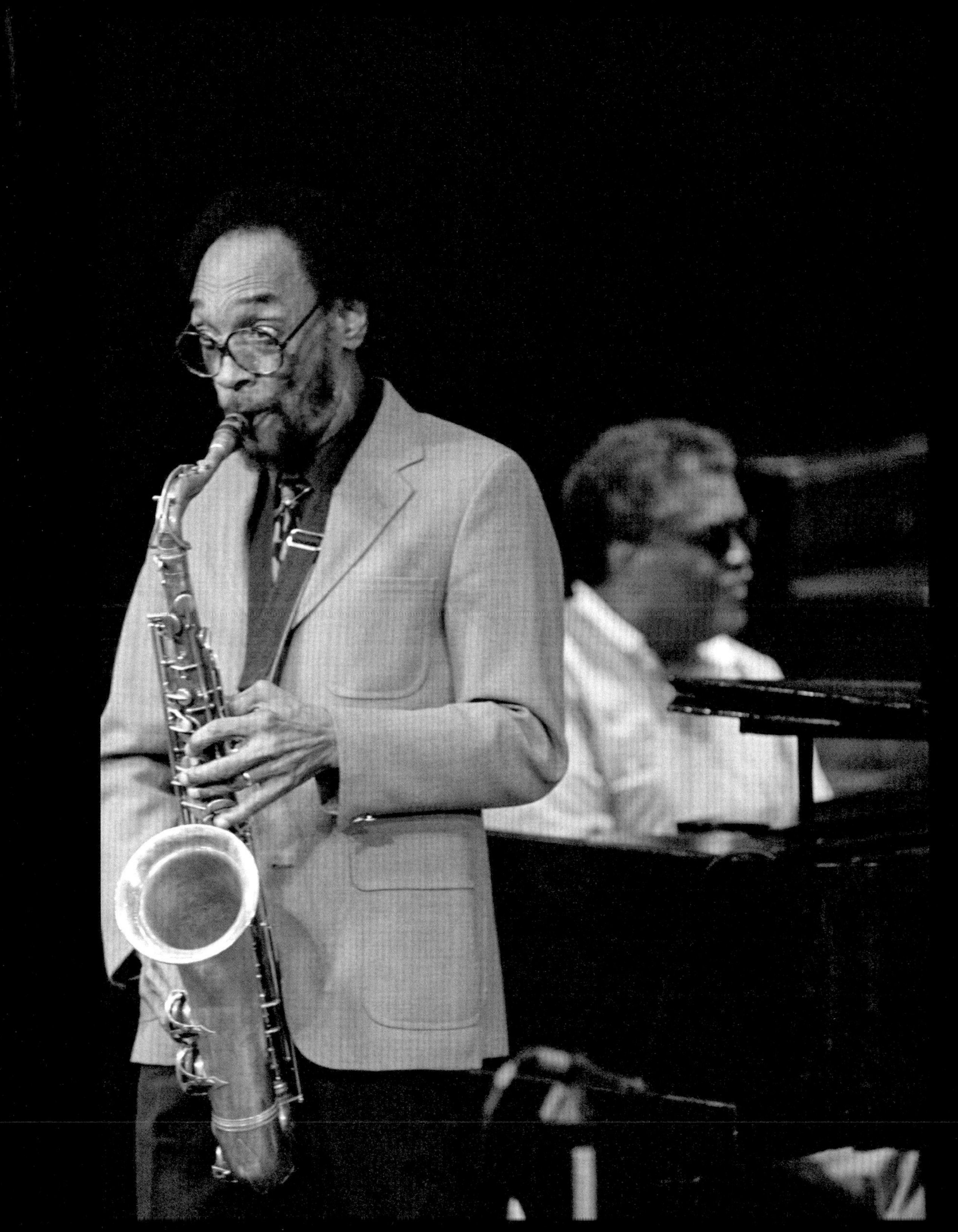

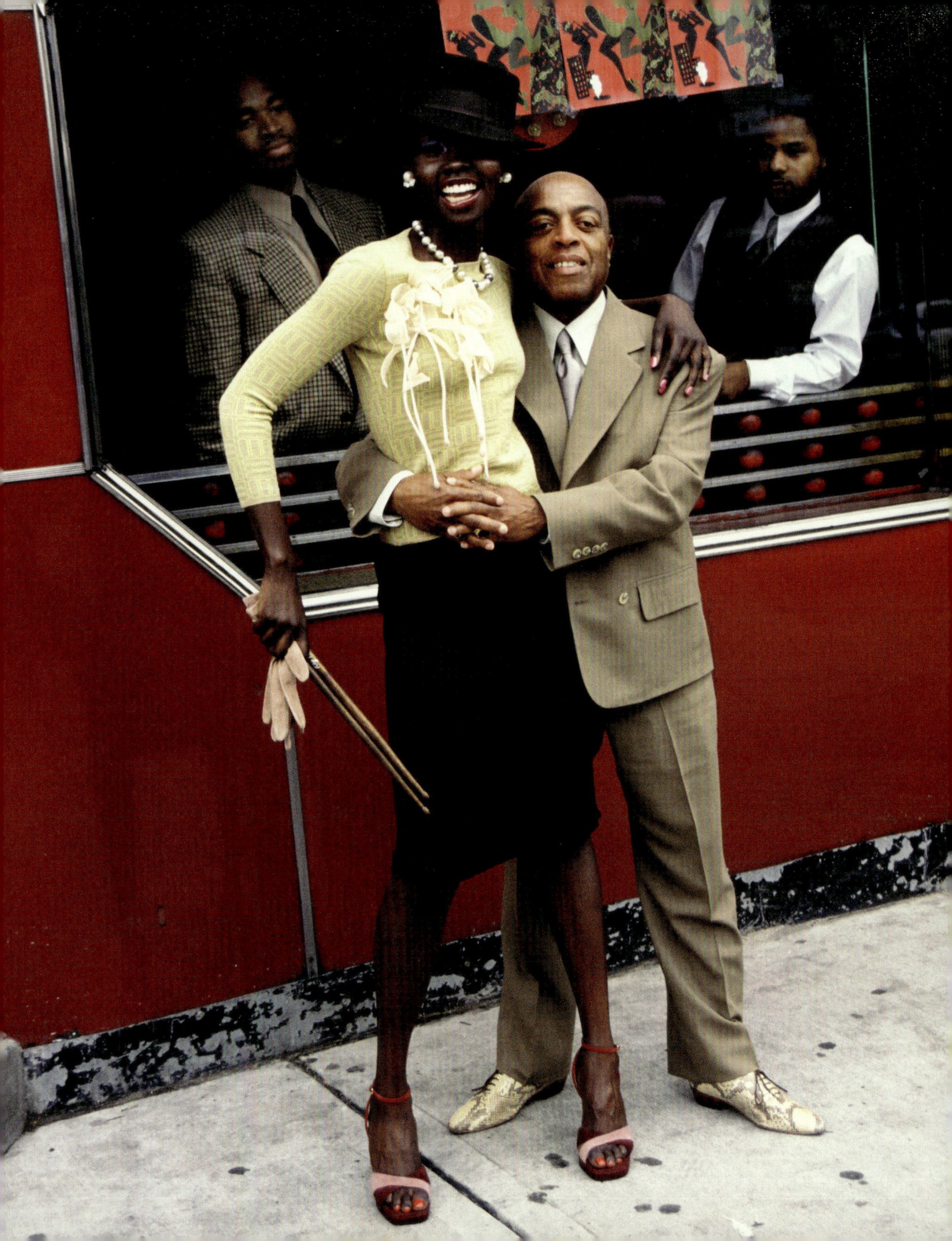

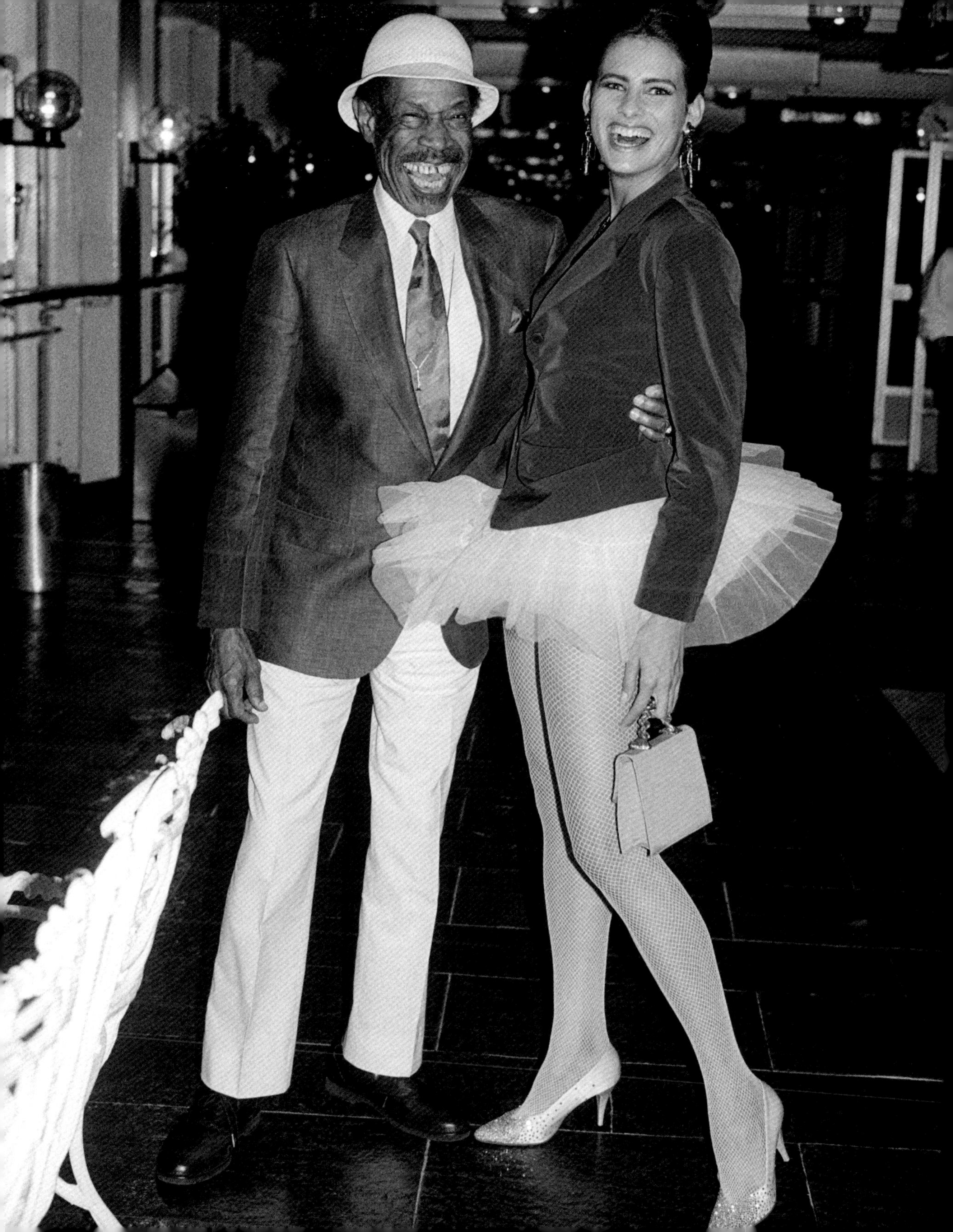

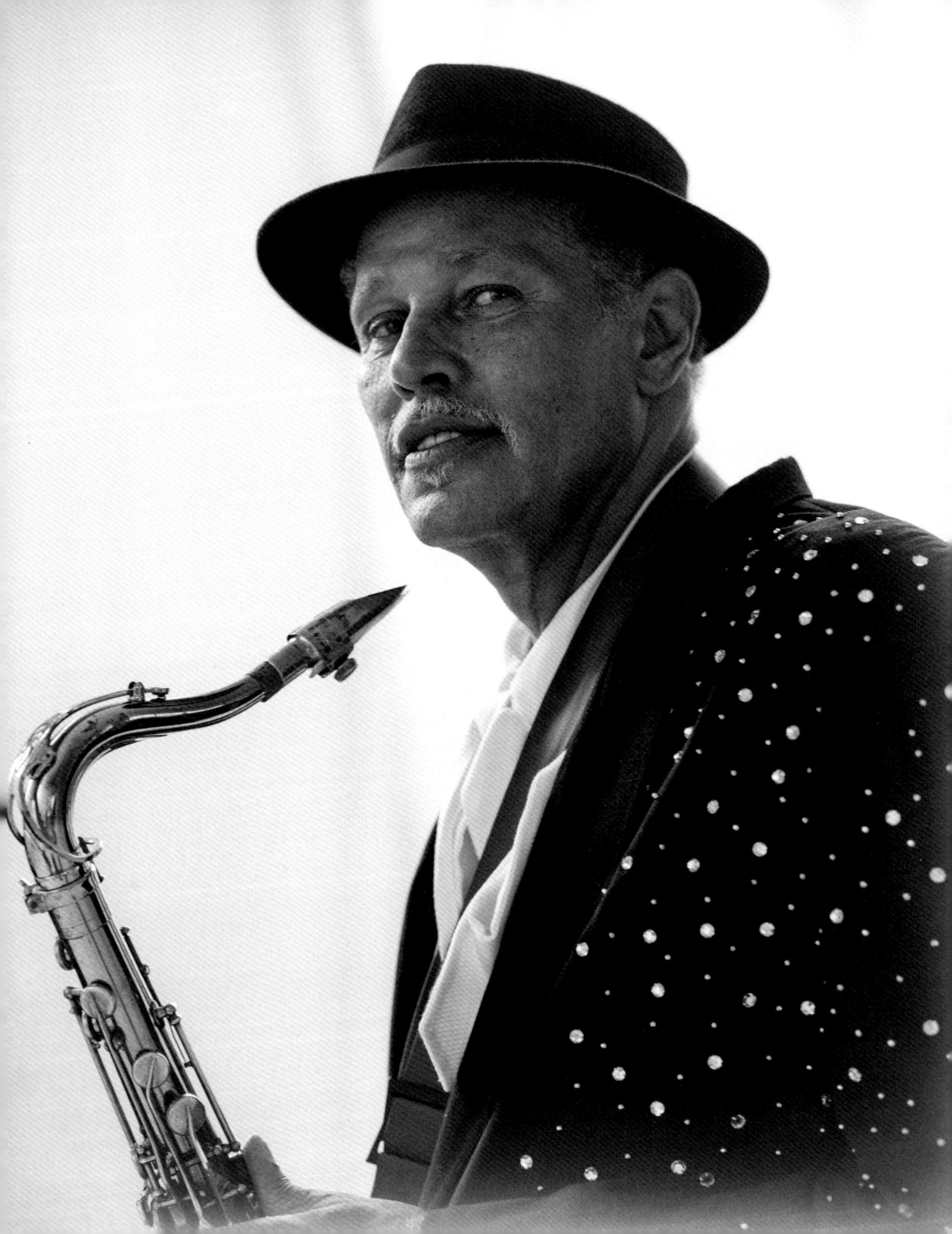

"Dexter Gordon was a favorite of mine for a long time. He was good at being modern and old-fashioned at the same time and he was known for dressing well. As a photographer I always wanted to take his picture because if you can look good and play well then you've got it all."

Dexter Gordon
1987, New York City

(preceding pages)
Roy Haynes
2000, New York City

Al Grey
1990, SS Norway

(following pages)
Dexter Gordon
1988, SS Norway

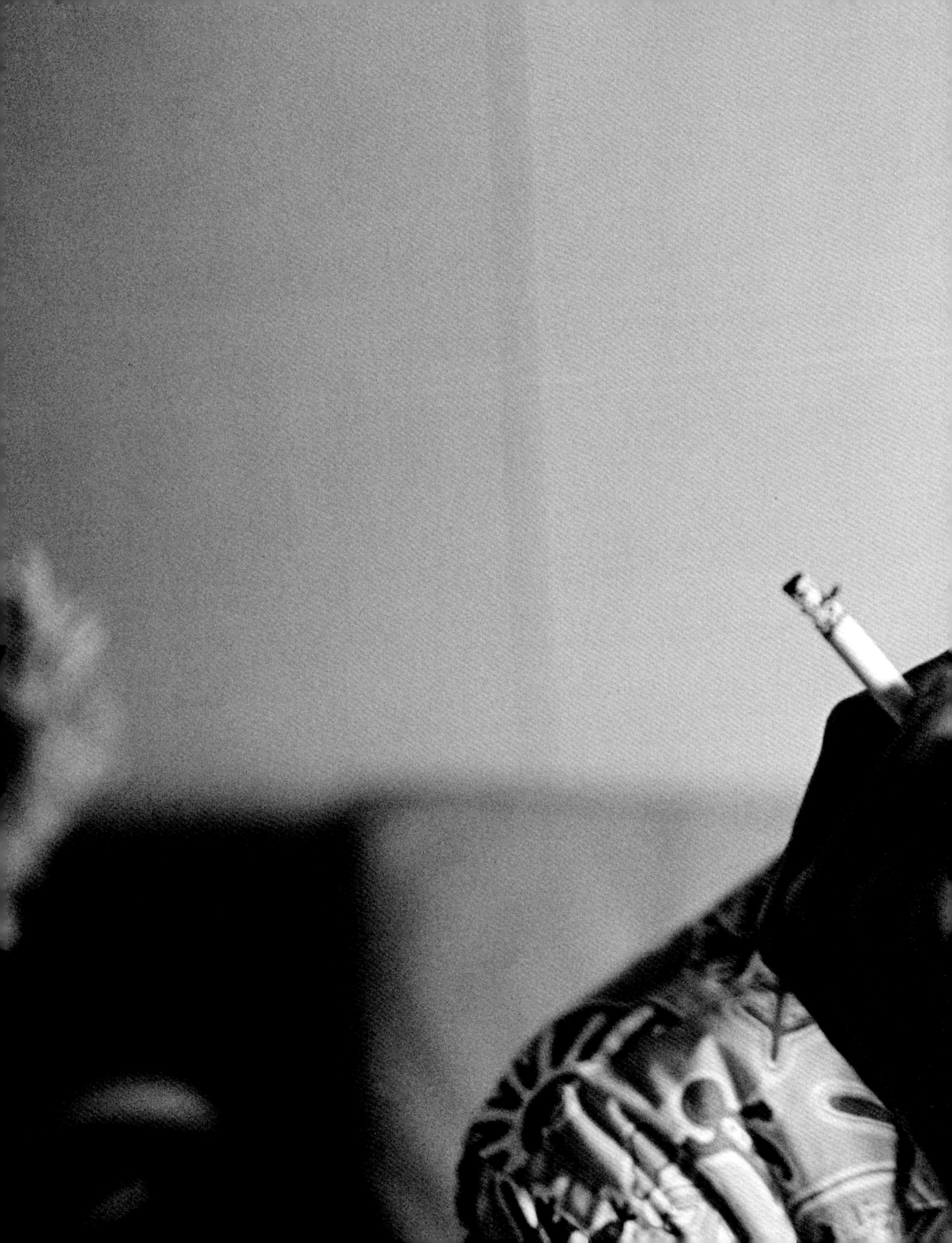

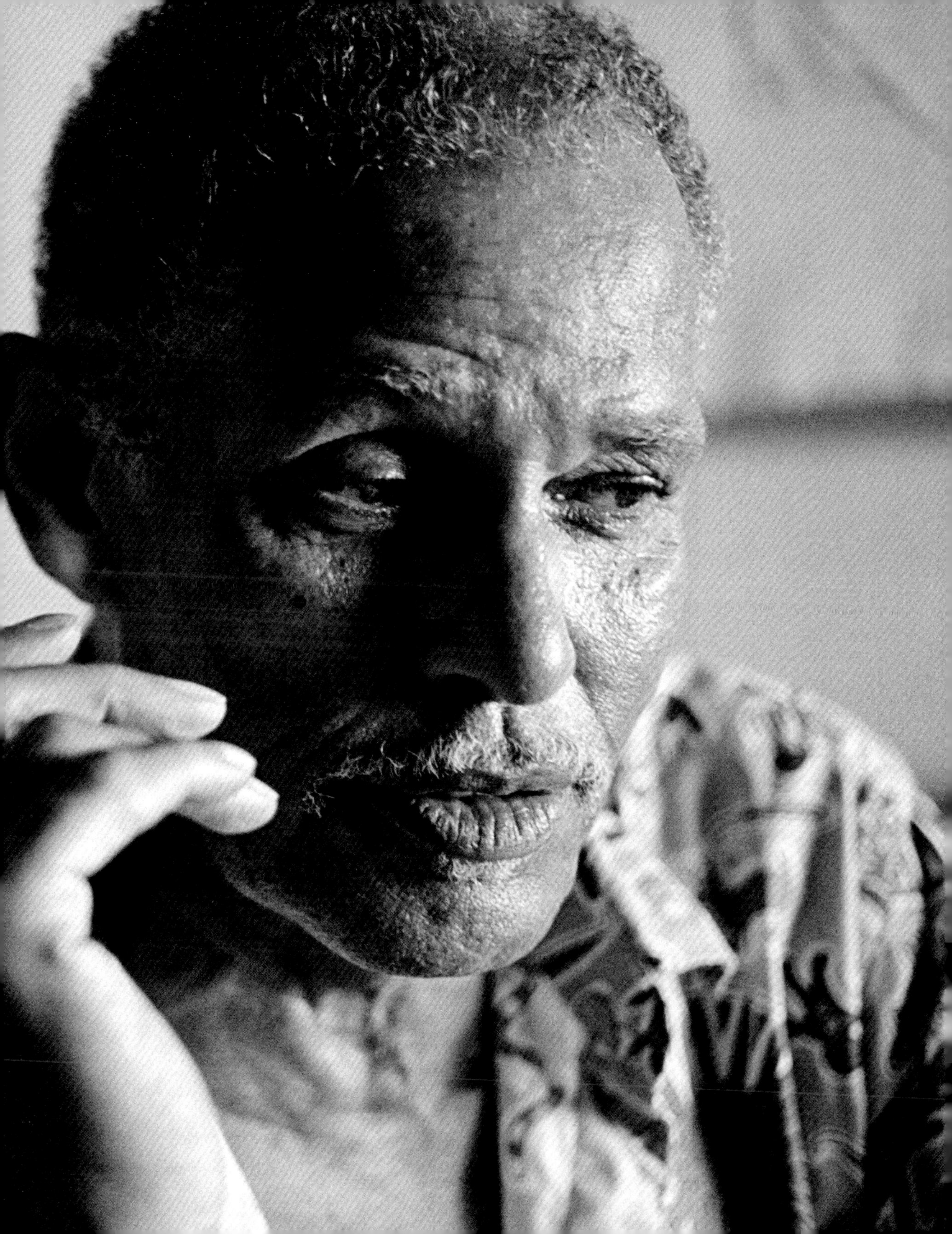

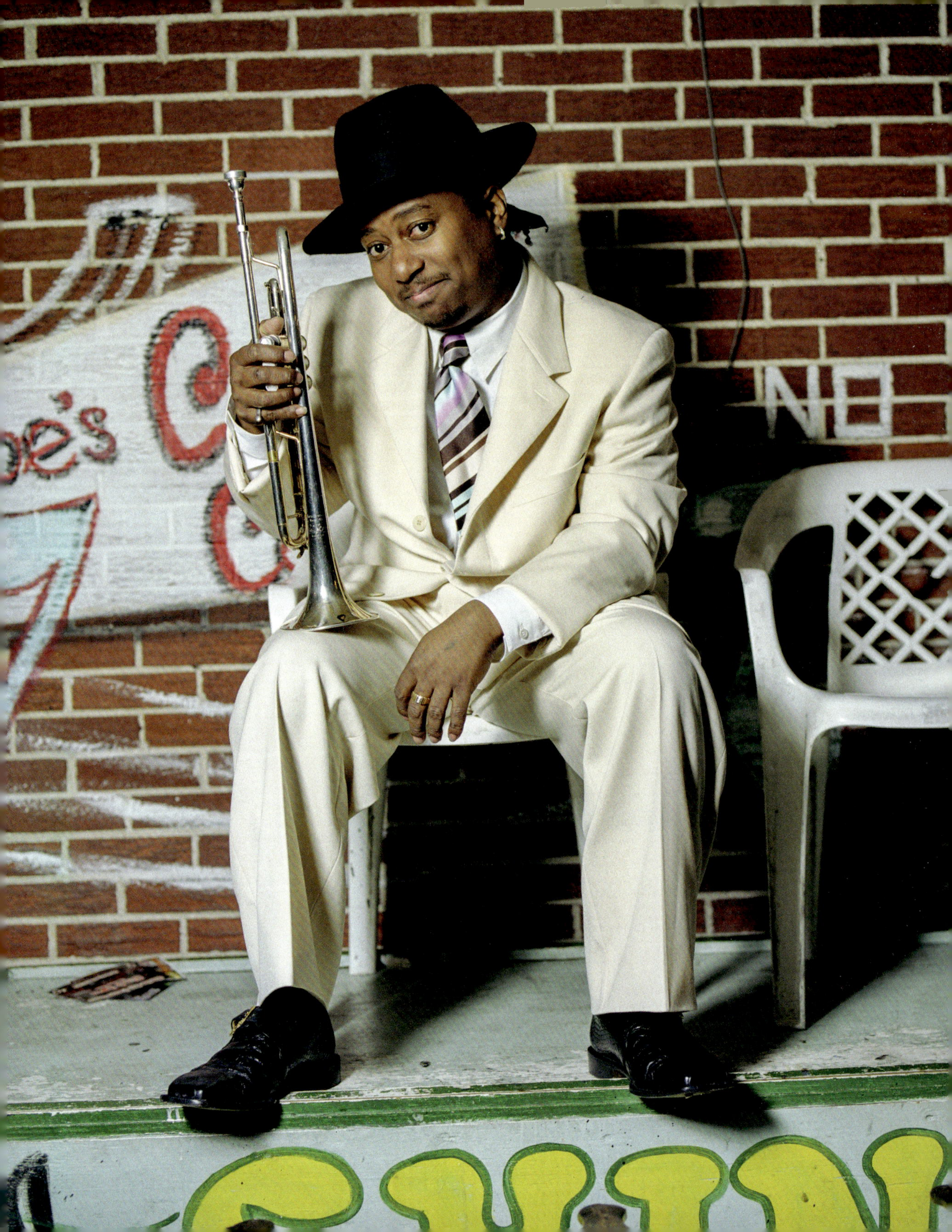
NO

Kermit Ruffins
2001, New Orleans

(following pages)
George Benson
1987, New York City

Illinois Jacquet
1990, New York City

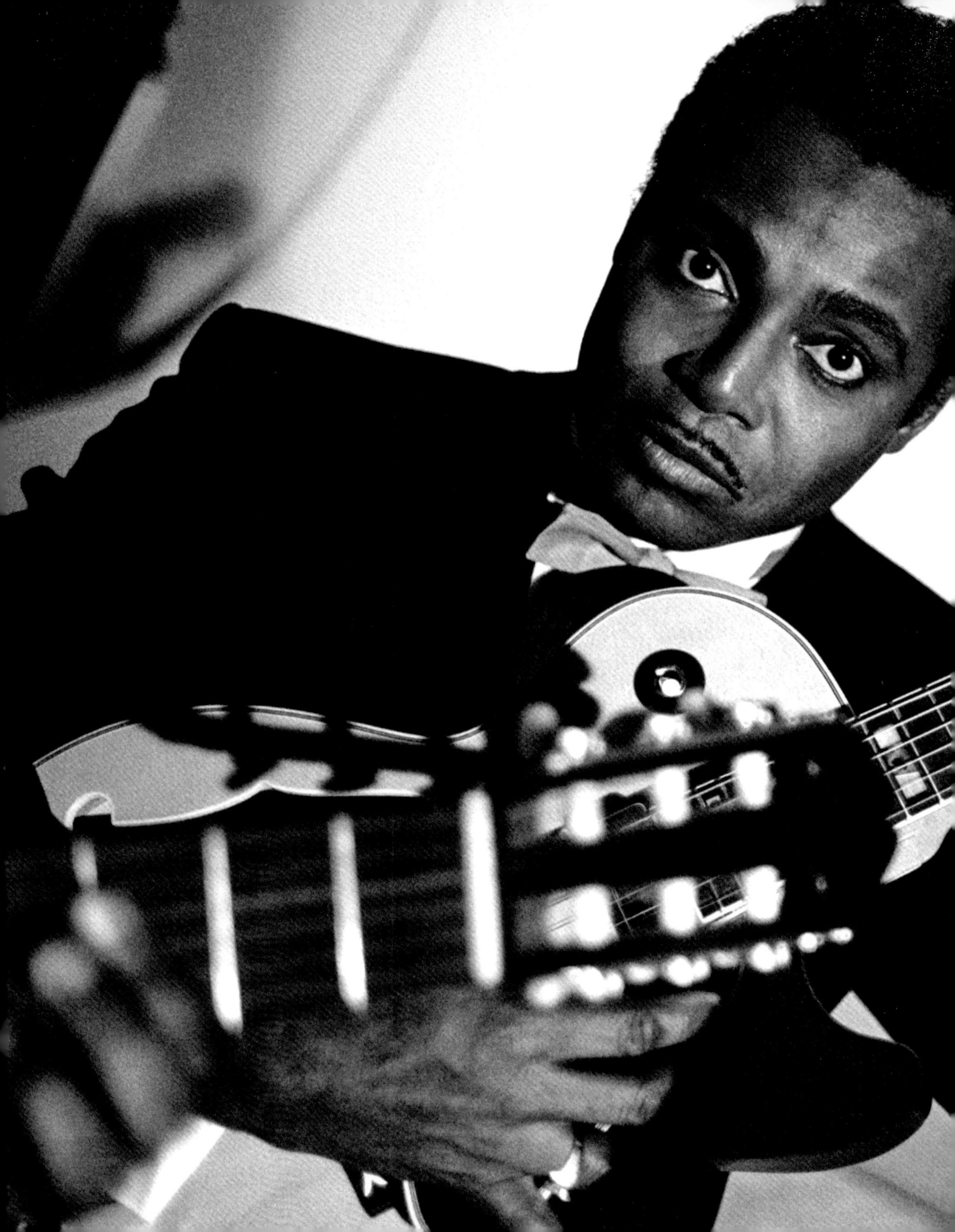

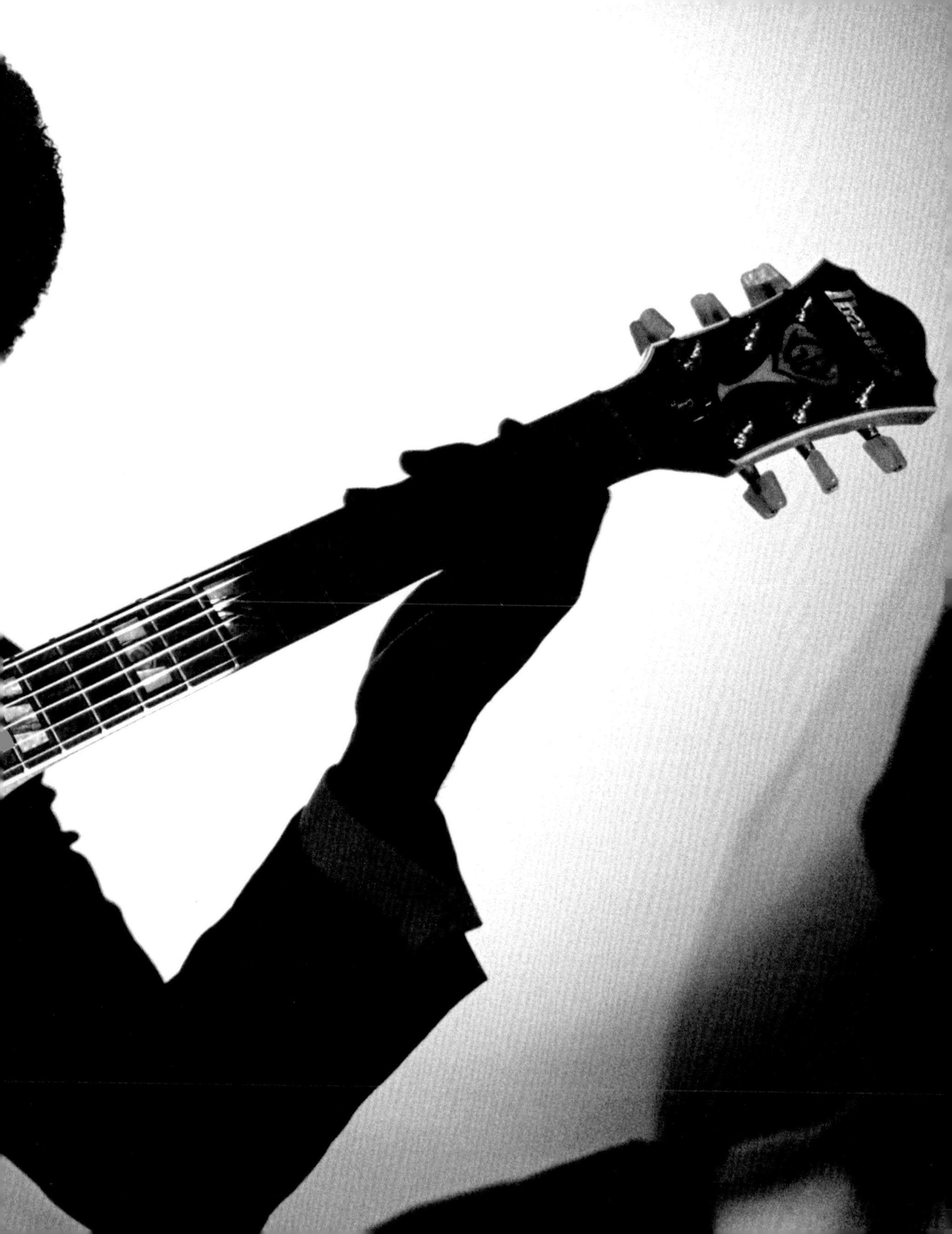

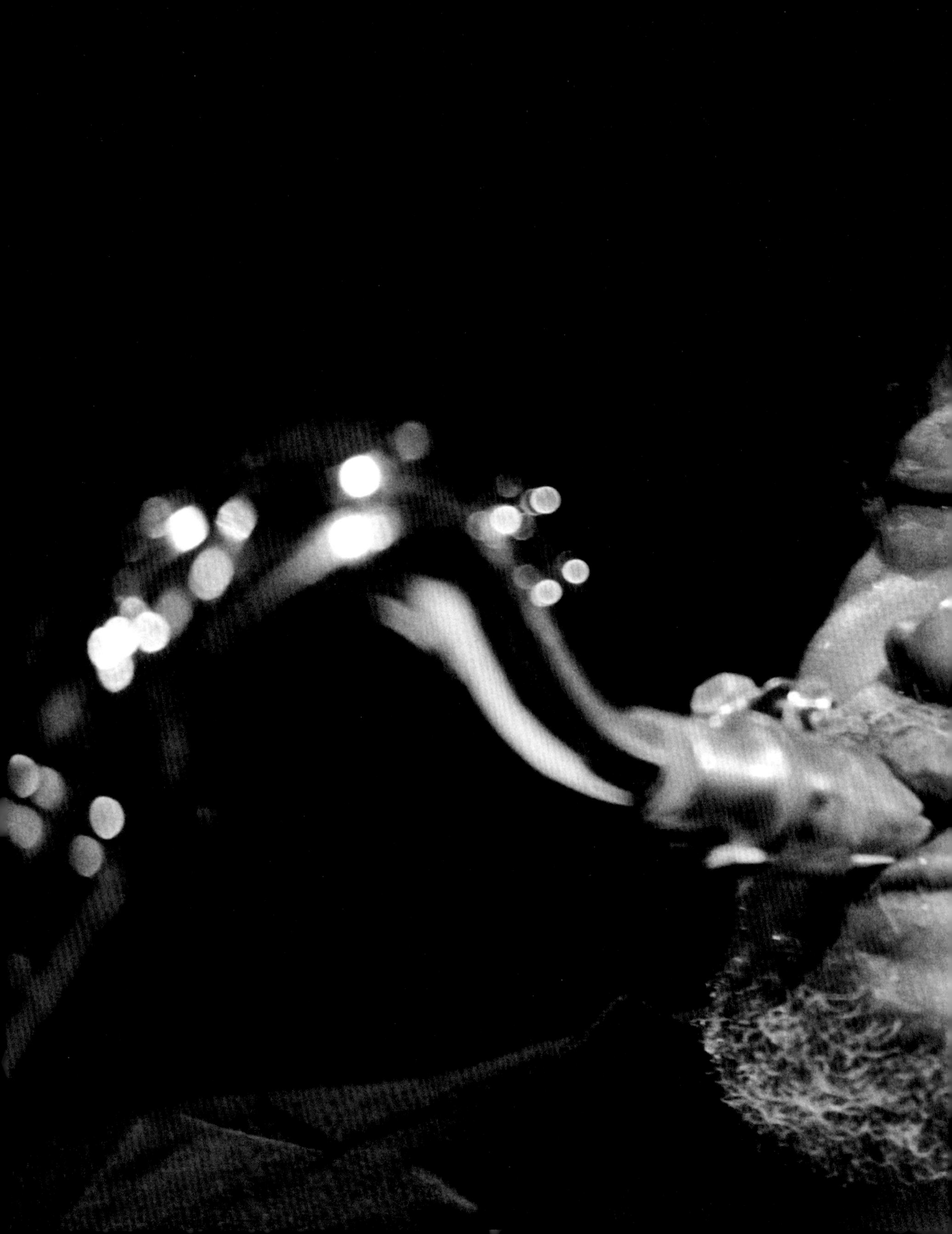

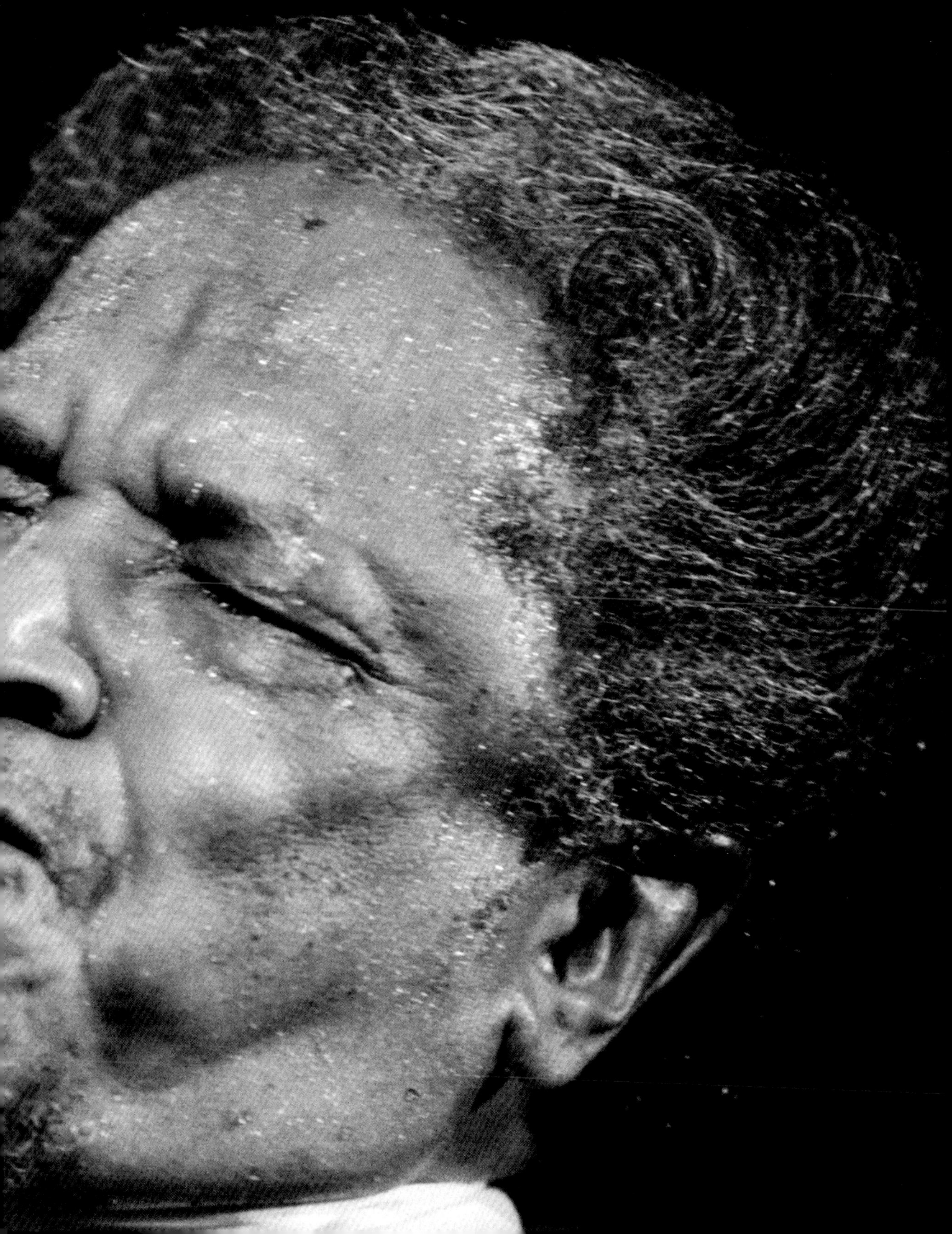

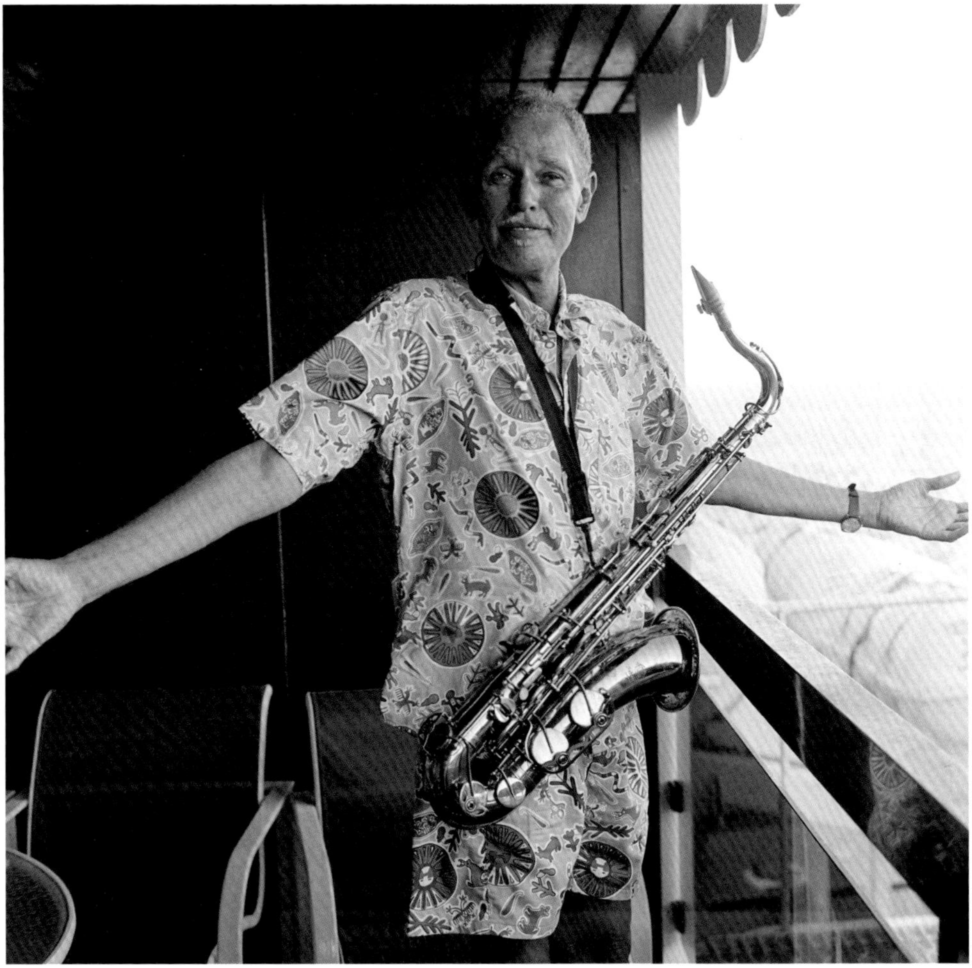

SPECIAL THANKS

Wynton Marsalis, Hank O'Neal, James Carter, Roy Haynes, Walter Blanding, Michael Bowie, Don Byron, Sonny Rollins, Joshua Redman, Cecil Payne, George Benson, Liya Kebede, Milt Hilton, Jeny Howorth, Dorothy Donegan, Jay McShann, Pat Metheny, Ornette Coleman, Aaron Neville, Dizzy Gillespie, John McLaughlin, Jimmy Scott, Jesse Davis, Illinois Jacquet, Lionel Hampton, Art Blakey, Dexter Gordon, Clark Terry, Christian Mcades, Ron Carter, Wycliff Gordon, Mona Hilton, Al Grey, Sam Newsome, Jon Faddis, Max Roach, Jerome Harris, Jack DeJohnette, Olu Dara, Michael Cain, Thelonious Monk Jr., Buddy Tate, Stefon Harris, Kermit Ruffins, Sam Rivers, Javon Jackson, Benny Carter, Jon Hendricks, Arnett Cobb, Tommy Flanagan, Kenny Baron, Doc Cheatham, Emilio Lyons, Selmer Factory, Jason Moran, Luther Lafatti, Courtney Pines, Bradford Marsalis, Jamal Haynes, Flip Phillips, Stafford Hunter, Amadou Diallo, Kenny Garrett, Anton Rooney, David Sanchez, and Jazz at Lincoln Center

Dexter Gordon
1988, SS Norway

ART DIRECTION:
MARIANNE HOUTENBOS
AOIFE WASSER

PHOTO EDITOR:
MARIANNE HOUTENBOS

TEXT EDITOR:
SALLY TAYLOR

PRINTING & PRODUCTION:
ELIZABETH COVINTREE

David Sanchez
2000, New York City

(following pages)
Dorothy Donegan
1991, SS Norway

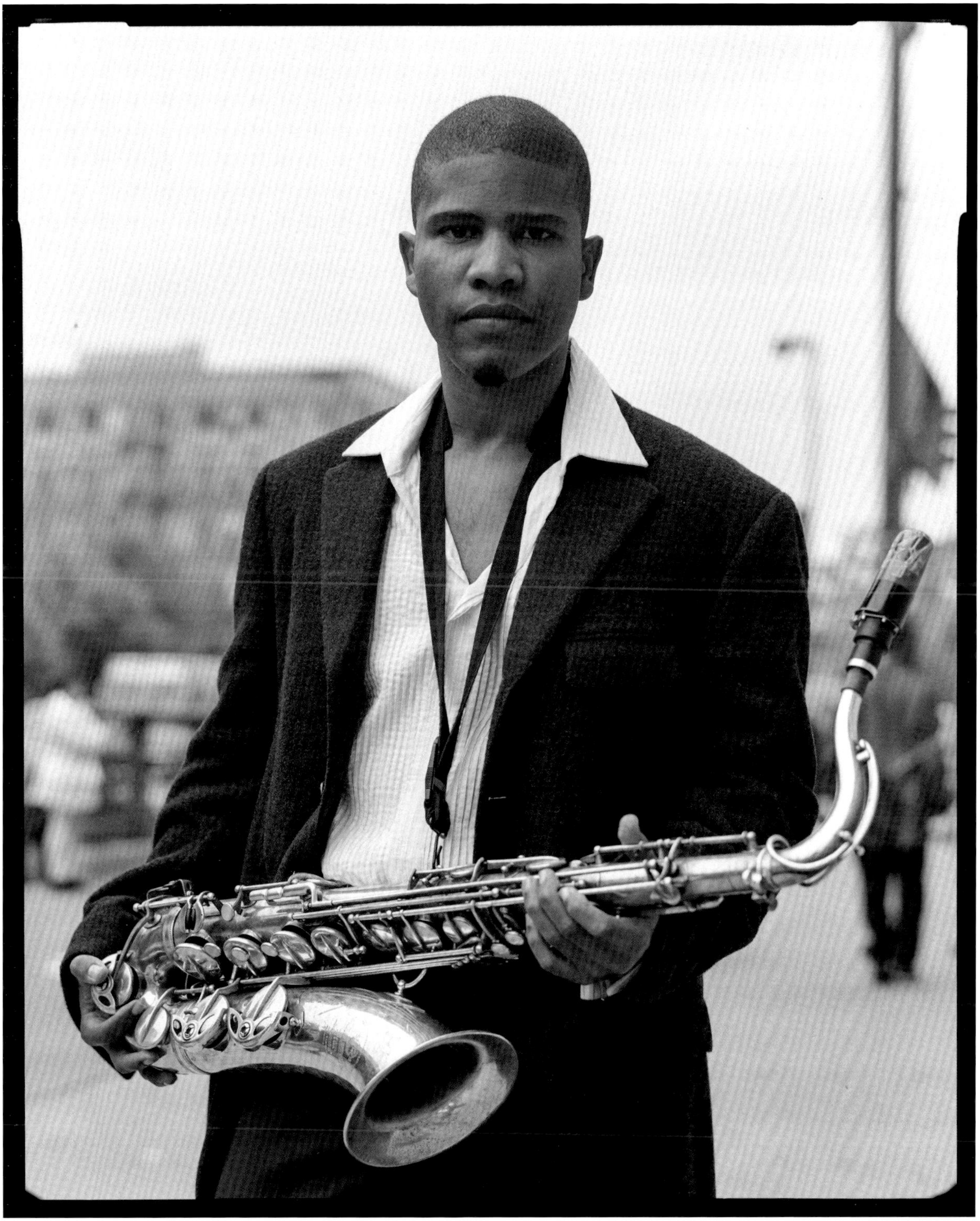

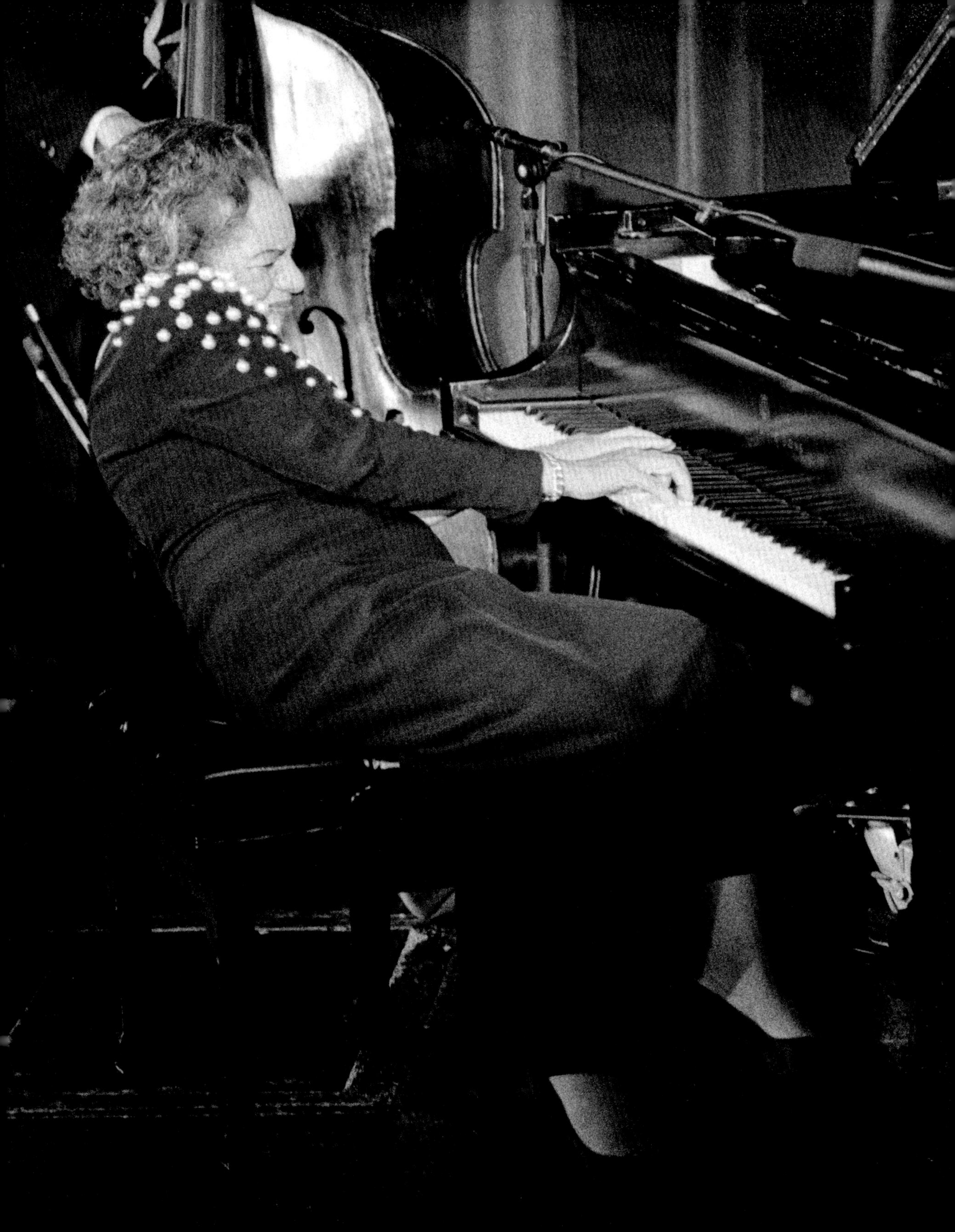

JAZZ
Arthur Elgort
(Cover) **Illinois Jacquet**, 1990, Paris

Book Design by
Marianne Houtenbos and Aoife Wasser

Published by Damiani
info@damianieditore.com, www.damianieditore.com

Printed in May 2018 by Grafiche Damiani – Faenza Group SpA, Italy.

ISBN 978-88-6208-608-0

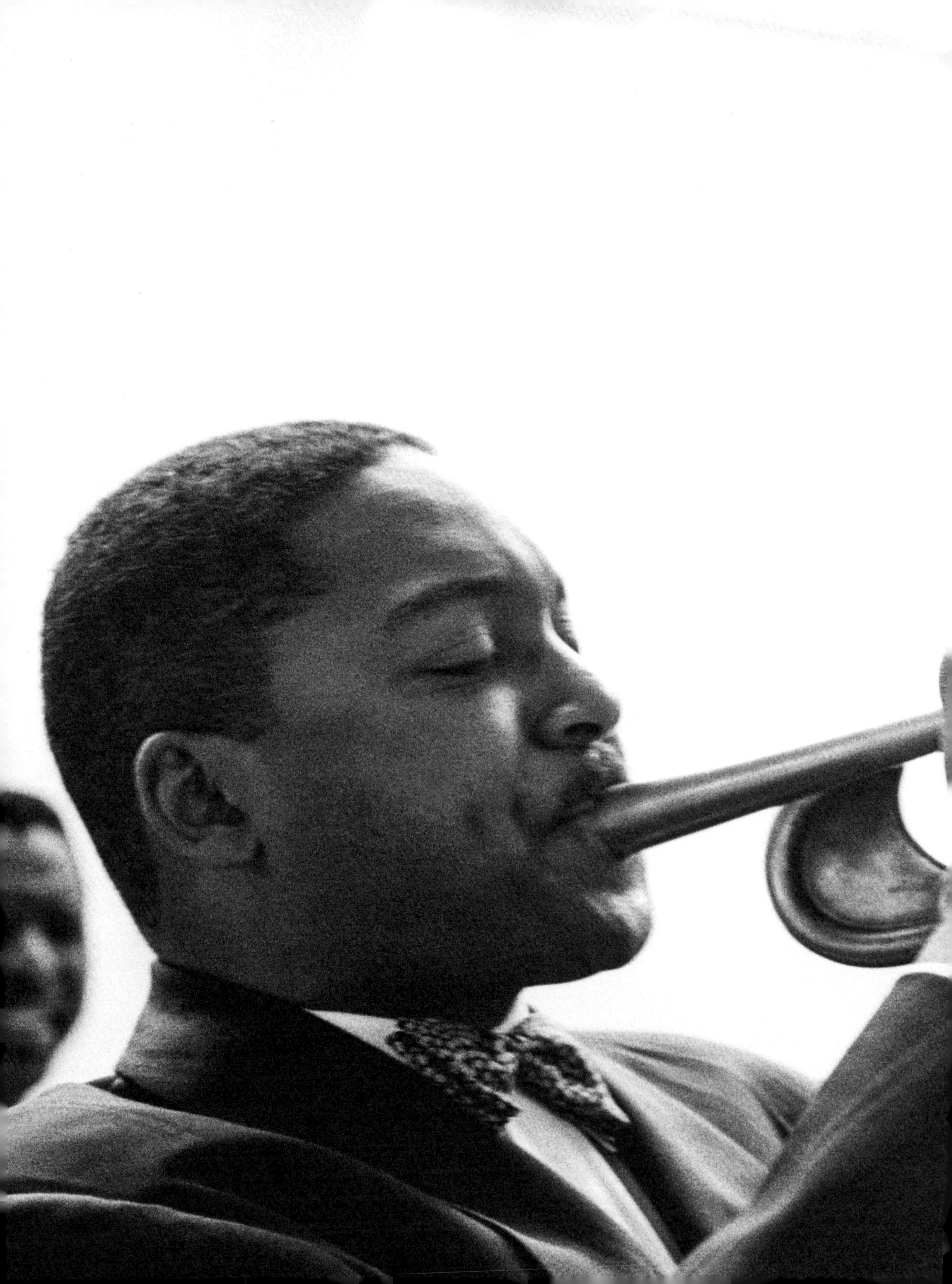